When Wright is Wrong

When Wright is Wrong

A Reformed Baptist Critique of N. T. Wright's
New Perspective on Paul

PHILLIP D. R. GRIFFITHS

RESOURCE *Publications* · Eugene, Oregon

WHEN WRIGHT IS WRONG
A Reformed Baptist Critique of N. T. Wright's New Perspective on Paul

Resource Publications
An Imprint of Wipf and Stock Publishers
199 W. 8th Ave., Suite 3
Eugene, OR 97401

www.wipfandstock.com

PAPERBACK ISBN: 978-1-5326-4919-6
HARDCOVER ISBN: 978-1-5326-4920-2
EBOOK ISBN: 978-1-5326-4921-9

Manufactured in the U.S.A.   JANUARY 8, 2019

Contents

Preface

TOM NICHOLAS WRIGHT CAN be described as the public face of what has become known as the new perspective on Paul. He is certainly the most popular, and most vocal, of its proponents. Through his many works, he has taken his new message to millions of Christians. He has that rare gift of communicating in a manner that is both informative and entertaining. This, coupled with his academic credentials, has caused many Christians to reassess their understanding of the nature of the atonement, especially justification by faith alone.

In this short work, as well as examining why I believe Wright's understanding of justification by faith alone is out of kilter with what the Scriptures teach, I examine his position on other related doctrines, for example, the essential difference between the old and new covenants, the nature of Old Testament sacrifices, life after death, the kingdom of God, and the penal verses *Christus Victor* theories of the atonement.

At the heart of the disagreement between Wright's position and that of Reformed Baptists is the way we view the covenants. The view argued for here maintains that all believers from both testaments have been saved in virtue of the new covenant in Christ. I show that the old and new covenants are not, as the paedobaptists would have us believe, different administrations of the one covenant of grace, but two separate covenants; each with its own particular blessings and punishments. Appreciating this will be vital for understanding what I believe to be Wright's inconsistency in the way he views the different covenants, for example, he tells us that Jesus fulfilled the old covenant, and then applies that covenant's temporal blessings to the new covenant, thereby, confusing the type with the antitype.

Wright's position can be very difficult to understand and, on occasions, one might think that I am charging him with something he does not actually believe. However, taking the work as a whole, I hope

I have shown that there are some fundamental differences between our positions, differences that go to the very heart of what Reformed Baptists believe.

I have on a number of occasions asked myself if I'm guilty of confirmation bias. This occurs when one gravitates toward those views one agrees with and avoids those that may call what one believes into question. Sometimes it occurs unconsciously, where one tends not to see the facts that may challenge one's understanding. Reading Wright has caused me to stop a number of times to consider whether his position is correct. Whether I am missing something. I have tried hard to see things from his perspective. I realize that no one is without prejudice, that no one can approach a text with complete candour. I have concluded that while I might be charged with confirmation bias, I am, nevertheless, convinced that the view expressed in this book is what Scripture teaches.

Some might wonder why, as a Baptist, I make use of works written by Reformed paedobaptists. I do this because on the majority of issues we are in full agreement. Indeed, much of the Second London Baptist Confession of 1689 mirrors that of the Westminster Confession. Again, some may wonder why I allude to theologians from a bygone age e.g., John Owen, John Gill etc., believing that theology has moved on. I reject this idea. The so-called new paths are not better than those hewn out by our predecessors, and, without doubt, the essentials of the Faith were articulated by men like Owen in a manner that is sadly lacking in much contemporary theology.

I have learned much from reading Wright and agree with a lot of what he has had to say. Some reading this work may well wonder why I have not said more about the positives. The reason I have not done so is simply that I want to concentrate on those parts of his teaching where there is disagreement. To spend time examining those areas in which we agree would involve a much longer book.

I have avoided *ad hominem* arguments[1]. These tend to be employed to shore up weak arguments. Let me also say that I would not hesitate to say that Wright is a Christian, but I would argue that he has gone astray in regard to certain doctrines. I would even say that in regard to living the Christian life, the way Wright conducts himself is an example we should all seek to emulate.

---

1. Arguments that attack the person rather than the arguments.

As I read over the work, my mind keeps informing me of other things I should have included. However, no work can cover all, and while this work might be imperfect, it is my desire that, while it will not convince all, it will engender greater thought and Bible searching on the issues covered.

Just one more thing. I have edited this work myself. When doing this there is always a tendency to read what one assumes to be written rather than what is actually on the page. I am certain there are times when I have done this. I trust there won't be too many typos, and I apologize beforehand for any that I may have missed.

Introduction

WHENEVER AND WHEREVER THE truth is believed and proclaimed controversy inevitably follows. Throughout its long history, the church has been engaged in a battle against those who have sought to undermine its core beliefs. The battle intensified following the so-called Enlightenment in the 18th century. This effectively laid the foundations for the contemporary skeptical paradigm. Man considered himself to have come of age, to have attained a level of maturity that necessitated the abandonment of thousands of years of servitude to what was considered outworn, external, and superstitious dogmas. The Enlightenment ushered in, especially in the Western world, an increasing willingness to reject anything that does not conform to the supposedly rationalistic paradigm. Today, to a large extent, external authority has been abandoned, instead, everything is to be subjected to the touchstone of reason. Man now considers himself to be the final arbiter in both things spiritual and temporal.

Many Christians have little or no knowledge of the origin of the present skepticism, and, perhaps, in most cases, are not even conscious of its presence, yet, in many churches, it has percolated into the innermost recesses of the Faith. Increasing numbers are turning their backs on confessional Christianity, abandoning many of evangelical's fundamental truths that speak of a supernatural dimension, for example, the virgin birth, Christ's miracles, the resurrection and the nature of his person etc.

The new perspective on Paul seems to adopt an approach to Scripture which attempts to have the best of both worlds with its eclectic acceptance and application of modern rationalistic methods to understand Scripture. This is exhibited in the way some of its proponents have reservations about Scripture's inerrancy and infallibility, as originally given. N. T. Wright, for example, although he still holds Scripture in high regard, seems ready to relegate such notions to the waste-paper bin of history:

> ... the insistence on an 'infallible' or 'inerrant' Bible has grown
> up within a complex cultural matrix (that, in particular, of mod-
> ern North American Protestantism) where the Bible has been
> seen as the bastion of orthodoxy against Roman Catholicism
> on the one hand and liberal modernism on the other. Unfortu-
> nately, the assumptions of both those worlds have conditioned
> the debate. It is no accident that this Protestant insistence on
> biblical infallibility arose at the same time that Rome was insist-
> ing on papal infallibility, or that the rationalism of the Enlight-
> enment infected even those who were battling against it.[1]

If, as Wright tries to show, the divisions that exist between Protestants
and Roman Catholics concern nothing more than a misunderstanding
regarding external boundary markers, then ecumenical unity becomes a
real possibility. If it can be shown that we are all members of one family
and that the doctrine of justification by faith alone concerns ecclesiology rather soteriology, there is no reason why Protestants and Catholics
should simply acknowledge each other as brothers and sisters in the one
Faith. Wright informs us that:

> Many Christians, both in the Reformation and the counter-
> Reformation traditions, have done themselves and the church
> a great disservice by treating the doctrine of 'justification' as
> central to their debates, and by supposing that it describes that
> system by which people attain salvation. They have turned the
> doctrine into its opposite. Justification declares that all who be-
> lieve in Jesus Christ belong to the same table, no matter what
> their cultural or racial differences.[2]

Error does not enter the church wearing a slogan pronouncing its
aberrant teachings, no, all too often a large proportion of what is taught
may be correct, yet on the back of this, usually in a slow piecemeal fashion, hijacking aspects of truth, error percolates into the church's inner
sanctum. The result has been incalculable damage, with many weaker
Christians becoming confused and depressed, and in some cases, even
leaving the church. In my own country of Wales, the so-called land of
revivals, one only needs to compare church attendance today with what
it was as little as twenty years ago. There seems to have been an inexo-
rable seepage, to the point where many once-thriving meeting places[3]

1. Wright, *Simply Christian*, 183.
2. Wright, *What Saint Paul Really Said*, 158–9.
3. In Scripture, the church is always the people, the congregation of the saved. It is

(churches) have been converted into comfortable houses, bingo halls, or even mosques. Although it is not possible to know how much of this is the result of false teachings, these have certainly played a part, denuding the word of God of its life-changing power.

Many evangelicals have become loath to even consider sharing and defending their faith, in the words of David Wells:

> Modernity has been hard at work reducing evangelical faith to something that is largely private and internal. Belief has shrunk from being a contemporary confession of God's truth in the church and beyond to being simply a part of personal identity and psychological makeup. Many evangelicals quietly assume, perhaps even without much thought, that it would be uncouth and uncivil to push this private dimension too noticeably or noisily on others or into the public square.[4]

This reluctance, coupled with a marked degree of ignorance, has made the church vulnerable, serving only to facilitate the entry of aberrant teachings.

It is, therefore, imperative for the church to be ever vigilant, always prepared to test every teaching against the benchmark of Scripture. Unity must never be at the expense of sound doctrine. Unfortunately, this warning is to a large extent going unheeded. Half-truths are in fashion, where many Christians speak of love at the expense of wrath, mercy at the expense of justice, and declare peace, peace, where there is no peace. They eschew anything negative and, believe, quite wrongly, that they are following in the footsteps of Jesus when what they have effectively done is open the door to a multitude of erroneous teachings. In their quest for unity, at almost any price, the nature of what constitutes the church has been undermined.

To counter this we need to bear in mind the words of Donald Bloesch, "In our striving for church unity, we must not lose sight of our mandate to counter doctrinal error, for nothing subverts the cause of unity more than a latitudinarianism which signifies giving up on real church unity in favor of mutual tolerance."[5] What the apostle said to the Corinthians is certainly applicable for today's church: "For if someone comes and proclaims another Jesus than the one we proclaimed, or if

---

never a bricks and mortar building

4. Wells, *God in the Wasteland*, 27.

5. Bloesch, *The Future of Evangelical Christianity*, 152.

you receive a different spirit from the one you received, or if you accept a different gospel from the one you accepted, you put up with it readily enough" (2 Cor 11:4).

One of the most worrying trends in the modern church is the fascination with novelty. Jude spoke of the Faith that was "once and for all delivered," yet many hanker after that which is considered "new," believing themselves to have discovered something that previous generations had missed. Perhaps this interest in novelty is the result of an anxiety caused by dwindling numbers, and the apparent lack of enthusiasm shown by many that do regularly attend church. I fear that all too often the desire to more effectively communicate with our post-modern world is causing many to embrace beliefs and methods that are unscriptural.

The sad truth is, as Wells puts it: "The evangelical world, in fact, is now coming apart because its central truths, what once held it all together, no longer have the binding power that they once had and, in some cases are rejected outright with no following outcry."[6] We need to realize that new is not necessarily better and that we should follow the old and tested paths rather than those newly hewn paths that, in spite of their enticement, ultimately lead away from the true gospel of Christ.

From the Gnostics in the early church to the liberalism of the 18th and 19th centuries, heresy has taken many forms. In just the last few decades we have witnessed, amongst other things, New Covenant Theology, The Emerging Church, Federal Vision, and its close relative, the New Perspective(s) on Paul. What makes these particularly dangerous is that they are being put forward and defended by those with evangelical credentials.

It should be stressed that the perpetrators of these new teachings are not consciously seeking to discard the old, rather, they earnestly believe in what they are doing. Erroneous doctrine is held, usually, by honest and very conscientious believers, and one should bear this in mind when attempting to refute their teachings. For example, N. T. Wright is not putting forward his novel understanding of the apostle Paul's teachings because he wants to cause controversy, but because he genuinely believes his position to be the right one. One must not, as many evangelical Christians have done, think of the new perspective[7] as something of marginal importance. It represents a paradigm shift, one that changes the entire

6. Wells, "Forward," 13.
7. New Perspective on Paul will from hereon be referred to as NPP.

complexion of Pauline theology, and, of course, this affects one's understanding of the entire Bible.

To date, most of the works critiquing the new perspective have been written from a Presbyterian/paedobaptist position. I, however, want to approach it from a Reformed Baptist stance. In so doing I will seek to show that the new perspective on Paul has misidentified the true Israel, confusing the old and new covenants and has consequently attributed what belonged to spiritual Israel, that Israel within Israel, to carnal or ethnic Israel. I will also seek to show, in keeping with previous critiques, only from a Reformed Baptist position, how the NPP embraces aberrant views on doctrines that touch the very heart of what we Reformed evangelicals believe, for example, the way it undermines justification by faith alone, denying the imputation of Christ's righteousness, and takes issue with what we believe Paul meant by "the works of the law" etc.

Being a Reformed Baptist does not mean that I do not make use of works produced by Reformed paedobaptists. Indeed, the 1689 Second London Baptist Confession is in almost all aspects identical to the 1647 Westminster Confession, differing only in regard to covenant theology, church government, and the rightful recipients of baptism. So, whilst I very much disagree with the Reformed paedobaptist position in regard to the covenants,[8] and the recipients of baptism, I stand shoulder to shoulder with them on most doctrines.

In this short work, I attempt not only to offer a refutation of Wright's new perspective on Paul but also exhort Christians to, in the words of Jude, "contend for the faith that was once and for all delivered to the saints" (Jude 3).

06/20/2018.

---

8. Here I am alluding to those who espouse Reformed paedobaptism, for example, John Owen, Charles and A. A. Hodge, John Murray etc.

PART ONE

Methodology

IN PART ONE, I will seek to provide a general introduction to the NPP.[1] However, one cannot understand the significance of this without knowing something about what is now called the old perspective or Lutheran view. I shall, therefore, start by briefly examining this position. This will be followed by looking at some of the main thinkers within the NPP. Here I will limit myself to examining the works of Stendahl, Sanders, Dunn, and N. T. Wright. More weight will obviously be given to Wright's position, after all, this is a work about his understanding of the new perspective.

Although in part one I will confine myself to describing the views of NPP proponents, when examining Wright's position, I will interject criticism, explaining to the reader why I disagree with some of his conclusions. Further criticism will be provided in part two where I shall examine certain passages of Scripture.

Because I am approaching this from a Reformed Baptist covenantal position, it will be necessary to explain its understanding of the covenant of works that God made with the first Adam, along with subsequent covenants, namely, those made with Abraham, Moses, and the new covenant in Christ. In the second part of this work, while I concentrate on texts drawn from Paul's letters to the Romans and Galatians, I will, however, also seek to address some other texts employed by Wright, for example, 1 Corinthians 1:30 and 2 Corinthians 5:21.

It will also be necessary to examine other motifs in Wright's new perspective, for example, the idea that being saved is not about going to heaven when we die, that Israel at the time of Christ was still in exile etc. Finally, I will, contrary to what Wright claims, seek to show that penal substitution lies at the very heart of Christ's victory over sin and that

1. Although I refer to this in the singular, it needs to be borne in mind that there are many new perspectives.

3

the *Christus Victor* model should be understood within the context of Christ's propitiatory offering.

HERMENEUTIC PRINCIPLE.

It is essential to understand the nature of the various covenants because a misunderstanding here will affect other areas of theology. For example, the Reformed paedobaptist belief that the old and new covenants are of the same substance causes them to conclude that water baptism has replaced circumcision, and, of course, if the latter included children then so too must the former, and this significantly changes the way one views the makeup of the church.

God always deals with his people through covenant, and when interpreting a given text or passage one should consider which of God's covenants the person(s) alluded to are under, for example, are they under the covenant of works or the covenant of grace? The old or the new covenant?

Scripture reveals two primary covenants– the covenant of works made with Adam and the new covenant made with Christ.[2] Both men are federal heads, all humanity was represented by Adam, and those whom God has chosen to save are represented by Christ. We are all either under the first Adam, and under the covenant of works, where we stand condemned because of sin or else under Christ, the second Adam, and under the new covenant. There is no alternative or third position.

There is only one covenant of grace and this is the new covenant. There is no other covenant, for example, the old covenant, for which Christ is the mediator, hence, to benefit from his mediatorial work one must belong to this covenant. All of God's people, whenever and wherever they may have lived, be it before or after Christ's redemptive work, have been the recipients of new covenant blessings. Therefore, central to my understanding of Scripture is the belief that there is no salvation outside of the new covenant, as John Frame succinctly states:

> [T]he work of Christ is the source of all human salvation from sin: the salvation of Adam and Eve, of Noah, of Abraham, of Moses, of David, and of all of God's people in every age, past, present, or future. Everyone who has ever been saved has been

---

2. Many speak of the covenant of grace, I will, however, refer to this as the new covenant because this is the only covenant where salvific grace is found.

saved through the new covenant in Christ. Everyone who is saved receives a new heart, a heart of obedience, through the new covenant work of Christ.[3]

Or as Woolsey puts it:

Christ was their Mediator too. Though his incarnation had not yet happened, the fruits of it still availed for the fathers. Christ was their head . . . So the men of God in the Old Testament were shown to be heirs of the new. The new covenant was actually more ancient than the old, though it was subsequently revealed. It was 'hidden in the prophetic ciphers' until the time of revelation in Christ.[4]

One objection frequently raised when one speaks of new covenant blessings being available before the covenant's ratification concerns the words uttered by Jeremiah when he alludes to the covenant that will be made in the future, being "after those days" (Isa 31:31; Heb 8:10). Clearly, if it was futuristic and "after those days" how could the fruits thereof be available to those who lived before "those days"? Understanding the answer to this question is vital for understanding the unity that exists in Scripture concerning the way of salvation. John Owen, who was arguably the greatest theologian the English speaking world has ever produced, anticipated this, explaining it in the form of a question and answer:

First, 'This covenant is promised as that which is *future*, to be brought in at a certain time, "after those days," as has been declared. But it is certain that the things here mentioned, the grace and mercy expressed, were really communicated unto many both before and after the giving of the law, long ere this covenant was made; for all who truly believed and feared God had these things affected in them by grace: wherefore their effectual communication cannot be esteemed a property of this covenant which was to be afterwards made.

Ans. This objection was sufficiently prevented in what we have already discoursed concerning the efficacy of the grace of this covenant before it was solemnly consummated. For all things of this nature that belong unto it do arise and spring from the mediation of Christ, or his interposition on behalf of sinners. Wherefore this took place from the giving of the first promise; the administration of the grace of this covenant did

3. Frame, *Systematic Theology*, 79–80.
4. Woolsey, "The Covenant in the Church Fathers," 42–43.

therein and then take its date. Howbeit the Lord Christ had not
yet done that whereby it was solemnly to be confirmed, and that
whereon all the virtue of it did depend.[5]

Before Christ came in the flesh, the new covenant existed in the
form of a promise, with its formal legal establishment occurring when
Christ completed his work. Those Old Testament individuals who believed in the promise were made partakers of new covenant blessings
because this covenant had a retrospective efficacy. From the first revelation of the promise in Genesis 15, salvation in the Old Testament was
always through the promise and participation in the new covenant. All
other covenants, e.g., those made with Abraham, Moses, and David, did
not alter the essential fact that salvation comes through believing in the
promise. They were, what we might call, subsidiary covenants.

My approach assumes that all other covenants are not as the paedobaptists would have us believe, simply different administrations of
the one covenant of grace, but conditional covenants, separate from the
covenant of grace or new covenant. These conditional covenants were dependent upon man's obedience for their temporal blessings; an obedience
he was incapable of providing. One can think of it as the 'carrot and stick'
principle. These conditional covenants held up the carrot of temporal
blessings upon obedience, with these serving as a type of the antitype that
is found in the new covenant. They served to show human inability, for if
man was incapable of attaining temporal blessings, then how much less
is he capable of attaining that which is spiritual and eternal. Inevitably,
Israel failed to abide by the covenantal conditions, and when her sin became overbearing to the point of endangering the nation, God, through
his prophets, would remind her of her covenantal responsibilities, and
the consequent temporal punishment. This punishment was the stick.
Even this temporal punishment served as a type, typifying that which
awaited those who refused to believe in the promised Messiah. What we
essentially have then is a covenant(s) whose conditions have to be obeyed
to secure blessings and the threat of punishment for failing to fulfill the
conditions. Israel would always fail and, in her failure, God would point
to another covenant, one in which all the conditions had been kept by the
Messiah spoken of in the prophets.

The problem with the Jews was that they afforded the subsidiary
covenants an efficacy they never possessed. These covenants spoke of

5. Owen, *Works*, 22, 147.

temporal curses and blessings, and were in themselves typical of the eternal blessings available to all those in the new covenant. Only, of course, with the latter, all the conditions have been fulfilled by Christ. The Jews wrongly believed the old covenant to be unto salvation, associating it with those eternal blessings that lay only in the domain of the new covenant. This is very much what we see in the new perspective, for example, in his exile motif Wright speaks of Israel's exile under the old covenant, and rightly says that this was the result of the Deuteronomic curse, but he then makes the mistake of interpreting Jesus' curse-bearing death in this context, while failing to emphasize the fact that Jesus' death and the reconciliation he has accomplished for both Jews and Gentiles was the antitype, that of which the Deuteronomic curse was but a type. The punishment or exile of Israel served to typify the exile Jesus saves his people from, which is nothing less than the separation from God under the original covenant of works. This is again a major weakness with the paedobaptist paradigm, believing the old covenant to be an earlier version or administration of the covenant of grace, they then ascribe to the old what only belongs to the new covenant, and thereby they invest the old with a degree of efficacy it never possessed. This will become more apparent as we proceed. It is important to keep in mind the fact that the only covenant of which Jesus Christ is the mediator is the new covenant, it, therefore, makes no sense to look for salvation outside of this covenant.

The Old Perspective

THE OLD PERSPECTIVE IS that understanding of salvation associated with the Protestant Reformers; men like Luther, Calvin, and Zwingli. It is often referred to as the Lutheran Perspective, principally because of the emphasis Luther placed on sin and justification in his answer to the question, "What must I, a sinner, do to be saved?" Along with the doctrine of total depravity, the most important doctrine to come out of the Reformation was Luther's rediscovery of justification by faith alone. This rediscovery was the spark that ignited the Protestant Reformation.

Luther's tumultuous life as an Augustinian monk and his quest to find acceptance with God came to an end when he understood that God had provided in his Son both the forgiveness of sins and a positive righteousness. On coming to a knowledge of the truth as revealed in Romans 1:17, "The righteous shall live by faith," Luther commented: "Then I grasped that the justice of God is that righteousness by which through grace and sheer mercy God justifies us through faith. Thereupon I felt myself to be reborn and to have gone through open doors into paradise . . . This passage of Paul became to me a gate to heaven."[1] It was justification by faith alone that became, as Calvin declared, "the main hinge on which religion turns,"[2] and by "religion" he meant the Protestant Faith.

The Reformers believed all humanity to be by nature sinful. All fell in Adam, and we have all inherited Adam's sin and sinful disposition. We are all guilty before God, not only because of the first or original sin but because of our own actual sins. It is because of sin that we are all estranged from God and exiled, and incapable of being reconciled to him by anything we might do. What is needed is for another to take our place and do what we are incapable of doing, thereby making God propitious

---

1. Bainton, *Here I Stand*, 49–50.
2. Calvin, *Institutes*. 3:11.1.

toward us by taking away his punishment, and, also, securing a righteousness without which, none can stand in the presence of the holy God.

The old perspective, or so Wright would have us believe, saw in first-century Judaism a legalistic religion, where the Jews believed that through their own works, or as Wright says, "pulling themselves up by their own moral bootstraps,"[3] they could achieve salvation. This, however, is something of a caricature. The Jews believed that they were God's special people because they were the recipients of the law, they were God's covenantal people. It was because of this that they believed their works were acceptable to God. They were, however, as we shall see, looking to the wrong covenant; one that offered no possibility of life, but only condemnation and death.

The law as revealed on Mount Sinai was a revival of the covenant of works made with Adam, only where there was a possibility for Adam to provide covenant obedience, there was now, since the fall of Adam, no such possibility; it is now a law, because of the weakness of the flesh, only unto death. This is shown in the manner in which the law was given, in "blazing fire and darkness and gloom and a tempest" (Heb 12:18). Indeed, so terrifying was the sight that Moses said, "I tremble with fear" (v.21). This all signified condemnation.

The Reformation view tells us that God sent his Son into the world to do what sinful man is incapable of doing. God himself became a man like us, yet without sin, to bring man unto himself. He was born in the natural way, born under God's law, in order that he might redeem his people from that law (Gal 4:4). He did this through his vicarious obedience to both the law's penal and preceptive demands. Traditionally this has been expressed in terms of Christ's active and passive obedience. This formula, if it might be referred to as such, is used simply to, "emphasize the two distinct aspects of our Lord's vicarious obedience."[4] In the former, Jesus met the preceptive demands of the law by perfectly obeying God's commandments. God the Father vented his holy wrath against sin by punishing his own Son. In his passive obedience, he offered satisfaction to the penal demands of the law by taking upon himself, as our vicar, the full weight of God's punishment. In the words of Murray, he "took care of our guilt and perfectly fulfilled the demand of righteousness."[5] One

---

3. Wright, *What St Paul Really Said*, 113. (subsequently referred to as *WSPRS*).

4. Murray, *Redemption Accomplished and Applied*, 15.

5. Ibid., 22.

does, however, need to be careful not to disassociate Christ's preceptive and penal obedience. As Turretin reminds us: "the two things are not to be separated from each other. We are not to say as some do that the 'satisfaction' is by the passive work of Christ alone and the 'merit' by his active work alone. The satisfaction and merit are not to be thus viewed in isolation, each by itself because the benefit in each depends upon the total work of Christ."[6] What we can say is that, in the words of Witsius: "from his very infancy, and through the whole course of His life, especially the close thereof, he endured all manner of sufferings, both in soul and body, humbling, nay, emptying himself, and being obedient to the Father unto death, even death of the cross…in time he fully performed for his people all that the law required in order to obtain a right to eternal life."[7] Shedd, again emphasizes the importance of Christ's active and passive obedience:

> When a criminal has suffered the penalty affixed to his crime, he has done a part, but not *all* that the law requires of him. He still owes a perfect obedience to the law, in *addition* to the endurance of the penalty. The law does not say to the transgressor: "If you will suffer the penalty, you need not render the obedience." But it says: "You must both suffer the penalty and render the obedience." Sin is under a *double* obligation; holiness is under only a *single* one. A guilty man owes both penalty and obedience; a holy angel owes only obedience.
>
> Consequently, the justification of a *sinner* must not only deliver him from the penalty due to disobedience, but provide for him an equivalent to personal obedience. Whoever justifies the *ungodly* must lay a ground both for his delivery from hell, and his entrance into heaven.[8]

It is because of God's holy nature that eternal life cannot be granted until the precepts of law have been perfectly fulfilled, nor can sin be forgiven without sin being atoned for. Jesus kept the law that Adam broke, the very law under which humanity stands condemned, as Calvin so rightly expressed, "For we hence infer, that it is from Christ we must seek what the law would confer on anyone who fulfilled it; or, which is the same thing, that by the grace of Christ we obtain what God promised in the law

---

6. Turretin, *Institutes of Elenctic Theology*, 448.

7. Witsius, *The Economy of the Covenants* 402.

8. Shedd, *Dogmatic Theology*, 2:539–540.

of works."[9] It is all of God, his redemptive work in his Son provides both his just verdict in regard to the sinner, and displays God's own justice. This is why Paul remarked that, in Christ, God is both the "just and the justifier of the one who has faith in Jesus" (Rom 3:26).

Though it might appear obvious, it must be clearly stated that Jesus' work would count for nothing if it remained external to us. In his mercy, not because he sees anything good in us, God chooses at a moment in time to call those for whom Christ died into fellowship with Jesus Christ (1 Cor 1:9). He regenerates the individual, taking away his heart of stone and replacing it with a heart of flesh (Ezek 36:26). Through God's gift of faith, God justifies the believer and adopts him into his family. This faith is itself the result of God's work in the heart, it is said to be a gift because it is nothing less than a natural consequence of the new birth in Christ (Eph 2:1–10).

Luther said that justification by faith alone was a teaching by which the church either stands or falls:

> The article of justification is the master and prince, the lord, the ruler, and the judge over all kinds of doctrines; it preserves and governs all church doctrine and raises up our consciences before God. Without this article, the world is utter death and darkness... If the article of justification is lost, all Christian doctrine is lost at the same time... This doctrine is the head and the cornerstone. It alone begets, nourishes, builds, preserves, and defends the church of God: and without it the church of God cannot exist for one hour...In short, if this article concerning Christ-the doctrine that we are justified and saved through Him alone and consider all apart from Him damned.[10]

If Jesus had only fulfilled the law's penal demands it would still be necessary to provide the necessary obedience to the law's preceptive requirements. In the believer's justification, there is a two-way transaction, exchange, or imputation. The righteousness that Christ secured by his perfect life in conformity to the law is imputed to the believer's account and the believer's sin is imputed to Christ. In the words of Calvin, "we explain justification simply as the acceptance with which God receives us into his favor as righteous men. And we say it consists in the remission of sins and the imputation of Christ's righteousness."[11] All of this happens

9. Calvin, Institutes, 2.17.5.

10. Luther, What Luther Says, 703.

11. Calvin, Institutes III. XI.2.

because God has by his Spirit, united the sinner with Christ, hence, on the basis of this union, all that Christ achieved becomes the possession of all who believe.

Justification is a forensic and declarative act, whereby the sinner is declared by God to be perfect on account of what Christ has done for him. Jesus could do this for his people because, in the words of Buchanan, "He identified Himself with His people and acted toward God as their substitute and representative. His legal liability on their account depended on His taking their law-place, and becoming answerable for them at the bar of divine justice."[12] The Second London 1689 Baptist Confession tells us that believers are "justified whole and solely because God imputes to them [reckons as their righteousness] Christ's righteousness. He imputed to them Christ's active obedience to the whole law and His passive obedience in death."[13]

It is important to bear in mind that the person who is declared justified is still, in himself, sinful; while the guilt of sin has been removed its pollution remains. It is the ungodly who are justified (Rom 4:5). Once justification is accomplished, then starts the process of progressive sanctification; that process by which the sinner is conformed to the very image of the glorified Christ. This will not be accomplished until the resurrection of the physical body on the return of Christ.

Justification is not simply, as Wright maintains,[14] a judge finding one to be in the right. It is, rather, an announcement, a forensic declaration that one is in the right because one is *in Christ*; the declaration is made in virtue of the sinner's identification with Christ. The judge then sees not the sinner's sin, but all that Christ achieved. The sinner is then viewed by God as being righteous because he has become part of Christ. This is why Paul can speak of a Messiah, "who of God is made unto us wisdom, and righteousness, and sanctification, and redemption" (1 Cor 1:30). This union with Christ is the source of the believer's justification, as Venema tells us, "the believer's justification on the basis of the imputation of Christ's righteousness is but a way of saying that the believer is justified

12. Buchanan, *Justification*, 299.

13. 1689 Baptist Confession of Faith 11:1.

14. Although Wright does not see those passages that speak of justification in terms of a righteousness secured by another and then imputed to the believer, he does, nevertheless, adopt more of a Reformation view of the believer's union with Christ from passages like Romans 6.

by virtue of his or her judicial connection with the work of Christ. Imputation is a corollary of union with Christ, not an alternative to it."[15]

Good works within the old perspective are always the result of salvation and never the cause. The believer was once a slave to unrighteousness, "to impurity and lawlessness" (Rom 6:19), however, following his
salvation in Christ, "having been raised with him through faith in the
powerful working of God" (Col 2:12), he is now a slave to righteousness
that leads to his sanctification (Rom 6:19). The believer now walks in
Christ, "rooted and built up in him, and established in the faith" (Col
2:7).

Although the believer's spirit has already been raised to newness
of life (Rom 8:11), his mortal body is still in its sinful state and will not
be renewed until the last day, when all past and present believers will
be given a body like unto Christ's glorified physical body. The believer's
journey in this world is marked by a tension between his resurrected
spirit and sinful body.[16] As the apostle says, "For the desire of the flesh
are against the spirit, and the desire of the spirit[17] are against the flesh,
for these are opposed to each other, and keep you from doing the things
you want to do" (Gal 5:17). I have, written spirit with a lower case, this is
because in this text Paul is speaking, not of the Holy Spirit, but his own
resurrected spirit. The believer is therefore called upon to put to death the
deeds of the body (Rom 6:19). He is in this life to produce good works in
presenting his body as a slave to righteousness that leads to sanctification
(Rom 6:19).

As will be shown later, Wright caricatures the old perspective, implying that it embraces a view of life after death that amounts to some
kind of vague, nebulous existence where eternity will be spent in an immaterial realm.[18] Nothing, however, could be further from the truth. We
look forward to a time when our spirits will be reunited with our glorified
bodies, bodies that will dwell upon a new earth in a new heavens.

---

15. Venema, *The Gospel of Free Acceptance in Christ*, 245

16. One must not confuse this with what the Gnostics believed. They considered
matter to be intrinsically evil. Christianity, on the other hand, sees our present physical
body as being polluted by sin, and we look forward to a time when it will be replaced
by a glorified sinless physical body.

17. In the ESV Spirit begins with a capital.

18. Wright, I believe, does believe in the intermediate state, but this is surprisingly
missing from his latest book, *The Day the Revolution Began."*

Concerning any future judgment, the believer will never be judged in regard to his justification. Justification is past-tense. It is something that is once and for all true for all those who are in Christ. Any future judgment will concern not the believer's position, but certain prizes for those already saved. There will never be, as Wright believes, a future justification based on the believer's post-salvation works.

The New Perspective(s)

IN REGARD TO THE NPP, I want to briefly look at the works of Krister Stendahl, E.P. Sanders, and James D.G. Dunn before I examine Nicholas Tom Wright's position in more depth. There are others who have directly or indirectly contributed to the NPP, for example, Claude Montefiore, George Foot etc. One of the difficulties with this subject is that there are many new perspectives, and they tend not to agree with each other. As J. Ligon Duncan put it: "There is no such thing as 'the New Perspective on Paul' if you mean a unified, uniform, comprehensive theory or mode of interpretation about which there has come to be a broad consensus of agreement."[1] It is because of this concern raised by Duncan that I will address only Wright's position.

KRISTER STENDAHL

In 1963 Stendahl delivered a very influential paper entitled *The Apostle Paul and the Introspective Conscience of the West*. According to Stendahl, the Western church started to go off the rails in its approach to Paul from the time of St Augustine, and this was very much compounded in the Protestant Reformation, as he puts it, "The Augustinian line leads into the Middle Ages and reaches its climax in the penitential struggle of an Augustinian monk, Martin Luther, and in his interpretation of Paul."[2] Error crept in because the wrong questions were being asked; questions that had to do with the individual's conscience and what the individual needed to do in order to be saved. He believes that "the West for centuries has wrongly surmised that the biblical writers were grappling with problems

---

1. Duncan, *Attractions of the New Perspective (s)*.
2. Stendahl, *Paul Among the Jews*, 85.

which no doubt are ours, but which never entered their consciousness."[3] The old perspective had been guilty of misreading Paul. According to Stendahl the "Reformation interpreters have read Luther's experience back into the writings of Paul, rather than comprehending Paul on his own terms," believing that "our conception of Paul is the product of medieval thought in the Western world that would have been completely foreign to those in the period of Second Temple Judaism."[4] Sanders comments that "Stendahl argued that . . . the usual (Lutheran) interpretation of Paul's view of righteousness by faith is historically erroneous since it understands the doctrine as freeing one from the guilt of an 'introspective conscience', while Paul had not suffered such a dilemma."[5]

Stendahl maintains that Luther's reading of what Paul said "has been reversed into saying the opposite to his original intention."[6] The Reformers misunderstood the Jewish problem, believing that they were attempting to achieve peace with God by their own works, essentially, justification by works, whereas Stendahl believes that Paul was concerned with something very different:

> The Problem we are trying to isolate could be expressed in hermeneutical terms somewhat like this: The Reformers' interpretation of Paul rests on an analogism when Pauline statements about Faith and Works, Law and Gospel, Jews and Gentiles are read in the framework of late medieval piety. The Law, the Torah, with its specific requirements of circumcision and food restrictions becomes a general principle of "legalism in religious matters." Where Paul was concerned about the possibility of Gentiles to be included in the messianic community, his statements are now read as answers to the quest for assurance about man's salvation out of a common human predicament.[7]

He sees little or no evidence in Scripture for the old perspective's interpretation of the law as something that makes men aware of their wretchedness. He states that "God's mighty hammer bringing complacent sinners to despair has little support in Paul. The roots of the notion are rather problems peculiar to the modern West."[8]

3. Stendahl, "The Apostle Paul", 95.

4. Cooper, *The Righteous One*, 3–4.

5. Sanders, *Paul and Palestinian Judaism*, 437.

6. Stendahl, "The Apostle Paul", 87.

7. Ibid., 86.

8. Westerholm, *Perspectives Old and New on Paul*, 149.

Stendahl rejects the more orthodox understanding of Paul's Damascene experience that insists it concerned his conversion or rebirth and associates it more with the apostle's call to preach the gospel to the Gentiles, "There is not- as we usually think-first a conversion, then a call to apostleship; there is only the call to work among the gentiles."[9] While Paul's great concern was the inclusion of the Gentiles, "his statements are now read as answers to the question for assurance about man's salvation out of a common human predicament."[10] When Paul spoke about justification his chief concern was the church's identity and to show that the law should not be imposed upon the Gentiles. He was most certainly not thinking about how the individual might be saved and inherit eternal life.

E. P. SANDERS

Stendahl's work, "like a cloud no bigger than a man's hand, gave promise of the coming storm. The storm broke with the publication in 1977 of *Paul and Palestinian Judaism.*"[11] This effectively provided the impetus for the development of the NPP.

Sanders maintains that in order to understand the New Testament's relationship to Judaism one must first understand the Judaism of the time. To this end, Sanders researched Second Temple Judaism, a period from BC 200 to AD 200. He saw the old perspective as being wrong, principally because it has been based on a Judaism from a later age. Regarding justification, he is of the opinion that "Many Christians, both in the Reformation and the Counter-Reformation traditions, have done themselves and the church a great disservice by treating the doctrine of 'justification' as central to their debates, and by supposing that it described the system by which people attained salvation." [12] When, therefore, the old perspective interprets Paul in regard to doctrines like justification by faith, it is, so he would have us believe, guilty of anachronism. In other words, the old perspective is charged with interpreting Paul's letters in the context of a Judaism that did not exist in the first century. Not only this, but Sanders maintains that our understanding of the New Testament owes much to Medieval Roman Catholicism.

---

9. Stendahl, "The Apostle Paul", 84–5.

10. Ibid., 86.

11. Neill and Wright, *The Interpretation of the New Testament*, 372.

12. Wright, *WSPRS*, 158–9.

The Reformers, men like Luther, Calvin, and Zwingli saw Roman Catholicism as a legalist religion, one based on good works. He tells us that "Luther's problems were not Paul's, and we misunderstand him if we see him through Luther's eyes."[13]

They then took this understanding and applied it to the Judaism of Paul's day. Their view of first-century Judaism was then, in the words of Sanders, the result of "the retrojection of the Protestant-Catholic debate into ancient history, with Judaism taking the role of Catholicism and Christianity the role of Lutheranism."[14]

From his research into Palestinian Judaism Sanders saw a very different Judaism from the Reformers legalist portrayal. He saw Paul arriving at a solution, namely, salvation in Christ before he became aware of man's plight. He essentially reversed the traditional understanding, so instead of believing that Paul became aware of sin and condemnation before he turned to Christ, he was, rather, reconciled with Christ before he turned his attention to the law. In the words of Venema, "Paul's understanding of the human plight was a kind of by-product of his view of salvation."[15] So the apostle's view of sin was shaped by his understanding of the salvation he recognized in Christ, where "Paul, in effect, starts from the basic conviction that Christ is the only Saviour of Jews and Gentiles and on this basis develops a doctrine of law and human sinfulness corresponding to it."[16]

He is of the opinion that Paul criticised the law because salvation is only found in Christ, however, having said this, he embraced a very different understanding of the Jewish relationship to the law from that of the old perspective. Paul does not criticise the Judaism of his day for believing in the possibility of keeping the law. By this, he did not mean a perfect obedience to God's moral law, but an acknowledgment that whilst the Israelites did break the law, they were, by correctly administering the sacrificial system, granted the forgiveness for their transgressions. So the keeping of the law relates not to perfect obedience, as the Reformers believe, but to the proper administration of the Mosaic administration.

---

13. Sanders, *Paul A Very Short Introduction*, 58.

14. Sanders, *Paul and Palestinian Judaism*, 57.

15. Venama, *Gospel of Free Acceptance*, 101.

16. Ibid., 101.

Sanders saw in Judaism a religion of grace and coined the term "covenantal nomism". He identifies essentially eight characteristics of first century Judaism.

> The 'pattern' or 'structure' of covenantal nomism is this: (1) God has chosen Israel and (2) given the law. The law implies both (3) God's promise to maintain the election and (4) the requirement to obey. (5) God rewards obedience and punishes transgression. (6) The law provides the means of atonement, and atonement results in (7) the maintenance or re-establishment of the covenantal relationship. (8) All those who are maintained in the covenant by obedience, atonement and God's mercy belong to the group which will be saved. An important interpretation of the first and last points is that election and ultimately salvation are considered to be by God's mercy rather than human achievement.[17]

Although Israel entered the covenant solely on account of God's grace, staying in the covenant was dependent on obedience to God's law, "Salvation is by grace but judgment is according to works; works are the condition of remaining 'in' but they do not earn salvation."[18] According to Wright, Sanders thus, "at a stroke, cut the ground from under the majority reading of Paul, especially mainline Protestantism."[19] Sanders summarizes covenant nomism as "one's place in God's plan . . . established on the basis of covenant and that covenant requires as the proper response of man his obedience to his commands, while providing means of atonement from transgression."[20]

If, however, as Reformed Baptists believe, this covenant made with Israel is a different covenant from the covenant of grace, being a type of the latter, then Sanders position is undermined. I hope to show that the grace of God in choosing Israel, its redemption from Egypt and being given Canaan, served to typify the grace unto spiritual redemption in the new covenant. Although, in its application, the new was before the old covenant. Thus, while the covenantal stipulations were a type promising temporal blessings on the condition of obedience, these served to highlight the work of the antitype, namely the obedience of Christ in the new covenant. It is my contention that Sanders, and those who follow him,

17. Sanders, *Paul and Palestinian Judaism*, 17.
18. Ibid., 543.
19. Wright, *WSPRS*, 19.
20. Sanders, *Paul and Palestinian Judaism*, 75.

are wrong because of the way they apply what belongs only to the new covenant in Christ to those who knew only the jurisdiction of the conditional old covenant. It amounts from a failure to appreciate that these are two radically different covenants, and whilst the old pointed to the new covenant, it contained promises of conditional temporal blessings which were always beyond the reach of those under its regime.

Although Sanders, and other advocates of the NPP, correctly maintain that Second Temple Judaism had nothing in common with Pelagianism, they fail to consider its resemblance with semi-Pelagianism. One cannot argue with the fact that Sanders' view comes pretty close to this. Semi-Pelagianism is the belief that salvation involves both works and grace, where the people are by grace placed in the land, but the continuance of land possession is based on their works. Grace plus works is at the very heart of Roman Catholic soteriology, it should, therefore, be borne in mind that the Reformers were far from wrong when comparing Second Temple Judaism and Roman Catholicism.

Whereas the Reformers placed justification in the context of soteriology, Sanders considered it more in terms of ecclesiology. It had to do not with whether one was saved, but with whether one was included amongst God's people; with whether one was in the covenant. Essentially, then, it was about the identification of the church. Justification is not, as the old perspective would have us believe, concerned with the imputation of righteousness, but rather, with who is "in" the new covenant community. The Jews were using "the works of the law," to maintain their exclusivism, namely, laws about food, circumcision etc., to prevent Gentiles from becoming members of the new covenant or being justified.

The Jews considered themselves as belonging to God's people to the exclusion of the Gentiles simply because they were in possession of the law, and their problem lay in their failure to appreciate the fact that with the new covenant there was now a "new way of entrance into the number of God's covenant people, a way equally open to Jews and Gentiles who put their faith in Jesus Christ."[21] From this, it appears, one can glean that Sanders considered the new covenant as commencing only after Christ, and, in keeping with the paedobaptist paradigm, wrongly maintains that before the arrival of the new covenant there was a way unto God through the old covenant.

---

21. Venema, *Gospel of Free Acceptance in Christ*, 103.

The righteousness of God is given a very different interpretation from that of the Reformers where it is something that is imputed. Rather, it has to do with maintaining one's status as a member of God's covenantal people. Sanders tells us that, "In Paul's usage, to 'be made righteous' ('be justified') is a term indicating, getting in, not staying in the body of the saved. Thus, when Paul says one cannot be righteous by works of law, he means that one cannot, by the works of the law 'transfer to the body of the saved'. "[22] The problem with the Jews was not their legalism but their exclusivity, believing that the Gentiles could not achieve covenantal status without embracing certain aspects of the law, such as its dietary requirements and circumcision.

The phrase "works of the law" is not, in the words of McGrath, "to be understood (as Luther suggested) as the means by which the Jews believed they could gain access to the covenant; for they already stood within it. The works of the law are to be seen as an expression of the fact that the Jews already belonged to the covenant people of God, and were living out their obligations to that covenant."[23] This assumption that the Jews were God's special people is a recurrent theme, and, as we shall see, it is a theme that fails to adequately distinguish between that earthly typical redemption that occurred in the exodus with that spiritual redemption that comes only through Christ.

It is worth pausing here to ask whether Sanders' take on Second Temple Judaism is correct. Wright fully accepts what Sanders said about the type of Judaism that existed at the time of Christ. If one can, however, show that Sanders was wrong in his deductions about Second Temple Judaism the foundation of the new perspective will be shown to have been built upon sinking sand. The question is: Did some within Second Temple Judaism believe in a works righteousness? Were the Reformers more right, than wrong? There is, in fact, a lot of evidence to show that works righteousness was present. We see this in the Apocrypha in, for example, *2 Esdras*, which includes *4 Ezra* in chapters 3-14. In *Ezra* we find a number of references to a works-based righteousness:

> For you have a treasury of works laid up with the Most High. (*4 Ezra* 7:77)

---

22. Ibid.

23. McGrath, *IUSTITIA DEI*, 28.

> The Day of Judgment is decisive and displays to all the seal of truth . . . For then everyone shall bear his own righteousness or unrighteousness. (4 Ezra 8:77)
>
> For the righteous, who have many works, laid up with you, shall receive their reward in consequence of their own deeds. (*4 Ezra 8:77*)

Another work within Second Temple Judaism is the *Testament of Abraham*. Again, we find references to works righteousness:

> The two angels on the right and on the left recorded. The one on the right recorded righteous deeds, while the one on the left recorded sins. The one who was in front of the table, who was holding the balance, weighed the souls (*T. Ab. A* 12:12-13).
>
> The Commander-in-Chief said, "Hear, righteous Abraham: Since the judge found its sins and its righteous deeds to be equal, then he handed over neither to judgment nor to be saved, until the judge of all shall come . . . If [one] could acquire one righteous deed more than one's sins, one would enter in to be saved. (*T. Ab. A* 14:2–4).

In the *Psalms of Solomon* we are told that:

> The Lord is faithful to those who truly love him, to those who endure his discipline, to those who live in the righteousness of his commandments, in the Law, which he has commanded for our life. The Lord's devout shall live by it forever. (*Psa. Sol.* 14: 1–3).
>
> Our works are in the choosing and power of our souls, to do right and wrong in the works of our hands, and in your righteousness you oversee human beings. The one who does what is right saves up life for himself with the Lord, and the one who does what is wrong causes his own life to be destroyed. (*Psa. Sol.* 9: 4-5)

There are many similar texts[24] in, for example, and various Rabbinic literature, the Dead Sea Scrolls etc. What is interesting is the way Sanders tries to brush these texts aside, unsuccessfully, I might add. In regard to Ezra, while he acknowledges that it does present a works righteousness, he seems to suggest that because it is polemic in nature, written against the backdrop of Roman oppression, it cannot be considered as a true representation. Again, while acknowledging the fact that there are texts

---

24. Wright places significant emphasis on a text known as 4QMMT. For a discussion of this see Tom Holland's *Tom Wright and the Search for Truth* pp. 316–331.

from the period that provide evidence contrary to his position, he nevertheless, views these as not reflecting the Jewish beliefs from the times, "It is true that there are some sayings which do indicate that God judges strictly according to the majority of a man's deeds . . . this can by no means be taken as Rabbinic doctrine."[25] It seems to me that Sanders has done a kind of balancing act with the texts, suggesting that if those that refer to grace outnumber those that speak of a works righteousness, it is only the former that should be considered as providing a true understanding of Second Temple Jewish beliefs.

Sanders's confidence that his ideas about covenantal nomism clearly represents what was consistently believed in Second Temple Judaism is far from watertight, and his conclusions are ambiguous. Imagine one 2000 years into the future doing research into Christianity in the 21st century, only to conclude that the majority of Christians espoused the beliefs of Roman Catholicism, and then interpreted all the evidence accordingly, this is essentially what Sanders has done to the Judaism of Jesus' day. One can only endorse the words of D. A. Carson:

> But covenantal nomism is not only reductionistic, it is misleading, and this for two reasons. Firstly, deploying this one neat formula across literature so diverse engenders an assumption that there is more uniformity in the literature than there is . . . Sanders's formula is rather difficult to falsify, precisely because it is so plastic that it hides more than it reveals, and engenders false assumptions that lose the flavour, emphases, priorities, and frames of reference of these diverse literary corpora . . .[26]

D. G. DUNN

Like Sanders, Dunn agrees that the standard Reformation understanding of 1st century Judaism was wrong, believing the "picture of Judaism to be drawn from Paul's writings is historically false."[27] He, on the whole, accepts Sanders understanding of Second Temple Judaism. However, he does not see eye-to-eye with Sanders on everything, for example, Dunn takes a more positive position concerning "the works of the law." In all,

---

25. Sanders, *Palestinian Judaism*, 143.

26. Carson, *Justification and Variegated Nomism*, 544.

27. Dunn, *The New Perspective on Paul*, 101.

Dunn essentially takes from Sanders that which he considered good, and incorporates this into his own ideas.

Agreeing with Sanders that the apostle's reference to the "works of the law", did not mean works of the legalistic righteousness one associates with the Reformers, he, unlike Sanders, concludes that the apostle in referring to "the works of the law" had in mind a kind of boundary marker; one that served to distinguish between who was in God's community and those who were not. Apart from the moral law, Dunn tells us that there were "other works of the law which from early times particularly marked out Israel's set-apartness to God and separation from the nations."[28] In this regard, he alludes especially to circumcision, Sabbath keeping, and food laws. To back up his understanding he makes reference to extra-biblical sources, for example, the Dead Sea Scrolls. So whilst he acknowledges that the works of the law "does, of course, refer to whatever the law requires," however, when comparisons are made between Israel and the nations, "certain laws would naturally come more into focus than others", in particular, "circumcision and food laws."[29] Elsewhere he states that the works of the law "functioned as identity markers . . . to identify their practitioners as Jewish in the eyes of the wider public."[30] We will see more of this when we examine Wright's understanding of particular texts.

Interestingly, Dunn acknowledges that prior to Christ's arrival people were justified by faith, that from man's side salvation is "wholly and solely of faith."[31] Yet, having said this he appears to associate God's people with those within the old covenant. To quote Westerholm, "The law spelled out how those who were already God's people were to live within the covenant. Its righteousness was this 'secondary righteousness,' to be practiced by those already in possession of 'primary righteousness' based on faith."[32] The problem I have with this is simply that Dunn is here associating salvation with the old covenant, making the assumption that all Israel was somehow in possession of a "righteousness based on faith."

Again, like Sanders, Dunn has a very different understanding of Justification from that of the Protestant Reformers. In the words of Venema:

28. Ibid., *The Theology of Paul the Apostle*, 356.

29. Ibid., 358.

30. Wright, "The New Perspective on Paul", 192.

31. Dunn, "The Theology of Galatians" 83.

32. Westerholm, *Perspectives Old and New*, 190.

Because Paul's doctrine has its roots in the traditional Jewish understanding of God's 'righteousness' as his covenant faithfulness, he uses the term, 'to be justified', to refer to God's gracious acknowledgement of his covenant people. Though Judaism also taught Justification by faith, the Christian gospel fulfils and surpasses Judaism by teaching that God *now* graciously acknowledged *all who believe in Christ* as his covenant people. The gospel announces that God in his righteousness has declared that all who believe in Christ, whether Jews or Gentiles, are acceptable to him. Justification is by 'faith alone' in the sense that faith in the crucified and risen Christ is now the *chief badge* of covenant membership.[33]

It is important to note that in recent years Dunn has come to see the weakness of his position and now believes that when Paul refers to "the works of the law" he means all that the law requires.[34]

N. T. WRIGHT

Nicholas Thomas (Tom) Wright is undoubtedly the greatest publicist for the new perspective, and it is principally his views I want to examine before criticising them in the light of Baptist covenant theology. Wright is a New Testament scholar who has authored over fifty books. He is currently Distinguished Research Professor of New Testament and Early Christianity at St Andrews University in Scotland. He has held a number of prestigious roles in the Church of England, and prior to his present position, he was, for seven years, Bishop of Durham. His position in the Church of England provided him with an essential vehicle for the dissemination of scholarly debates to the man in the pew, and he has, in the words of Waters, "done more than any other single individual to mediate NPP exegesis into the mainline and evangelical churches."[35] He possesses that rare gift of making complex ideas intelligible and extremely interesting. This has enabled him to bridge the gap that usually exists between the rarefied world of academia and the average churchgoer. Wright claims to be thoroughly evangelical. His credentials were clearly manifested in his work on the resurrection.[36] He said in an interview, "My only agenda

33. Venema, *The Gospel* 114.

34. See Garwood P. Anderson, *Paul's New Perspective* 46.

35. Waters, *Justification*, 119.

36. Wright, *The Resurrection of the Son of God*, London, SPCK, 2003.

here is to be as close as I can possibly get to what Paul actually says. And I really don't care too much what the different later Christian traditions say. My aim is to be faithful to Scripture here."[37] No evangelical would disagree with this. It is somewhat ironic that Wright's position concerning two justifications and the idea of imputed righteousness are similar to the 17th century Puritan Richard Baxter (1615–91).

When Wright is discussed, people tend to converge to polar extremes, to quote Schreiner, "Some are inclined toward an uncritical adulation of his scholarship, while others to an uncritical denigration."[38] Wright has a lovely engaging writing style, and secondly, he makes one think and ask questions about one's own position. Many have been convinced by his arguments due to the forthright way he puts his points across. I was somewhat surprised, especially in light of Wright's refusal to believe in God's wrath, and the imputation of righteousness, to find Tom Holland saying in reference to Wright's many books, "These works have assured many that he is a trustworthy teacher of the church and that for the most, the early suspicions concerning his proposals concerning justification have evaporated."[39] It is because of this that many readers can come away believing the case to be settled, especially if they are not grounded in Reformed theology. What Carl Trueman said about the new perspective's understanding of Luther is relevant here:

> The story is told of Bernard Shaw being taken to see the lights of Las Vegas late one night. 'It must be beautiful' he commented, 'if you can't read.' I confess that the New Perspective approach to Luther strikes me a little that way. It too must be beautiful, but only if you don't know the primary texts. Its portrait of the Reformer certainly appears persuasive and impressive but that is because of the confidence with which it is presented to an audience whose culture generally considers novelty a good thing and tradition to be bad. A close examination of his theology in context reveals this portraits [sic] manifest deficiencies and palpable errors.[40]

Wright puts his points across with a marked degree of rhetorical flourish that encourages the unwary and unsuspecting reader to accept what he says. Again, many find themselves agreeing with Wright because

37. Wright, Transcript of interview by Trevin Wax.

38. Schreiner, *Faith Alone*, 240

39. Holland, *Search for Truth*, 34-35.

40. Trueman R. Carl, *A Man More Sinned Against than Sinning?*

they have been swayed by his academic credentials. They assume that he must, because of these, have researched all there is to research, and that such a man's approach is candor personified. Such a person, however, does not exist, not only in the field of theology but in any discipline. We also need to bear in mind that there is nothing new under the sun. So-called new theologies are usually, on closer examination, reworked versions of what has gone before. The Christian needs to realize that the truth of God's word is revealed not to the clever or the wise but to the foolish and that God uses the foolish to confound the wisdom of the wise (1 Cor 1:18–24).

Evangelicals then listen to what Wright has to say, and it is this that makes his thoughts on Paul dangerous. I say dangerous because error is mixed in with much that is right (excuse the pun). Surprisingly, as well as Tom Holland, Wright's work has been endorsed by a number of evangelicals, for example, Peter Enns, a professor at Westminster Theological Seminary, Philadelphia, in positively reviewing a two-volume work of Wright's sermons could write, "I recommend these volumes without reservation to all who wish to know better the biblical Christ and bring the challenge of this Christ to those around them."[41] He was suspended from the seminary in 2008 because he had differing views about inspiration. George Grant could say when reviewing *What Saint Paul Really Said*, Wright "weighs the evidence and finds that only historic biblical orthodoxy has sufficiently answered the thorny questions of the apostle's contribution to the faith.... Mr. Wright pores over the New Testament data with forensic precision to add new weight to a conservative theological interpretation."[42] For an evangelical to say this is something of a mystery, to say the least. This, again only serves to confuse the average Christian, and to give Wright's teaching a degree of legitimacy within evangelical circles.

If any should consider the NPP to be more of an annoyance, what might be called: a storm in a teacup" than a serious threat, they should bear in mind the words of Kim Seyoon:

> Since the Reformation, I think no school of thought, not even the Bultmanian school, has exerted greater influence upon Pauline scholarship than the school of the New Perspective. With its radical reinterpretation of Paul's gospel, especially the

41. Enns, Peter, "Book Review" 328.
42. Grant, George, "Books: Revisiting the Apostle"

doctrine of justification, on the basis of Ed P. Sanders's definition of Second Temple Judaism as covenantal nomism, the New Perspective in many respects overturning the Reformation interpretation of Paul's gospel. The potential significance of the school for the whole Christian faith can hardly be exaggerated.[43]

The very fact that one can read Wright's works, e.g., *What Jesus Really Said*, and be no wiser at the end of the book; that one can expend so many words and still leave many readers confused should be a sign that something is askew. While I would not go as far as John Macarthur, his words speak for many of Wright's readers: "I have read his writings and they are a mass of confusing ambiguity, contradiction, and obfuscation, academic sleight of hand. I cannot tell you what he believes."[44]

When reading Wright one should bear in mind that heresy never enters the church under a placard declaring itself to be a deviant teaching, but usually on the back of an orthodox teaching, and even then when one is least expecting it. Wright says much that Reformed believers can wholeheartedly agree with, yet, like the Trojan Horse, error is allowed to creep in unawares, as it has done in many evangelical churches, contaminating some of Protestantism's most cherished beliefs. This has especially been the case in some Presbyterian churches in North America. I would have to agree with Eveson that Wright's "interpretation of the Pauline texts is arguably the strongest challenge to the traditional Protestant approach that has yet appeared."[45]

The new perspective tends to employ the same terminology as Reformed Protestantism, but changes the meaning. Many get caught out by this because they only hear what they believe to be orthodoxy.

Wright is not slow in criticizing the old perspective, yet he does not interact with any of the primary sources. For example, while he does not shy away from criticizing the Reformers, he never appears to interact with their teachings. One will find in Wright's work very little in regard to actual quotes from the Reformers' many works. One can only draw the same conclusion as Fesko, namely, that when Wright "does allude to its teachings he usually does so with superficial caricature. Because Wright does not examine primary sources and their historical setting, his claims of distortion lack cogency; they are suspended in mid-air apart from any

---

43. Seyoon, *Paul and the New Perspective*. XIV.

44. MacArthur, John MacArthur Refutes False Teacher.

45. Eveson, *The Great Exchange*, 126.

factual foundation."[46]This may well be because "For NT scholars, the history of interpretation usually starts somewhere in the early nineteenth-century with little to no attention given to the previous eighteen hundred years of church history."[47]

Although he does not see eye-to-eye with Sanders and Dunn on everything, the main trajectory of Wright's thought is similar. He tells us that Sanders's new take on Paul "dominates the landscape [of Pauline studies], and, until a major refutation of his central thesis is produced, honesty compels one to do business with him. I do not myself believe that such a refutation can or will be offered; serious modifications are required, but I regard the basic point as established."[48]

He accepts Sanders's views when they fit with his purpose. Wright says that "one of the great ironies in Sanders' position is that he has never really carried through his reform into a thorough rethinking of Paul's own thought. He contents himself with a somewhat unsympathetic treatment of Pauline themes."[49] It appears that Wright sees himself as having picked up the mantle and considers himself to be a modern-day Luther, ushering in a new Protestant Reformation.

WRIGHT AND THE RIGHTEOUSNESS OF GOD.

In traditional Protestantism, the "righteousness of God" manifests itself in two ways. First, it denotes God's righteous anger against sin, for example, as manifested in Romans 1-3. Secondly, it represents God's faithfulness to the new covenant in that God himself has achieved through the work of his Son a righteousness for all who believe. What Wright considers to be the main motif, namely, God's faithfulness to his covenant promises, the old perspective takes as a given and it is found in Christ's fulfillment of the original covenant of works.

Wright is of the opinion that the Reformed school has "systematically done violence to that text for hundreds of years, and . . . it is time for the text itself to be heard."[50] He believes it is wrong to perceive of righteousness as something that can be given or imputed to another. Rather,

46. Fesko, *Deficiencies in Wright's Theology*,
47. Fesko, "John Owen . . .", 18.
48. Wright , *WSPRS*, 20.
49. Ibid., 19.
50. Wright, *WSPRS*, 51.

God's righteousness must be seen as representing his unfailing loyalty to his covenantal promises:

> God's 'righteousness', especially in Isaiah 40-55, is that aspect of God's character because of which he saved Israel, despite Israel's perversity and lustiness. God has made promises; Israel can trust those promises. God's righteousness is thus cognate with his trustworthiness on the one hand, and Israel's salvation on the other. And at the heart of that picture in Isaiah there stands, of course, the strange figure of the suffering servant through whom God's righteous purposes are finally accomplished.[51]

God's righteousness is then covenant orientated; it is God demonstrating his faithfulness to his covenant. He initially chose Israel to be his people; a people who were to be a light to the nations, and, although Israel failed in its mission, God, however, has remained faithful, and he has through Jesus, the faithful Israelite, done what fallen humanity was incapable of doing.

Of course, both Reformed Baptists and paedobaptists believe in God's faithfulness to his covenant; it is what God secured in his Son's preceptive and penal obedience to his covenantal requirements. None would disagree with Wright in maintaining that there must be covenant faithfulness before there can be salvation. As we will see, however, Wright's idea of covenant faithfulness and that of Reformed Baptists is markedly different. The latter's understanding of the old perspective takes umbrage with him because, not only has he mixed up the covenants, but he has essentially limited God's faithfulness, separating it from his faithfulness to himself as the just God, denying entirely the imputation imputation of God's righteousness in Christ.

WRIGHT AND JUSTIFICATION

Justification for Wright is very different from what one finds in orthodox Protestantism. It is not concerned with how sinners find favor with God, indeed, it is not even about soteriology, but, rather with ecclesiology, with the identification of those who are in the covenantal family. Furthermore, justification has nothing to do with the imputation of righteousness, but with God finding one to be in the right because one is counted among the covenant people.

51. Ibid., 113.

Carl Trueman, while he does not specifically mention Wright, clearly has him in his sights when referring to the new perspective's deviant understanding of justification:

> To put it bluntly, it seems to me that the current revision of the doctrine of justification as formulated by the advocates of the so-called New Perspective on Paul is nothing less than a fundamental repudiation not just of that Protestantism which seeks to stand within the creedal and doctrinal trajectories of the Reformation but also of virtually the entire Western tradition on justification from at least as far back as Augustine.[52]

Wright believes the Reformers saw in first century Judaism a people who were seeking acceptance with God through their good works, and, no doubt, he would fully endorse the words of Duncan:

> At the heart of the NPP's critique of both Protestant and Catholic teaching interpretation of Paul is the charge that Reformational-era theologians read Paul via a medieval framework that obscured the categories of first century Judaism, resulting in a complete misunderstanding of his teaching on justification. The ideas of "the righteousness of God," "imputation," and even the definition of justification itself-all these have been invented or misunderstood by Lutheran and Catholic traditions of interpretation.[53]

Again, Wright agrees with Alister McGrath in his two-volume work on justification, where he states the doctrine:

> Has come to develop a meaning quite independent of its biblical origins, and concerns the means by which man's relationship with God is established. The church has chosen to subsume its discussion of the reconciliation of man to God under the aegis of justification, thereby giving the concept an emphasis quite absent from the New Testament. The 'doctrine of justification' has come to bear a meaning within dogmatic theology which is quite independent of its Pauline origins.[54]

Are we seriously to believe that the old perspective's understanding of justification is "independent of its Pauline origins"? That "Imputation is nowhere to be found, in either the teaching of Paul or anywhere else in

52. Truman, "The Portrait of Martin Luther".
53. Duncan, "The Attractions of the New Perspectives on Paul," 16–30.
54. McGrath, *Iustitia Dei. A History of the Doctrine of Justification*, Vol. 1, 1–2.

the New Testament? I have no doubt that McGrath's words fit a number of views on this doctrine from the church's long history, however, I find it hard to accept that such a critique can be applied to the Reformed position. One could well ask what it is that makes McGrath's interpretation true, while others, as qualified as him, argue the opposite? While I agree that there is more to our salvation than justification, for example, regeneration, adoption etc., which, it should be noted, the Reformers would not deny, it is Wright's understanding of this doctrine that falls short of the mark. He tells us that: "I want my people to understand and hear the whole word of God, not just the parts of it that fit someone's system."[55] I don't believe there is any who would not acquiesce with this. However, at the subconscious level, it is very difficult, if not impossible, for one to put aside all previous ideas. One finds that Wright has contorted the word to make it fit his own system; effectively he has taken a preconceived idea and has galloped through the New Testament with it.

Although agreeing with the Reformers that justification is expressed forensically in the terms of the law court, Wright denies any two-way exchange:

> In the Hebrew law court, the judge does not give, bestow, impute, or impart *his own "righteousness"* to the defendant. That would imply that the defendant was deemed to have conducted the case impartially, in accordance with the law, to have punished sin and upheld the defenceless innocent ones. "Justification" of course means nothing like that. "Righteousness" is not a quality or substance that can thus be passed or transferred from the judge to the defendant. The righteousness of the judge is the judge's own character status, and activity, demonstrated in doing these various things. The "righteousness" of the defendants is the status they possess when the court has found in their favour. Nothing more, nothing less. When we translate these forensic categories back into their theological context, that of the covenant, the point remains fundamental" the divine covenant faithful is not the same as human covenant membership.[56]

To be accepted by God there must be both the forgiveness of sin, and also the imputation of that which Christ secured by his active obedience. This is why the believer's possession of Christ's righteousness lies at the

---

55. Wright, *WSPRS*, 167.
56. Wright, "Romans and the Theology of Paul" 3:38–39.

heart of the Reformed Baptist understanding of justification. The words of Owen are particularly pertinent here

> It is not enough to say that we are not guilty. We must also be perfectly righteous. The law must be fulfilled by perfect obedience if we would enter into eternal life. And this is found only in Jesus (Rom 5:10). His death reconciled us to God. Now we are saved by his life. The perfect actual obedience that Christ rendered on earth is that righteousness by which we are saved. His righteousness is imputed to me so that I am counted as having perfectly obeyed the law myself. This must be my righteousness if I would be found in Christ, not having my own righteousness which is of the law, but the righteousness which is of God by faith (Phil 3:9).

The holy character of God cannot, as Wright claims, just find in favor of the sinner, he can only do this if an actual righteousness is present. To do otherwise would be to undermine his holiness. Again, to quote Owen:

> For that any may be reputed righteous—that is, be judged or esteemed to be so—there must be a real foundation of that reputation, or it is a mistake, and not a right judgment; as any man may be reputed to be wise who is a fool, or be reputed to be rich who is a beggar. Wherefore, he that is reputed righteous must either have a righteousness of his own, or another antecedently imputed unto him, as the foundation of that reputation. Wherefore, to impute righteousness unto one that hath none of his own, is not to impute him to be righteous who is indeed unrighteous; but it is to communicate a righteousness unto him, that he may rightly and justly be esteemed, judged, or reputed righteous.[57]

Maintaining Christ's redemptive work to have only secured the forgiveness of sins is to grossly misconstrue the true nature of justification. In the words of John Murray:

> . . . it is prejudicial to the grace and nature of justification to construe of it merely in terms of remission. This is so to such an extent that the bare notion of remission does not express, nor does it of itself imply, the concept of justification. The latter means not simply that the person is free from guilt but is accepted as righteous; he is declared to be just. In the judicially constitutive and in the declarative sense he is righteous in God's

---

57. Owen, *Works*, 5, 166.

sight. In other words, it is the positive judgment on God's part that gives to justification its specific character.[58]

The righteousness that God bestows on those in Christ occurs instantaneously, being a forensic declaration that one is now considered both forgiven and righteous. It is a consequence of being placed into Christ. This righteousness must not be confused with that which the apostle refers to in texts like Romans 8:3–4, where the righteousness is not forensic, but concerns the believer's progressive sanctification. In regard to justification, the only ones who may dwell in his presence are those who meet the necessary criteria, namely, possessing righteousness and being forgiven for sin, as the Psalmist said, "O LORD, who shall sojourn in your tent? Who shall dwell on your holy hill? He who walks blamelessly and does what is right and speaks truth in his heart" (Ps 15:1–2). Wright, however, maintains that forgiveness and membership of the covenant is sufficient:

> Paul can assume that "reckoning righteousness apart from works and "not reckoning sin against someone" are equivalents. The covenant, we must always remind ourselves, was there to deal with sin; when God forgives sin, or reckons someone within the covenant [=justifies], these are functionally equivalent. They draw attention to different aspects of the same event.[59]

He holds no punches in regard to the imputation of righteousness, maintaining it to be impossible, even nonsense:

> To imagine the defendant somehow receiving the judge's righteousness is simply a category mistake. That is not how the language works . . . If and when God does act to vindication his people, his people will then, metaphorically speaking, have the status of 'righteousness. That makes no sense all.[60]

He again states:

> If we use the language of the law-court, it makes no sense whatsoever to say that the judge imputes, imparts, bequeaths, conveys or otherwise transfers his righteousness to either the plaintiff or the defendant. Righteousness is not an object, a substance or a gas which can be passed across a courtroom.[61]

---

58. Murray, *Collected Works*, 2, 218.

59. Wright, *The letter to the Romans*, 493.

60. Wright, *WSPRS*, 99.

61. Wright, *WSPRS*, 98–99.

We must not forget that any analogy can be taken to extremes and cari-catured. We need to heed the words of Carson, commenting on a popular caricature of the courtroom analogy:

> In certain crucial ways, human law courts, whether contempo-rary or ancient Hebrew courts, are merely analogical models and cannot highlight one or two crucial distinctions that are necessarily operative when the judge is God. In particular, both the contemporary judge and the judge in the Hebrew law court is an administrator of a system. To take the contemporary court: in no sense has the criminal legally offended judge . . . the crime has been 'against the state' or 'against the people' or 'against the laws of the land.' In such a system, for the administrator of the system, the judge, to take the criminal's place would be pro-foundly unjust; it would be a perversion of the justice required by the system, of which the judge is the sworn administrator. But when God is the judge, the offence is always and necessarily against him. He is never the administrator of a system external to himself; he is the offended party as well as the impartial judge. To force categories of merely human courts onto these uniquely divine realities is bound to lead to distortion.[62]

Wright has forced categories that are applicable to human courts onto the court of God, this has resulted in a gross distortion of justifica-tion. Campbell cuts to the chase, aptly summing up the implications of Wright's understanding of justification:

> For all its laboured originality, this theory completely fails to escape the gravitational pull of the religion of self-justification. Wright's basic thrust is that justification is no legal fiction: the believer is righteous, but when all is said and done it is our own personal righteousness. It is inherent, not imputed. We are asked to stand on the rock of our own covenant-keeping. Could that have given Martin Luther peace? Could it give any of us peace? On the contrary, our hope would ebb and flow with every rise and fall in the tide of our personal spirituality.[63]

To suggest that the righteousness which justifies is like an object, sub-stance or a gas[64] is to grossly misconstrue the teaching. It needs to be emphasized that it is not God's intrinsic or essential *righteousness* that is

---

62. Carson, "Atonement in Romans" 132.

63. Campbell, *A Faith To Live By*, 166–167.

64. Wright, *WSPRS*, 98.

imputed to the believer, but the righteousness secured by Christ in his redemptive work. In Wright's depiction of the courtroom, there is only the judge and the defendant in attendance, when, in fact, there are three persons, a judge, a defendant, and a third party, who is Christ. Indeed, the "Reformers and their heirs labored the point that it is Christ's successful fulfilment of the trial of the covenant representative that is imputed or credited to all who believe. His meritorious achievement, not God's own essential righteousness, is imputed."[65] Unlike God's own essential righteousness, that righteousness secured by Christ's covenantal obedience did not always exist. It is the result of what the third-party in the court has done on behalf of the defendant, and it is this that constitutes that which is imputed. About Wright's deficient portrayal of justification, Horton states, "Wright's account so far does not seem to allow for an inheritance to be actually given to anyone in particular. Justification may be forensic (that is, judicial), but there can be no transfer of assets, if you will, from a faithful representative to the ungodly."[66]

Wright again tells us that justification arises out of the believer's covenant membership. It is a declaration that one is in covenant with God. The problem with this is, to use the proverbial saying, "it puts the cart before the horse." He limits justification to a relationship that has already been established when it is justification is that establishes the relationship. There can be no membership of the new covenant without it, as Gathercole tells us, "God's act of justification is not one of recognition but is, rather, closer to creation. It is God's determination of our new identity rather than a recognition of it."[67]

Those who are justified have peace with God, "therefore, since we have been justified by faith we have peace with God through our Lord Jesus Christ. Through him we have also received access into this faith in which we stand, and we rejoice in the hope of the glory of God" (Rom 5:1). Such justification did not only apply after Christ, for Paul uses Abraham as an example. If, as Wright maintains, justification means that one belongs to the covenant, and if this was the position of Israel, then he seems to be saying that all had peace with God. To put this in the form of a syllogism:

- Justification means one is a member of the covenant

65. Horton, *Covenant and Salvation*, 104.

66. Ibid., 105.

67. Gathercole, "The Doctrine of Justification in Paul" 229.

- Being a member of the covenant means having peace with God
- All Israelites were members of the old covenant
- Therefore, all Israelites had peace with God

Yet we know that it was only the remnant who had peace with God, even though all Israel belonged to the old covenant. Far from knowing the peace of God, the nation found itself under God's wrath.

GOD IS JUST

Many ask the question: "Is not God unjust for allowing an innocent party to be punished for the sins of others?" Christ was innocent, and to maintain, as some do, that God then punished our sins in his flesh is to call God's justice into question because a righteous judge would not punish an innocent party for the sins of another, "He who justifies the wicked and he who condemns the righteous are both alike an abomination to the LORD" (Prov 17:15).

Caricaturing the analogy occurs when one makes a like-for-like comparison of the things being compared without allowing for the differences that might exist between them. For example, the human court analogy can only go so far in drawing out certain principles. It must not be pressed too far. There are aspects of God's judgment that simply do not fit with our human categories. When Jesus was punished in our stead he was not an unrelated third-party. It is not as if one who is separate from us suffered for our wrongdoing. No, Christ, because of our union with him and his union with us, became liable for the consequences of our sins. It is a union which ensures that God the Father views Christ and his people as constituting one body, Christ being the head, and we his members. As John Owen puts it:

> [God] might punish the elect either in their own persons, or in their surety standing in their room and stead [as their substitute]; and when he is punished, they also are punished [in their representative]: for in this point of view the federal head and those represented by him are not considered as distinct, but as one; for although they are not one in respect of personal unity, they are, however, one,-that is, one body in mystical union, yea one mystical Christ;-namely, the surety is the head, those

represented by him the members; and when the head is punished, the members also are punished.[68]

In the application of redemption, our union with Christ was communicated to us when God effectively called us into fellowship with himself at
a point in time (1 Cor 1:9). Having said this, in another sense, one can say
that our union with Christ began before the foundation of the world in
the covenant of redemption, "Blessed be the God and Father of our Lord
Jesus Christ, who has blessed us in Christ with every spiritual blessing
in the heavenly places, even as he chose us in him before the foundation
of the world, that we should be holy and blameless before him. In love
he predestined us for adoption to himself as sons through Jesus Christ,
according to the purpose of his will" (Eph 1:3-5). It is important to realize
that we have been blessed because, even before our salvation, we were in
some sense "in Christ." God the Father gave a people to the Son (John
6:37–39), and it was for these that Christ carried out his redemptive
work. All those whose names are written in the book, as it were, are those
for whom Christ suffered and died. This is why, even before our union
with Christ in time, Jesus could justly suffer for his people's sins because
the union that exists between him and his people makes him liable for his
people's sins and righteousness.

One also needs to take into account that in the death of Christ the
Father was not an entirely separate being, an onlooker, so to speak. He
was not like the human judge who remains distanced from the acts of the
accused. The Father too suffered in the death of Christ. This is something
of a mystery; one that lies in the union that exists between the persons of
the Trinity. One must, of course, avoid modalism, which teaches that the
one God can appear in three different modes, where the Son can become
the Father etc., this leads to patripassionism, a teaching which maintains
that it was the Father who died upon the cross. I point this out because it
is often not taken into consideration when human analogies are used in
speaking about Christ's sufferings. For example, Wright, in criticising the
human categories of the law court metaphor does tend to caricature the
analogy, not sufficiently expressing the limits of such language, the fact
that it can at best be compared to looking through opaque glass into the
mind of God.

Justification should not be viewed in isolation from the believer's
union with Christ. They must go together. The idea of a judge somehow

68. Owen, *Works*, 10, 598.

walking across a courtroom and giving something of his own to the defendant is, to say the least, liable to misunderstanding. It is at best a somewhat imperfect attempt to capture an aspect of what justification involves. Wright overplays the human aspect, not alluding to the fact that God's courtroom is very different from that of which we are familiar with. Talking in human terms, if I do a good work for someone else, say, serve a prison sentence so that the person in question does not have to, I will always remain external to the person. This is not what happens in justification. The believer is in possession of Christ's actual righteousness because he is in Christ. In my simple example, for it to bear any resemblance to justification, one would have to say that not only did I serve the prison sentence, but that the person on whose behalf I did so must be looked upon by the appropriate authorities as if he actually served the sentence with me. This could not occur because, unlike with the relationship that exists between the believer and Christ, there cannot exist the necessary union between us. So, of course, righteousness cannot be given to one who is external from the giver; it can, however, become one's very own in virtue of a person being made at one with him who possesses the righteousness. This is why the apostle keeps using the phrase "in Christ," it is because of being "in him" that the believer possesses all that belongs to him. Our union with Christ and our resulting justification exist in a dimension unavailable to human courts in that it is the result of the Spirit's supernatural activity whereby we are engrafted into Christ, where we possess all that he achieved in his redemptive work.

Furthermore, in a human court, if the judge pronounces a guilty criminal innocent it is because he has made a mistake. It is a mistake based on his lack of knowledge about the crimes of the accused. This, however, cannot happen in God's law court because God is omniscient. He will never acquit the guilty. If he did he would be a very unjust judge. That he does so is entirely because of the fact that when he looks upon the sinner he sees Christ's righteousness and sacrificial death. He sees this rather than the sinner because the sinner is in Christ's body; flesh of his flesh, blood of his blood. One does not separate Christ, the head from the body, and neither must one separate justification from union with Christ.

Again, Wright does not see justification as a one-time past event in the believer's life, but simply the first of two justifications. So while acknowledging the believer's present justification, he emphasizes an eschatological aspect or a future justification. Although one may be considered as presently or provisionally justified, with the final verdict being brought forward, one's works now begin to play a role. They do so to the point where one's future justification will be based on these works, on the life one has lived. He is essentially applying to the Christian what Sanders said about Israel, where God by his grace rescued Israel and placed her within the land; having done so he made her continuance in the land dependent upon works, in a similar manner the believer is placed in the covenant community, but abiding there depends on his works.

Wright is somewhat remiss in not adequately explaining how those within the nation were saved in the time preceding Christ's arrival, and in discerning the different covenants and their respective ends. He leaves one asking a number of questions. Is he saying that prior to Christ's arrival salvation was possible by keeping the law? Is he telling us that faith became the badge of covenantal membership only for New Testament believers? He does, however, state, that "Those who adhered in the proper way to the ancestral covenant charter, the Torah, were assured in the present that they were the people who would be vindicated in the future."[69] What does he mean by "ancestral covenant charter"? This is where he appears to mix up or confuse the covenants. If he has the old Mosaic covenant in mind he is remiss of the fact that no salvation was available under this covenant. Paul, in the third chapter of his second letter to the Corinthians, "contrasted his own ministry with the ministry of Moses. Moses ministry was incapable of bringing life, what it did bring condemnation; the apostle refers to the law as a "ministry of death" (2 Cor 3:7). Indeed, if it were possible to bring in a law life, then righteousness would have been by the law (Gal 3:21–22). As Holland reminds us: "Whatever Rabbinic Judaism thought of Israel's status, Paul's point seems diametrically opposed to it. The law is not evidence of acceptance, but of separation. Israel was a prisoner to sin."[70] Paul's own ministry, on the other hand, brings righteousness and life. Wright, it seems, is here making the classic paedobaptist blunder in affording the old covenant an efficacy it never possessed. Israel was never expected to keep the covenant even to secure temporal blessings, let alone anything related to the spiritual realm. Joshua was under no illusions about Israel's position, telling the people that they were "not able to serve the LORD" (Josh 24:19).

69. Wright, *WSPRS*, 119.

70. Holland, *Contours of Pauline Theology*, 209.

CONTINUING EXILE AND THE LAW

One of the central planks of Wright's position is the idea that the Israel of Jesus' time was still in exile.[71] If he means the nation was disqualified from those blessings we read of in Deuteronomy 27–30 because of its disobedience he is unquestionably correct. Wright, however, goes further, believing that when Jesus became a curse, as we read of in Galatians 3:13, he did so with only the Jewish exile in mind. He sees Jesus as having brought to an end Israel's exile, and in so doing misses the essential fact that any exile Israel may have been under was but a type of the exile which all humanity is born into as a result of Adam's sin. Holland correctly distinguishes between these two exiles:

> The Jews when sent into exile received fully what they deserved. Once they suffered what God saw was appropriate (Isa 51:17), then he delivered/redeemed them. But Paul is not talking about salvation at a temporary level where it was possible to be punished and the past put behind. Rather he means an eternal exile from the presence of God, a totally different exile from anything depicted in Israel's history . . . The nature of the exile caused by Adam is of a different dimension and order, and required an act of cosmic redemption. The nature of this exile is of such significance that the offender cannot possibly make atonement.[72]

Although there is no longer any need for typical Israel, humanity's exile under the covenant of works has not gone away. All people remain, unless they believe in Christ, under God's condemnation because of their transgressions and sins.

It was only a minority from within the nation, the remnant, who saw beyond the various sacrifices and believed in the one promised. Only these knew justification. The country they looked forward to in faith was a different country from that promised to earthly Israel. They desired a "better country, that is a heavenly country: wherefore God is not ashamed to be called their God, for he hath prepared for them a city" (Heb 11:16). They looked not to those conditional promises as found in Deuteronomy 27–29, that were part of the old covenant and spoke only of the type, rather, they looked to the new covenant expressed in the promise, and benefited from the spiritual and eternal blessings secured by Christ, the antitype. True Israelites, the true children of Abraham, "all died in faith,

71. For example, see *Revolution* 105–6.
72. Holland, *Contours of Pauline Theology*, 170.

not having received the promises, but having seen them afar off, and were persuaded of them, and embraced them, and confessed they were strangers and pilgrims on the earth" (Heb 11:13).

Concerning "the works of the law" Wright takes the same position as Sanders in regard to covenantal nomism, and adopts Dunn's understanding that the works of the law are concerned with boundary markers, i.e., the apostle does not have in mind a legalistic keeping of the law in an attempt to gain God's favor, but those aspects of the law that certain Jews were using to exclude Gentile membership of the covenant, namely, dietary laws, circumcision, the Sabbath and other holy days. One of the problems with this view, although not what Wright articulates, but his references to Israel certainly imply it, is that it assumes that Israel of old was a justified people and that these boundary markers marked them out as such. The Jews were all circumcised, they kept their holy days and the Sabbath, and this marked them as being in the covenant. Again, because of Wright's mono-covenantal position, it seems that he deems the new covenant to be a continuation of the old covenant, only in the new covenant Jesus, as the faithful Israelite, has kept the covenant that Israel was supposed to keep but didn't. It is a position that fails to appreciate the fact that these external regulations marked Israel out as being a people under, not the covenant of grace, or new covenant, but the temporal and conditional old covenant.

The law's function was not to vouchsafe acceptance before God but to show that without perfect conformity to its moral demands there could be no acceptance. To quote Holland, "The law is not evidence of acceptance, but of separation. Israel was a prisoner of sin."[73] The apostle advised the Jerusalem Council in Acts 15:6–11, saying that the law should not be imposed on the Gentiles, Why? because it was a yoke that they were unable to bear. Clearly, he is not speaking of "boundary markers" because these could hardly be considered as being too difficult to bear, as Holland tells us, "It would have been inconceivable for a Jew not to be circumcised, so it would have been meaningless to say that the Jews were not able to bear it. The same would be true of the other boundary markers, dietary law, and Sabbath keeping."[74]

The problem with Wright's position, as with all new perspectives on Paul, is that he relies on Second Temple Judaism to understand

73. Ibid., 209.
74. Ibid., 210.

justification and the role of the law. It may be an extreme example, but if a thousand years from now one wanted to know about the Triune God one would not go to those documents provided by today's Jehovah's Witness to explain it. By the same token, in wanting to understand the New Testament and the place of the law, one should not go to Second Temple Judaism. This is because there were a variety of different views being propounded by the Judaism of the time. As I said in the case of Sanders, the danger is that one might take one of these views, perhaps the wrong one, and seek to interpret the Scriptures accordingly. I'm not saying that we cannot learn much from Second Temple Judaism, but I am saying that great care must be taken when one tries to interpret the Scriptures in the light of this.

WRIGHT, CALVIN AND, THE REFORMATION.

Before moving on, I want to briefly examine what Wright has to say about Calvin and the imputation of righteousness. He clearly believes his position on justification to be something akin to that of the Reformer:

> As with Calvin himself, and many subsequent Reformed theologians, Sanders saw that Paul's doctrine of justification meant what it meant within the idea of 'participation', of 'being in Christ'.[75]
>
> The irony is that at this point Sanders and others, including the present writer, are standing firmly in line . . . with Calvin himself, though it is from would-be Calvinists that some of the sharpest criticism has come.[76]
>
> The idea of imputed *righteousness*, whether of God himself or, as some constructs, of Christ himself, is not the only way of addressing the question. The idea of 'imputed righteousness' was in any case, a latecomer to Reformation theology.[77]

So is Wright's position "firmly in line with" the great Reformer? In regard to the believer's "participation" and "being in Christ," one would have to say yes. One must be fair to what Wright is saying, he maintains that because of believers' union with Christ, they are in possession of all that Christ's work achieved.

75. Wright, *Paul and His Recent Interpreters*, 67.
76. Ibid., 119.
77. Ibid., 120.

The sticking point concerns the meaning of justification, and one would have to say that Wright's position is far removed from that of Calvin. This is because he fails to acknowledge imputation; something that lay at the heart of the Reformer's understanding of justification. He tells us that contemporary Calvinists consider justification as a first-order doctrine in our salvation, when, in fact, it is of secondary importance. He states that "from reading many today who claim Calvin's heritage but would be shocked to find 'justification' as a 'secondary crater.'"[78] Calvin, however, does not consider justification as a secondary anything, rather, he sees being "in Christ" and justification as soul mates. Yes, one can correctly say that justification is the result of the believer being in Christ, however, one cannot be saved without being justified, and one cannot be justified without being "in Christ." So important was justification for Calvin that he considered it "the main hinge on which religion turns."[79] This is because there can be no peace with God without it. Both our union with Christ and our justification, although we separate them logically, in terms of chronology, occur simultaneously, with one being no more important than the other. To call justification a "secondary crater" is to misunderstand Calvin

I find Wright's statement, "The idea of 'imputed righteousness' was, in any case, a latecomer to Reformation theology" rather bazaar, to say the least. Does he perhaps think that it is something Calvin and the other Reformers[80] did not fully endorse? In all probably the concept was introduced to Luther in 1519 by his close companion Philip Melanchthon. He was a Greek scholar, and it was his study of the New Testament that convinced him that the Greek word *dikaioo* meant, not as the Latin maintained, to make righteous intrinsically, but to declare righteous. It was a forensic act that takes place outside the sinner and amounts to a legal declaration by God that the sinner is righteous. It is based on the imputation of Christ's righteousness to the sinner, with the sinner's sin imputed to Christ.

---

78. Ibid.

79. Calvin, *Institutes XI*, 3: 1.

80. Luther also believed in a righteousness that is imputed to the believer, see, R. Scott Clark's article entitled: "Iustitia Imputata Christi: Alien or Proper to Luther's Doctrine if Justification?" in *Concordia Theological Quarterly*, Vol. 7:3/4, July/October 1976, pp. 269-310. In this Clark examines Luther's mature writings and unambiguously shows that he believed in the imputation of Christ's righteousness to the believer.

A cursory look at what Calvin said about justification should dispel any notion that it was a latecomer to the Reformation:

> Therefore, we explain justification simply as the acceptance with which God receives us into his favour as righteous men. And we say that it consists of the remission of sins and the *imputation of Christ's righteousness*.[81]
>
> He is said to be justified in God's sight who in both reckoned righteous in God's judgment and has been accepted on account of his righteousness.[82]
>
> Now he is justified who is reckoned in the condition not of a sinner, but of a righteous man.[83]
>
> On the contrary, justified by faith is he who, is excluded from the righteousness of works, grasps the righteousness of Christ through faith, and clothed in it, appears in God's sight not as a sinner but as a righteous man.[84]
>
> Therefore, "to justify" means nothing else than to acquit of guilt him who was accused, as if his innocence were confirmed. Therefore, since God justifies by the intercessions of Christ, he absolves us not by the confirmation of our own innocence but by the imputation of the righteousness of Christ, so that we who are not righteous in ourselves may be reckoned such in Christ.[85]

Calvin could not have expressed his belief in justification and the role that Christ's righteousness plays, more clearly. The above quotes should suffice to show that Calvin adhered to the traditional Protestant understanding of imputation.

81. Calvin, *Institutes* III, XI, 2.

82. Ibid., III, XI, 2.

83. Ibid.

84. Ibid.

85. Ibid., III, XI, 4.

The Covenant of Works

ACCORDING TO WRIGHT, "COVENANT theology is one of the main clues, usually neglected, for understanding Paul."[1] This again strikes me as something of an odd statement, especially in light of the fact that both Reformed paedobaptists and Baptists ascribe to covenant theology, and, indeed, base their entire understanding of God's dealings with man in a covenantal context. What Wright obviously means is that the old perspective has not adopted his understanding of covenant theology.

Reformed covenant theology was not invented in the 16th and 17th centuries, but refined and systematised. Wright, however, seems only too willing to distance himself from this, and, indeed, admits that he has done little reading in this area: "Like many New Testament scholars, I am largely ignorant of the Pauline exegesis of all but a few of the fathers and reformers. The Middle Ages and the seventeenth and eighteenth centuries had plenty to say about Paul, but I have not read it."[2] He caricatures the covenant of works, which he refers to as a "works contract."[3] In its place, he speaks of "a covenant of vocation,"[4] as if this is something that is neglected by the covenant of works proponents. Nothing, however, could be further from the truth. The epithet, "unbiblical," as I hope to show, is more applicable to Wright's position.

A covenant is essentially a mutually agreed promise that is based upon the fulfillment of certain conditions. It essentially has three parts: first, there is a promise made, second, the conditions are stipulated, and thirdly, there is a penal sanction laid down in case one party fails to abide by the conditions. God entered into a covenant with the first man, Adam,

1. Wright, *Climax of the Covenant,* xi, 1.
2. Wright, *Paul: In Fresh Perspective,* 13.
3. Wright, *Revolution,* 75.
4. Ibid., 73–87.

telling him that he could eat from any tree in the garden except the tree of the knowledge of good and evil (Gen 3:16,17). While not called a covenant in Scripture, it clearly had the necessary ingredients. Wilhelmus a Brakel provides a succinct definition of the covenant God made with Adam:

> The covenant of works was an agreement between God and the human race as represented in Adam, in which God promised eternal life upon condition of obedience, and threatened eternal death upon disobedience. Adam accepted both this promise and this condition.[5]

The covenant was based on the representative federal principle, the actions of our first parents had repercussions for all their posterity. When they became disobedient, God deemed us all likewise disobedient (Rom 5:12:16–17).

Concerning the 17th Century understanding of the covenant of works as put forward in the Westminster Confession, Wright states:

> Such a view of the relationship between God and humans is a travesty. It is unbiblical. It insists on taking us to a goal very different from the one held out in scripture. It ignores, in particular, the actual meaning of Israel's scriptures, both in themselves and as they were read by the earliest Christians. And it insists on a diagnosis of the human that is, ironically, trivial compared with the real thing.[6]

To call such a position a "travesty" and "unbiblical" when it has been espoused by godly men who have spent a lifetime in the Scriptures can be construed as arrogance.[7] Have they really taken it to a "goal very different from the one held out in scripture"? I don't think so. The bible is unambiguous, informing us that humanity became separated from God and placed under a curse as a result of the first Adam's disobedience. The ultimate goal of redemption is that sinners be reconciled to God, becoming a new humanity; one that is a perfect divine image bearer, living upon a new earth, within a new heaven, serving the Lord forever. To say that the old perspective's diagnosis of the human condition is trivial is itself the result of trivializing what Reformed Protestants believed.

5. Wilhemlus a Brakel, *Our Reasonable Service*, 1:355.

6. Wright, *Revolution*, 76.

7. As I have already said, while this appears arrogant, it stems from Wright's faith in his exegesis of the text. He is certainly not being deliberately arrogant.

As he so often does, Wright tends to speak disparagingly of the old perspective on a number of points before going on to say something that the old perspective fully endorses. Wright tells us that "what the bible offers is not a 'works contract' but a covenant of *vocation*. The vocation in question is that of being a genuine human being, with genuinely human tasks to perform as part of the Creator's purpose for this world."[8] He then goes on to state that, "the diagnosis of the human plight is not simply that humans have broken god's moral law—though this is true as well. This law breaking is a symptom of a much more serious disease."[9] I know of no Reformed believer who would not wholeheartedly agree with this. Since the Fall humanity has turned away from that which God called it to, worshiping the things created rather than the Creator. Individual sins are the result of humanity's fallen condition, one where the principle of sin reigns in the heart. As far as a "works contract" and "vocation" are concerned, the Scriptures speak of a vocation that is dependent on the fulfillment of a "works contract" in order to overcome the enmity that exists between God and man. It is not a question of either/or. Before sinners can embark on that vocation, or their God-given calling, where they can offer unto God their bodies in living and acceptable sacrifice, there must first be the fulfillment of certain conditions. Conditions that require perfect righteousness and a propitiatory substitutionary death.

Prior to sin, the law was unto life; it was for the justification of the righteous. Adam had been created in God's image and after his likeness (Gen 1:27), with the law of God written upon his heart. In his original righteousness, this law served to vouchsafe that all was well. Had Adam succeeded in keeping the stipulation he would have obtained eternal life for both himself and his posterity. He would have partaken of the tree of life that is now available for all believers because Christ, the second Adam, has succeeded where the first Adam failed (Rev 2:7; 22:2). When Adam[10] failed he had then to face punishment. God said to him, "for in the day that you eat of it you shall surely die" (Gen 2:17).

All of humanity is then exiled from God, unless, of course, they have been reconciled on account of Christ's completed work. When we consider Christ's work in reference to exile it is this exile one should bear in mind, not any exile that the nation of Israel experienced. As already

---

8. Ibid., 76.

9. Ibid., 77.

10. By Adam I mean Adam and Eve, our first parents.

said, when Wright alludes to Israel's exile he fails to emphasize the fact that the nation's exile was but a type of that exile that applies to all humanity because of Adam's sin.

It is important to bear in mind that the covenant of works has not gone away. God still demands perfect obedience and the punishment of sin. Man is spiritually impotent and at enmity with the God who created him, and there is no way back to God for fallen man through his own efforts, for truly, as the Psalmist says, there is no one who is righteousness before God (Psa 143:2). John Bunyan aptly portrays the relationship that now exists between the sinner and the law:

> The law was now only unto death; it was powerless to do otherwise. With the entrance of sin man lost his first estate and was banished from God's presence, God "drove out the man, and at the east of the garden of Eden he placed the cherubim and a flaming sword that turned every way to guard the way to the tree of life" (Gen 3:24). Death here meant estrangement from God. Immediately there was spiritual death, and eventually, physical or bodily death. The law, as it is a covenant of works, doth not allow any repentance unto life, to those that live and die under it. For the law being once broken by thee, never speaks good unto thee, neither doth God at all regard these, if thou be under that covenant, not withstanding all thy repentings, and also thy promise to do so no more. 'No,' saith the law, 'thou hast sinned, therefore I must curse thee, for it is even, and I can do nothing else but curse, every one that doth in any point transgress against me.' Gal. iii. 10. "The break my covenant, and I regarded them not, saith the Lord." Heb. viii. 'let them cry, I will not regard them; let them repent, I will not regard them: they have broken my covenant, and done that in which I delighted not; therefore by that covenant I do curse, and not bless; damn, and not save; frown, and not smile; I reject, and not embrace; charge sin, and not forgive it.[11]

Not only have we sinned in Adam, but we all sin daily. For there to be reconciliation it would be necessary not only to keep God's commandments perfectly, but also pay the penalty for sin. For all those living before Christ's death, it was only those who embraced the promise who were removed from their obligation to provide obedience to the covenant. About such as these, Owen states: "When this is actually embraced, that the first covenant ceaseth towards them, as unto its curse, in all its concerns as a

---

11. Bunyan, *The Doctrine of the Law and Grace Unfolded*, 502–3.

covenant, and obligations unto sinless obedience as a condition of life because both of them are answered by the mediator of the new covenant."[12]

With sin's entrance and the imposition of God's curse, God's image in man has been largely erased, although a vestige of this remains.
Prior to Sinai, although the Ten Commandments had not been explicitly
revealed as they would be later on the two tablets of stone, the requirements of what the law demanded were nevertheless written upon man's
conscience, or, as Paul says, "they have the works of the law written upon
their hearts" (Rom 2:15). This is essentially what has been called natural law. This amounted to an innate knowledge of what God demanded,
along with the knowledge that this was something impossible for sinful
humanity to provide. It would require the intervention of another, none
less than the very Son of God himself. As Augustine commented: "just
as Adam became a cause of death to those who are born of him, even
though they have not eaten of the tree, the death brought on by the eating, so also Christ was made a provider of righteousness for those who
belong to Him, even though they are entirely lacking in righteousness."[13]

12. Owen, *Works*, 22, 79.
13. Augustine, *Contra Julianum*, 305.

The Application of Salvation

BEFORE ABRAHAM

THE FIRST GLIMMER OF light occurred shortly after the first Man's sin. At the critical moment, when Adam expected to hear only the sentence of death, the Lord pronounced the fact that he was going to interpose on man's behalf through one who would be born of woman (Gen 3:15). This first promise "implied that God, instead of appearing *against* them as their enemy, was to interpose *for* them as their friend; that He had formed a purpose of grace and mercy towards them."[1] One may well find Adam among the congregation of the saved, providing he embraced the promise in faith. While prior to his fall Adam was a federal head of all his offspring, the promise was to be embraced on an individual basis. As Coxe puts it:

> It must be noted that although the covenant of grace was revealed this far to Adam, yet we see in all this there was no formal and express covenant transaction with him. Even less was the covenant of grace established with him as a public person or representative of any kind. But he obtained interest for himself alone by his own faith in the grace of God revealed in this way, so must those of his posterity be saved.[2]

Throughout the Old Testament period, this promise would become progressively more explicit; culminating in the appearance of the one promised with the formal legal establishment of the new covenant. Although the first promise was somewhat obscure, "it contained enough to lay a solid foundation for faith and hope towards God, and it was the first

1. Buchannan, *The Doctrine of Justification*, 26.
2. Coxe, "*A Discourse of the Covenants*," 57.

beam of Gospel light on our fallen world."[3] Salvation was only available
by believing this promise, and, as Denault reminds us, "As a result all
those who were saved since the creation of the world were saved by virtue
of the New Covenant which was in effect as a promise."[4]

There was a considerable time span from the fall of Adam to the arrival of Abraham. In this time, both before and after the flood, God's offer
of salvation was present and people were being saved. In those relatively
dark days, the promise was universal in that it was not chiefly revealed
to a particular nation; there was no distinction between Jew and Gentile.
Although the new covenant only existed in the form of a promise, in the
words of Owen, "It wanted its solemn confirmation and establishment by
the blood of the only sacrifice which belonged to it . . . Before this was
done in the death of Christ, it had not the formal nature of a covenant or
a testament."[5] The way of salvation, however, was the same as it is today.
Those who believed became recipients of new covenant blessings because
of its *retrospective efficacy*. All those who believed were effectually called,
regenerated by the Spirit, justified by faith and adopted into the family
of God. The only badge of membership, if one can call it that, was faith.
Those so-called "boundary markers" as the NPP refers to them, did not
apply then, and when they later did so they only related to the conditional covenant made with Israel, with its temporal blessings that were
dependent upon the people's obedience to the law.

Consider the case of Abel. How was he saved? Was the way of salvation different then from what it is today? Was it different from what it was
under the old covenant? I emphasize this because it is crucial to the case
against Wright and the way he views Israel. Abel knew right from wrong
because he had knowledge of the law's requirements upon his heart. He
was by nature a child of wrath, separated from God because of both his
own and Adam's sin. In Hebrews we are told that "By faith Abel offered to
God a more acceptable sacrifice than Cain, through which he was com-
mended as righteous, God commending him by accepting his gifts. And
through his faith, though he died, he still speaks" (Heb 11:4). No doubt
his sacrifice was acceptable to God because it was of a bloody nature,
suggesting that he, by a revelation of the Spirit of Christ, saw from afar
the blood of Christ. In faith, he would have been united to Christ and

3. Ibid., 27.

4. Denault, *The Distinctiveness*, 71.

5. Owen, *Works*, 22, 74.

made a partaker of the blessings Christ achieved in his redemptive work. And, one must remember that this was before the existence of the nation.

Old Testament saints obviously did not possess the knowledge about Christ's work that we have today; they were very much looking through a glass darkly. These saints believed the promise that God would at some future time rescue fallen man. In the age preceding the new covenant's consummation in Christ's completed work, the Holy Spirit, whom Peter calls "the Spirit of Christ" (1 Pet 1:11), was at work in regenerating his people, generating faith and uniting believers to Christ. We see the gospel going forth prior to the flood in the case of Noah. Peter tells us that it was the same Spirit of Christ who later raised Christ from the dead, who through Noah "preached to the spirits in prison" (1 Pet 3:19). Through this prophet's word God "condemned the world", yet those who believed "became heir of the righteousness which is by faith" (Heb 11:7).

The Reformed Baptist covenantal paradigm displays unity in its simplicity. There is no covenant duality within the new covenant. Salvation has always been the same, namely by exercising faith in Christ, the mediator of the new covenant. It is usual for many, if not most, Reformed theologians, when examining the way covenantal blessings in the Old Testament, refer to the "covenant of grace." In this work, I have, on the whole, done the same. It is, however, something I have not been completely comfortable with. This is because the term is not employed in the Scriptures, and also because no one has ever been saved but by the new covenant. It seems, therefore, more reasonable to say that all believers were members of the new covenant.

With God there is no favoritism, one child is not favored over another on the basis of what its parents may believe, except, of course, of finding itself in a privileged position in regard to the hearing of the gospel. Unlike Israel where all were members of the old covenant, children of believers do not become members of the new covenant simply in virtue of being born into a certain family. God is Spirit and those who worship him do so in spirit and in truth (John 4:24). The only way into Christ is by the new birth, by becoming a new creation; having a new heart of flesh. The church of God is, and always has been, the body of Christ, and Christ as the head of his church is transforming it into the image of his glorified humanity. About all the saints of God John Calvin surprisingly states:

> The children of the promise [Rom. 9:8], reborn of God, who have obeyed the commands of faith, working through love [Gal. 5:6], have belonged to the New Covenant since the world began.

This they did, not in hope of carnal, earthly, and temporal things, but in hope of spiritual, heavenly, and eternal benefits.[6]

I say surprisingly because Calvin was a paedobaptist, and the majority of Reformed paedobaptists maintain that the new covenant did not become operative until consummated by Christ.

GOD'S COVENANT WITH ABRAHAM

According to paedobaptists, the old and new covenants are not radically different from each other. The new covenant is deemed to be of the same substance as the old covenant, although a fuller and more extended version; with salvation being available under the old covenant as it would later be available under the new covenant. So we effectively have one covenant of grace applied under different administrations. What Dabney said about the new covenant applies to most paedobaptists, Wright included: "We understand that the new dispensation is an extension of the old one, more liberal in its provisions, and its grace."[7]

The Reformed Baptist position completely rejects this. We do not see the old covenant as being one of grace, and, although it contained elements of grace, there was certainly no salvation under it. Salvation is found only in Christ, the mediator of the new covenant. The Second London Baptist Confession tells us something about those in the new covenant:

> All believers are a holy and sanctified people, and that sanctification is a spiritual grace of the New Covenant, and an effect of the love of God manifested in the soul, whereby the believer presseth after a heavenly and evangelical obedience to all the commands, which Christ as head and king in His New Covenant hath prescribed to them.[8]

By "all believers" is meant all the saints of God from both before and after Christ's finished work. As Owen reminds us, "the covenant of grace was contained and prepared only in the promise, before it was solemnly confirmed in the blood and sacrifice of Christ, and so legalized or established

---

6. Calvin, *Institutes*, 2.11.10.

7. Dabney, *Lectures in Systematic Theology*, 786.

8. *Baptist Confession of Faith*, XXIX.

as the only rule of worship for the church."[9] As there is only one covenant unto salvation revealed in both testaments, so there has only ever been one true church:

> Hence it was, that at the coming of the messiah there was not one Church taken away and another set up in the room thereof, but the Church continued the same in those that were the children of Abraham according to faith. The Christian Church is not another Church, but the very same that was before the coming of Christ, having the same faith, and interest in the same covenant.[10]

It is most important to understand the case of Abraham because it will be pivotal for understanding why the Reformed Baptists disagree not only with Wright, but also Reformed paedobaptists. Their error is to confuse the covenant promised to Abraham, through which his faith was counted as righteousness, with the covenant that was concluded or established with him sometime later. To quote Pascal, "The Covenant of Grace was revealed to Abraham, but the formal covenant that God concluded with him was not the Covenant of Grace."[11] Spiritual blessings come through the promise, and Abraham himself was justified because he believed this promise, not through any covenant that was established with him.[12] Wright appears to mix up these two posterities, speaking of Israel as one homogenous people and then maintaining that it was this Israel Jesus came to save. He fails to see that, where salvation is concerned, it was only Abraham's spiritual offspring who were God's true people and who were counted amongst the saved..

Of course, at that time the new covenant, existing only as a promise, did not have those outward modes of worship that we see in the New Testament, namely, baptism and the memorial service of bread and wine. However, it was through the same faith in the promise that believers were enabled to participate in the blessings of the new covenant that would be ratified in Christ's work. It was through this covenant that all Old Testament saints were made citizens of the spiritual heavenly Jerusalem, and were seated in heavenly places in virtue of their participation in the work of Christ.

9. Owen, *Works*, 22, 82.

10. Hutchinson, *A Treatise Concerning the Covenant and Baptism*, 33.

11. Denault, *The Distinctiveness*, 116.

12. I show later why I consider the covenant in Genesis 15 to be of grace.

Sometime after Abraham had been justified by faith, a conditional covenant was made with him, and this was the covenant of circumcision. We see the conditional side of this covenant for unless one was circumcised one would end up being cut off from the people (Gen 17:14), which essentially meant death. Entrance into this covenant was essentially based on ethnicity, while entry into the promised new covenant was based on faith, to quote Hamer, the new covenant "employs a different 'technology'–a faith-based affinity union with the Bridegroom Messiah, Abraham's distant seed, not a blood union with his grandson Jacob."[13] The apostle draws out the essential differences between circumcision of the flesh that was accorded to the natural conditional seeds of Abraham and the new covenant in a number of his letters, e.g., 2 Corinthians 3. All Israelites were circumcised, because they were born to the right parents, whereas, baptism is only for those who exercise faith.

> The analogy between circumcision and baptism is plain. Infants were eligible for the former because every one of the children of Israel was, by his natural birth, within the terms of God's promise to Abraham, Isaac, and Jacob. No work of God in an Israelite was needed to make him one of the natural seed of Abraham. Natural birth made him an Israelite, and hence a proper subject for circumcision. But, to bring a sinner within the scope of the new covenant, ratified in the blood of Christ, a work of God in the heart is needed.[14]

There were then two separate covenants alluded to in the case of Abraham, one promised, the other established. There were two posterities, one spiritual, the other physical. The conditional covenant made with Abraham was made more explicit under Moses and was then referred to as the old covenant. Paedobaptists mix up the covenant promised to Abraham and the covenant concluded with him, this causes them to miss the essential point, namely, that from the loins of Abraham two peoples would come forth, one would consist of the Jews who were considered to be Abraham's seeds (plural). These are Israel according to the flesh. The other would consist of the seed, (singular), who is the Christ (Gal.3:16). The saved are counted as the same seed as Christ on account of their union with him. The old covenant was made with carnal Israel, with Abraham's seeds, while the new covenant concerned the seed in the singular, and it

13. Hamer, *The Bridgegroom Messiah*, 39.
14. Booth, *Paedobaptism Examined*, 265

was only those Jews who placed their faith in the promised seed (Christ) would correspond to spiritual Israel. As Coxe expressed it:

> Abraham is to be considered in a double capacity: he is the father of all true believers and the father and root of the Israelite nation. God entered into a covenant with him for both of these seeds and since they are formally distinguished from one another, their covenant interest must necessarily be different and fall under a distinct consideration. The blessings appropriate to either must be conveyed in a way agreeable to their particular and respective covenant interest. And these things may not be confounded without a manifest hazard to the most important articles of the Christian religion.[15]

Hodge, although a paedobaptist, clearly distinguishes between external Israel and true spiritual Israel:

> It is to be remembered that there were two covenants made with Abraham. By the one his natural descendants through Isaac, were constituted a commonwealth, an external community; by the other his spiritual descendants were constituted into a church, [invisible, of course, since that time, the only formal organisation was that of the law.] The parties to the former covenant, were God and the nation; to the other, God, and his true people. The promises of the national covenant were national blessings; the promises of the spiritual covenant (i.e., the covenant of grace) were spiritual blessings, as reconciliation, holiness, and eternal life. The conditions of the one covenant [the old] were circumcision and obedience to the law; the conditions of the other were, and ever have been, faith in the Messiah, as the seed of the woman, the Son of God, the Saviour of the world. There cannot be a greater mistake than to confound the national covenant with the covenant of grace, [that is, the old covenant with the new) and the commonwealth founded on the one, with the church founded on the other. When Christ came, the commonwealth was abolished, and there was nothing to put in its place. The church [now made visible] remained. There was no external covenant, nor promises of external blessings, on condition of external rites and subjection. There was a spiritual society, with spiritual promises, on condition of faith in Christ. The church is, therefore, in its essential nature, a company of

15. Coxe, "A Discourse of the Covenants", 72–73.

believers, and not an external society, requiring merely external profession as the condition of membership.[16]

These two strands should never be confused. To reiterate, what we see is, on the one hand, the old covenant made with carnal Israel, and on the other, the promise of the new covenant that concerns only God's elect. This dual aspect runs throughout the Old Testament. The temporal blessings we associate with the old covenant, and carnal Israel, that spoke of this-earthly blessings, served to typify the spiritual blessings available to spiritual Israel. Abraham, and all those of faith, on the other hand, looked not to the temporal sphere but to that which is eternal:

> Note that God promised to give the land of Canaan not just to Abraham's descendants but also Abraham himself. Yet Abraham never owned as much as a square foot of ground in the land of Canaan (cf. Acts 7:5) –except for the burial cave which he had to purchase from the Hittites (see Gen.23). What now was Abraham's attitude with respect to this promise of the inheritance of the land of Canaan, which was never fulfilled during his own lifetime? We get the answer to this question from the book of Hebrews. In chapter 11, verses 9–10, we read, "By faith he [Abraham] sojourned in the land of promise, as in a foreign land, living in tents with Isaac and Jacob, heirs with him of the same promise. For he looked forward to a city which has foundations, whose builder and maker is God." By "the city which has foundations" we are to understand the holy city or the new Jerusalem which will be found on the new earth. Abraham, in other words, looked forward to the new earth as the real fulfilment of the inheritance which had been promised to him—so did the other patriarchs.[17]

Failing to distinguish between these two strands, one will wrongly assume that all of Israelites after the flesh were God's true people. Wright appears to be saying that all Israel was justified even though they did not all have faith; this was a later badge of membership. The Scriptures, however, teach something different, for example, when Paul is explaining justification by faith, he alludes to the case of Abraham, showing that he too was justified in exactly the same way as New Testament saints (Rom 4:1–12). By failing to adequately differentiate between the two Israels, Wright speaks of Israel as one redeemed people, and then he assumes

---

16. Hodge, *Princeton Review*, October, 1853.
17. Hoekema, *The Bible and the Future*, 278.

that the curse-bearing significance of his death resides in Christ delivering this one Israel from its curse under exile. This kind of reasoning directly affects one's understanding of justification. If, as Wright maintains, to be justified means to be declared to belong to God's covenant community, then one would have to conclude that Israelites after the flesh were justified because they were members of such a community. However, the majority within ethnic Israel did not exhibit the badge of faith that showed they belonged to the new covenant where true salvation is to be found, so although they were from Israel they did not correspond to the true spiritual Israel.

The Sinaitic Covenant
(The Old Covenant)

THE EXILE THAT THE nation of Israel experienced under the Babylonians was but a type of the exile that all humanity is under, even from birth. The Jews effectively experienced a twofold exile. They were under exile as a nation because they failed to keep the old covenant, and, more importantly, they were exiled, with of rest of humanity, because of their position in the first Adam. Those Jews who had faith in the promise, while experiencing the nation's typical exile, were nevertheless reconciled to God in Christ, and it was only these who constituted the true Israel of God. Wright's mistake is that he starts with Israel rather than with Adam, and consequently, confuses the two Israels, failing to see the consistency through time as regards true church. He provides little or no explanation for the universal application of God's promise from Adam to Abraham, and he accords to carnal Israel a relevance it was never meant to have; attributing to it that which has only ever applied to the spiritual remnant within the nation.

Israel after the flesh experienced exile under the Babylonians because of its sin, yet those from within the nation who had been born of the Spirit would have been captive to no earthly power. The Son had set them free and they were free indeed (John 8:36). They had been reconciled to God because of the future death of his Son. So although outwardly, because they were among Abraham's ethnic seed, they experienced the temporal exile, they knew that in this world they were but pilgrims, and the Jerusalem they yearned for was something other than the earthly one. They may have been treated like children under age, not having that subjective understanding and deep assurance of their position that was given to God's people at Pentecost, however, objectively, in regard to their actual position in Christ, they were like their counterparts in the New Testament; they were saved by the same Spirit, on account of the same work of Christ.

It is because of this that I find Wright's insistence on a newly defined Israel somewhat incongruous. He believes, to quote Westerholm, "the fulfillment of God's covenant involves the redefinition of 'Israel as God's people along lines determined by grace, not race; by faith, not by the 'works' (or boundary markers) of Torah."[1] Of course, change did take place with the demise of the old covenant, for example, the barriers between Jew and Gentile were abolished, and the fullness of the gospel was to going forth to the Gentile world, this did not bring about a change within spiritual Israel.[2] God's true people in regard to their objective position in Christ has been the same from the beginning of faith. As far as the church was concerned, all that occurred was its extension with the bringing in of the Gentiles. It did not affect the fact that God's spiritual people were his new creation, but it did mean that the numbers who were incorporated into this new creation was going to significantly increase. With the coming of Christ God did not change the criterion for determining the identity of his true people. Before, during, and after the old covenant, to be God's true people, faith was and always will be, the only requirement. Wright appears to lump all of Israel together, thereby suggesting that all were God's people.

This can be seen in the way Wright views Paul's Damascus Road experience. The old perspective maintains that Paul, or Saul, as he was then known, underwent a conversion; he was born again and reconciled to the God he had formally been at enmity with. Wright's understanding of this is very different. Paul did not undergo a conversion, but simply a change in his perceptions concerning God's plan for the Gentiles. Paul was already in the covenant and saved. What he discovered in Christ was not a new life, but a new vocation. He was a faithful Jew who honored the Torah, and he was already justified, as Brian Roberson comments, "For Wright, this means that Paul didn't see himself then, or even later, as lost, in our understanding of the term, because Paul was secure in the knowledge that he was saved by grace and was now seeking to live a life pleasing to God in what is called 'covenantal nomism,' as were most of the Jews in Paul's day."[3] The problem with this is the assumption that

---

1. Westerholm, *Perspectives Old and New on Paul*, 181.

2. It did, however, provide the church, especially from Pentecost, with a much greater subjective understanding of its position.

3. Robinson, *Banner of Truth Magazine*, 2002.

Paul was already saved from his position under the old covenant. When the apostle said that none can be saved by the law, he was not alluding to something new, salvation was not at one time by the law and at a later stage through faith. No matter how hard an Israelite like Paul tried to keep the law, it was powerless to make him one of God's true people.

One must not think that ethnic Israel gave way to the New Testament church. I say this because the true church of God, one that consists of all the saved, has been in existence from the very beginning. In ethnic Israel, the true church consisted only of those who believed. The true Jew was not one who had been circumcised in his flesh only, but one who knew that circumcision of the heart (Rom 2:29). By failing to adequately separate the two Israels, Wright does not sufficiently acknowledge the fact that "not all who are descended from Israel belong to Israel, and not all are children of Abraham because they are his offspring" (Rom 9:7).

It should also be noted that paedobaptists, Wright included, believe the new covenant to have become operative, and its blessings accessible, only after Christ's completed redemptive work. They are then, logically speaking, left having to acknowledge salvation prior to Christ, for example, from Moses to Christ, as emerging from the old covenant whose mediator was Moses rather than Christ (Heb 3:2-5). Moreover, because the blessings referred to by Jeremiah 31:31-34 and Ezekiel 36:26-27 are only applicable to those in the new covenant one would have to conclude that these blessings were unavailable to all those who lived prior to the new covenant. Old Testament saints must then be excluded from blessings that, in actual fact, applied to all of God's people from the first person who embraced the promise. A somewhat precarious position to say the least.

Accepting Sanders view, Wright seems to be of the opinion that the Reformed Protestant position teaches some kind of pure legalism in regard to Judaism. I agree that there has been a tendency to believe that the Jews were doing their utmost to keep the law as a means of achieving salvation, it is not, however, the position put forward here. None would disagree that Israel was chosen and given certain blessings as a result of God's unmerited grace; God had after all, by his grace, rescued Israel from Egyptian bondage. He had led it safely through the Red Sea and across the Jordan, to quote Owen, "The land of Canaan was given to the posterity of Abraham by promise. And therefore doth God so often mind them of the freedom of it–that it was an act of mercy and sovereign grace."[4] So there was of course grace present because the type cannot represent the thing typified unless there be some likeness. However, having given Israel the land, God made Israel's prosperity and continuance in the therein conditional, and this is where the legal aspect becomes important since ethnic Israel's occupation depended on her obedience to the old covenant.

The covenant made with ethnic Israel was subservient to the new covenant in Christ but was in itself a very different covenant. Owen states:

> This covenant thus made, with these ends and promises [not exceeding the temporal boundaries of Canaan], did never save or condemn any man eternally. All that lived under the administration of it did attain eternal life, or perished forever, not by virtue of this covenant, as formally such. It did, indeed, revive the commanding power and sanction of the first covenant of works . . . And on the hand, it directed also unto the promise, which was the instrument of life and salvation unto all that did believe. But as unto what it had of its own, it was confined unto things temporal.[5]

Augustine says the same thing:

> That testament, however, which is properly called the Old, and was given on Mount Sinai, only earthly happiness is expressly promised. Accordingly . . . into which the nation, after being led through the wilderness, was conducted, is called the land of promise, wherein peace and royal power, and the gaining of victories over enemies, and an abundance of children and of fruits of the ground, and gifts of a similar kind are the promises of the Old Testament. And these, indeed, are figures of the spiritual blessings which appertain to the New Testament; but yet the man who lives under God's law with those earthly blessings for his sanction, is precisely the heir of the Old Testament, for just such rewards are promised and given to him, according to the terms of the Old Testament, as are the objects of his desire according to the condition of the old man.[6]

Augustine takes the word testament to be synonymous with covenant. Luther is of the same mind:

---

4. Owen, *Works*, 22, 321.

5. Ibid., 85.

6. Augustine, Proceedings on Pelagius, 13 (v).

> For the old testament given through Moses was not a promise of
> forgiveness of sins or of eternal things, but of temporal things,
> namely, of the land of Canaan, by which no man was renewed
> in spirit to lay hold on the heavenly inheritance. Wherefore also
> it was necessary that, a figure of Christ, a dumb beast should be
> slain, in whose blood the same testament might be confirmed,
> as the blood corresponded to the testament and the sacrifice
> corresponded to the promise. But here Christ says 'the new tes-
> tament in my blood' [Luke 22:20; 1 Cor. 11:25], not somebody
> else's, but his own, by which grace is promised through the Spirit
> for the forgiveness of sins, that we may obtain the inheritance.[7]

The Sinaitic law never saved or condemned any man in regard to his
eternal destiny because that was simply not that covenant's purpose. It
did, however, bear witness to the covenant that saved. The law and the
prophets bore witness to the gospel (Rom 3:21–22) with the gospel being
"manifested independently of the Mosaic covenant."[8] The law was like
a mirror into which the Jews could see their true sinful state. This would
encourage them to look to the new covenant and the promised Messiah
for salvation. Hence we have one covenant that condemns, and another
through which salvation becomes available.

Furthermore, while God's true people, those who constituted an
Israel within Israel, were subject to the law's temporary strictures, these
did not affect their eternal destiny. Edward Fisher tells us that:

> Were not Moses and Aaron, for their disobedience, hindered
> from entering into the land of Canaan, as well as others? Numb.
> XX. 12. And was not Josiah, for his disobedience to God's com-
> mand, slain in the valley of Megiddo? 2 Chron. XXXV, 21, 22.
> Therefore assure yourself, that when believers in the Old Tes-
> tament did transgress God's commandments, God's temporal
> wrath went out against them, and was manifest in temporal ca-
> lamities that befell them as well as others, Numb. Xvi, 46. Only
> there was a difference, the believers' temporal calamities had no
> eternal calamities included in them, not following of them; and
> unbelievers' temporal blessings had no eternal blessings includ-
> ed in them, and their temporal calamities had eternal calamities
> included in them, and following them.[9]

---

7. Luther, *The Babylonian Captivity of the Church.*

8. Johnson, *Kingdom of God,* 123.

9. Fisher, *Marrow of Modern Divinity,* 78.

Again, following Sanders, Wright refers to Israel as God's people and, as we have seen, attributes to the old covenant an efficacy it never possessed, attributing to the nation a status it did not have:

> Judaism in Paul's day was not, as has regularly been supposed, a religion of legalistic works-righteousness. If we imagine that it was, and that Paul was attacking it as if it was, we do great violence to it and to him. Most Protestant exegetes had read Paul and Judaism as if Judaism was a form of the old heresy Pelagianism, according to which humans must pull themselves up by their moral bootstraps and thereby earn justification, righteousness and, salvation. No, said Sanders. Keeping the law within Judaism always functioned without the covenantal scheme. God took the initiative, when he made the covenant with Judaism; God's grace thus precedes everything that people (specifically, Jews) do in response. The Jew keeps the law out of gratitude, as the proper response to grace-not, in other words, in order to *get* into the covenant people, but to *stay* in. Being "in" in the first place was God's gift. This scheme Sanders famously labelled as "covenant nomism" (from the Greek *nomos*, law). Keeping the Jewish law was the human response to God's covenantal initiative.[10]

Wright omits to say what the grace which Israel responded to was efficacious unto. Being placed within the land did not mean that Israel was counted among those whom Peter calls "a chosen race, a royal priesthood, a holy nation, a people for his own possession" (1 Pet 2:9). For Wright to suggest that obedience sprang solely out of gratitude is to believe that all Israel was already "in" when the truth was quite the opposite. Yes, they may have been "in" the old covenant, but most were excluded from the new covenant because of their unbelief. In *People of God* Wright states:

> The "works of Torah" were not a legalist's ladder, up which one climbed to earn the divine favour, but were the badges that one wore as the marks of identity, of belonging to the chosen people in the present, and hence the all-important signs, to oneself and one's neighbours, that one belonged to the company who would be vindicated when the covenant god acted to redeem his people. They were present signs of future vindication. This was how "the works of Torah" functioned within the belief, and the hope, of the Jews and particularly of Pharisees.[11]

10. Wright, *WSPRS*, 18–19.
11. Wright, *People of God*, 237.

If ethnic Israel did believe the Torah to be a sign concerning its future vindication, it was because it misunderstood the law's purpose. Contrary to what Wright claims, the Torah served to remind ethnic Israel that by its works, "works of Torah," no salvation was possible. In regard to Israel's present vindication, the Torah spoke of sin, punishment, and Christ, but it was itself impotent to bring about any necessary change of heart. Those who did believe did so solely on account of God's saving activity in their hearts. Believers, even then, were, by the Spirit, translated from the kingdom of darkness, where they lived in Adam, into the new covenant and the kingdom of Jesus Christ. Of course, many Jews misunderstood the Torah, wrongly believing it to be a covenant unto salvation, and wrongly believing themselves to be God's true people. They were presumptuous, expecting to benefit from the promises without doing the necessary obedience. Let me use a very simple illustration. Imagine that I buy a house for a couple, and place them in the house solely as a result of my free grace. I then say to them, "Keep the house tidy and make sure it is decorated and I will consider you to be true friends. If, however, you do not do this I will throw you out on the street." They agree to my terms, stating that they will do all that is required. If one year later I return to the house and find it looking like a pig-sty, the persons will not be my true friends and I will be justified in throwing them out onto the street. They will have clearly broken the terms of the covenant that I made with them. Wright, to use the illustration, is presuming that the couple had already completed my instructions just because they have occupied the house.

Israel under the old covenant was very much like the couple in the illustration. For carnal Israel to become God's people it had to be obedient, "Now, therefore, if you will indeed obey my voice and keep my covenant, you shall be my treasured possession among all peoples . . . and you shall be to me a kingdom of priests and a holy nation" (Ex 19:5–6). I am sure that many read this verse without noticing the all-important word, "if." Becoming God's people was entirely contingent on obedience. The nation was not to keep the law to show its gratitude for having become God's people, rather, the requirement to become his true people depended on Israel's faithfulness to the covenant. Israel after the flesh, however, would never keep the requirements of God's law. As Joshua stated shortly before his death, knowing Israel's sinful disposition, "You are not able to serve the LORD: for he is a holy God; he is a jealous God; he will not forgive your transgressions or your sins" (Joshua 24:19). Joshua clearly understood fallen human nature and the infinite holiness and justice of

God. There was, however, one who would come forth from the loins of Abraham, a second Adam, who would, as a propitiatory substitute, keep God's statutes, fulfilling the conditions of the covenant that the first Adam broke. Consequently, because of Christ's obedience, the words of Peter can be addressed to those Israelites who had faith in the promise. Only these became "a chosen generation, a royal priesthood, a holy nation, a people for his own possession" (1 Pet 2:9). In the Old Testament, these words (Ex 19:5-6) must be read within the context of the old covenant. For example, when God spoke of Israel being his treasured possession etc., if they were obedient, he was not an alluding to spiritual salvation, but was again speaking of the type, with its mundane blessings in order to suggest the possibility of becoming God's true people if only they embraced the promise in faith.

The great promise running through the Old Testament is that God will be a God to those who obey him and they shall be his people: Gen 17:7; Ex 6:7; Lev 26:12; Jere 7:23, 31: 11:4, 30:22; Ezek 11:20 etc. Usually, when this promise is declared the condition of obedience is present. For example, Leviticus 26, God tells Israel that should it keep his commandments he would not abhor the people but walk among them, being their God and they his people (vv. 11,12). In Jeremiah we read, "But this thing commanded I them, saying, Obey my voice, and I will be your God, and you shall be my people: and walk you in all the ways that I have commanded you, that it may be well unto you" (Jere 7:23). We find the same thing in Ezekiel, "That they may walk in my statutes, and keep mine ordinances, and do them, and I will be their God" (Ezek 11:20).

God is holy and jealous, and he cannot so much as look upon sin (Hab 1:13). He demands perfect obedience and punishment for all who fall short of his glory. As the words of Peter 2:9 only apply to those who believe in Christ, so too it was only for those Israelites who believed that this promise finds its fulfillment, only to this people can one say that truly God is their God, and they are his people. This is why Paul can declare that "all the promises find their yes in him" (2 Cor 1:20). This is because Christ fully honored the conditions of the covenant of works, also paying the penalty for our failing to do so, and since believers are in him, they too are deemed to have met all of that covenant's conditions, and have once and for all paid the penalty for sin.

The old covenant most certainly "did not constitute a new way or means of righteousness, life, and salvation; but believers sought for them alone by the covenant of grace, as declared in the promise."[12] Owen tells us:

> If reconciliation and salvation by Christ were to be obtained not only under the old covenant, but by virtue thereof, then it must be the same for substance with the new. But this is not so; for no reconciliation could be obtained by virtue of the old covenant, or the administration of it . . . all believers were reconciled, justified, and saved, by virtue of the promise, whilst they were under the covenant.[13]

The law is, of course, holy, the problem lies not with the law but human inability (Rom 8:3). In the case of Adam, once sin had entered in the law became powerless. The Sinaitic covenant was essentially a reiteration of the original covenant of works, as Owen, in reference to the Ten Commandments, tells us, Sinai "revived, declared, and expressed all, the commands of that covenant in the Decalogue."[14] There is, however, one very important caveat, there was now no possibility of obedience for Israel to secure temporal, let alone spiritual and eternal blessings. The New Testament leaves one in no doubt about the old covenant's impotence to save. It was the covenant the people broke (Heb 8:9). It was a letter that kills (2 Cor 3:6), a "ministry of death" (v.7). The law was a yoke upon the neck of the disciples, which neither the fathers nor the generation of Paul's day was capable of fulfilling (Acts 15:10). The law essentially came in alongside the promise, not to offer an alternative way to God, but to stir up sin and drive the sinner to despair, thereby encouraging sinful humanity to look to the promised Messiah and to be saved. About the Mosaic covenant Edward Fisher reminds us:

> But it was added by way of subserviency and attendance, the better to advance and make effectual the covenant of grace; so that although the same covenant that was made with Adam was renewed on Mount Sinai, yet I say still, it was not for the same purpose. For this was it that God aimed at, in making the covenant of works with man in innocency, to have that which was his due from man: but God made it with the Israelites for no other end, than that man, being thereby convinced of his weakness, might flee to Christ. So that it was renewed only to help forward and introduce another and better covenant; and so to

12. Owen, *Works*, 22, 82.

13. Ibid., 77.

14. Ibid.

be a manuduction unto Christ, viz: to discover sin, to waken the conscience, and to convince them of their own impotency, and drive them out of themselves to Christ.[15]

The new covenant is what the apostle calls "the ministration of righteousness" (2 Cor 3:9). All humanity finds itself in one of two positions, one is either under the "ministry of death" or "the ministry of righteousness," under Adam or under Christ. To be under the latter is to be in the new covenant and a recipient of better promises. As Owen states, "I take it for granted that no man was ever saved but by virtue of the new covenant and the mediation of Christ therein."[16]

Let me use a simple illustration to show how the law works. Imagine you want a car costing £100,000. You presently don't have the money to purchase it. Now suppose someone approaches you and says that they will lend you the money on condition that you meet the monthly payments of £4000. You are also told that if you don't make these payments you will end up in prison. You agree, signing the piece of paper making the contract formal. The only problem is you don't have any money. After a month you have broken the contract. Before you know it, because you cannot repay, you end up in prison with no prospect of release. From your prison cell, you realize your utter inability and you wish someone would pay the debt for you. It is only upon realizing your awful predicament that you will seek out the one who will ransom you and be your surety. Jesus is the one who came and honored all of the conditions of the covenant of works. He did not set it aside, neither did he change it, rather, he perfectly kept it for his people. Another illustration should further reveal the radical difference between the old and new covenants: imagine one man walking a long path carrying food which he distributes to the needy. After walking some distance, he is joined by a companion. This companion walks beside him, and calls out to the needy, pointing them to the man with the food. After walking with the man for some way, the companion leaves his side for good. This companion is like the old covenant. While he was there he did not in any way change the source of the food; it was the same both before, during, and after his companionship. In a similar manner, the old covenant does not change the source of new covenant salvific blessings in Christ under the new covenant.

15. Fisher, *Marrow of Modern Divinity*, 63.
16. Ibid., 70.

The law that was explicitly revealed under Moses was juxtaposed to the pre-existing promise in order to make the promise more prominent; essentially it served as a signpost that magnified the work of the approaching Messiah. This is why the apostle tells us that the law was a schoolmaster to bring people to the promise so that they might be justified by faith (Gal 3:24), and that it was "added because of transgressions, till the seed should come to whom the promise was made" (Gal 3:19). A schoolmaster is one who facilitates the gaining of knowledge, although the law cannot justify, it does point to the one who can. The law "declared the *impossibility of obtaining reconciliation and peace with God* any other way but by the promise. For representing the commands of the covenant of works, requiring perfect, sinless obedience under the penalty of the curse, it convinced men that this was no way for sinners to seek life and salvation by."[17] Again, Wright's error is to place too much emphasis on the law, the old covenant, to the point where the promise is itself made dependent on the law. One must add that much of what Wright says about the law is correct, however, the problems become evident when he appears to make contradictory statements, where he fails to differentiate between the conditional covenant made with Abraham, and later expanded at Sinai, and the unconditional covenant made with Abraham.

It has been common in Reformed circles to speak of the threefold law, namely, the moral law or Ten Commandments, the civil[18] or judicial law and the sacrificial law. As we saw with Sanders, the law could not have been legalistic in the way the Reformers had imagined, because through the sacrificial system forgiveness was possible, and, obviously, forgiveness meant there was something to be forgiven. They saw the law as a self-contained system, where going through the motions would suffice to secure God's blessings. If they sinned they would offer a sacrifice to cover their sin and all would be well, irrespective of whether they exercised the necessary faith in the Messiah. The bottom line is that they were placing their faith in the wrong covenant.

There were never any spiritual blessings afforded by the sacrificial system. The writer of Hebrews tells us that the sacrifices "were a figure of the time then present, in which they were offered both gifts and sacrifices that could not make him that did the service perfect, as pertaining to the conscience; [which stood] only in meats and drinks, and diverse

17. Owen, *Works*, 22, 79.
18. The civil law is essentially the application of the 10 Commands to daily life.

washings, and carnal ordinances, imposed [on them] until the time of the reformation" (Heb 8:9–10). Any blessings merited by obedience to the old covenant related to those we read about in Deuteronomy 27-30, and these were of an entirely temporal nature. Even these, however, could not be secured because Israel failed to perform the sacrifices in a meaningful way. Owen clearly distinguishes between the old and the new covenant when describing the law's twofold purpose

> Wherefore God in his mercy and patience, provided that by the sacred gifts and offerings atonement should be made for sin . . .There were two things to be considered in those sins which God had appointed that atonement should be made for. The first was, *the external temporal punishment which was due unto them*, according unto the place which the law or covenant had in the polity of the commonwealth of Israel. The other, that *eternal punishment* that was due to every sin by the law, as the rule of all moral obedience; for "the wages of sin is death." In the first of these, *the person of the sinner*, in all his outward circumstances, his life goods, his liberty, and the like was concerned. In the latter, his conscience, or the inward man alone was so. And as unto the first of them, the gifts and sacrifices mentioned, being rightly offered, were able in themselves, 'ex opera operato,' to free the sinner from all temporal, political inconvenience or detriment, so as that his life and inheritance should be continued in the land of Canaan, or his state preserved entire in the commonwealth of Israel. . . but as unto the latter, wherein conscience was concerned, he denies that they had any such efficacy.[19]

The old covenant and its many sacrifices suggested the possibility of temporal blessings for ethnic Israel should she be obedient to the Lord. In that the many sacrifices had an efficacy unto things external, they served to represent the sacrifice of him who was made known to those who exercised faith in the promise. To offer sacrifices without looking to the promise was, spiritually speaking, completely meaningless. Only those Israelites who believed, like their father Abraham, would have known cleansing of the conscience.

Wright tells us that "Romans and Galatians are all drawing on, and claiming to fulfill, two central passages in the Pentateuch: Genesis 15, where God established his covenant with Abraham, and Deuteronomy 30, where Israel is offered the promise of the covenant renewal after

19. Ibid., 249.

exile."[20]In this covenantal mix-up, Wright fails to appreciate that the blessings alluded to in Deuteronomy pertained only to the temporal, and then only unto that covenant made specifically with Israel. As I hope to show, those blessings spoken of in Genesis 15, unlike those in Deuteronomy, are all of grace, and it is this that Paul alludes to when he speaks of the promise in Galatians 3:16. So, essentially, what Wright takes to be one covenant, is, in fact, two different covenants, one national and conditional, holding out the promise of temporal blessings, the other, effective for both Jews and Gentiles, solely dependent of the obedience of Christ.

One will look in vain to see any covenant renewal for physical Israel with the completion of Christ's work. On the contrary, what we do see is the demise of the national covenant. Wright then makes a category mistake of believing Jesus to have fulfilled what Israel should have done, by his obedience to the old covenant. From this, he then wrongly speaks of Jesus' fulfillment of the old covenant as a necessary condition for securing blessings that are both spiritual and eternal. He fails to adequately differentiate between the old and new covenants, in making the new covenant blessings dependent on the old covenant he makes the antitype dependent on the fulfillment of the type. The covenant Jesus kept was the original covenant of works, the covenant which the Mosaic was patterned after, as the writer to the Hebrews informs us, "it was therefore necessary that the patterns of things in the heavens should be purified with rites, but the heavenly things themselves with better sacrifices than these (Heb 9:23). The old covenant sacrifices at best served as "a copy and shadow of heavenly things" (Heb 8:5). When the details of the covenant were revealed unto Moses he was instructed to make everything according to the copy of the original pattern (v.7). The original pattern was nothing less than the new covenant. Wright, therefore, errs in that he attaches to the copy and shadow that which should only apply to the substance.

Furthermore, the idea that Jesus kept the Mosaic covenant and in doing so put an end to Israel's exile immediately runs into a problem. For Jesus to have met the old covenantal conditions would have required a change in the terms of the covenant; something Scripture tells us cannot be done, as Paul tells us, even in regard to a covenant made by man, "no man disannulled, or addeth thereto." (Gal 3:15). How much more, we may ask, does this apply to a covenant made by God? Central to Jesus' work was his priestly role, yet Jesus' priesthood was very different from

---

20. Wright, *Justification*, 73.

that prescribed by the law. The law stipulated that all priests come from the tribe of Levi (Num 8:16–18), Jesus, however, was from the tribe of Judah, "For the one of whom these things are spoken belonged to another tribe, from which no one has ever served at the altar. For it is evident that our Lord was descended from Judah, and in connection with that tribe Moses said nothing about priests" (Heb 7:13–14).

If Jesus fulfilled the old covenant, because he was from a different tribe, his obedience was effectively illegitimate. Also, there was no eternal inheritance available by the Aaronic priesthood, "If therefore perfection were by the Levitical priesthood (for under it the people received the law,) what further need was there that another priest should rise after the order of Melchisedec, and not be called after the order of Aaron" (Heb 7:11). In the case of Jesus, there was a change in the priesthood and also a change in the law (Heb 7:12). He was "made, not after the law of a carnal commandment, but after the power of an endless life" (Heb 7:16). To contend then that Jesus' fulfillment of the old covenant is a necessary condition for those blessings that pertain unto spiritual and eternal redemption is *non sequitur*, the result of failing to compare like with like.

Again, if Jesus did keep the Mosaic covenant to end Israel's exile it is most unlikely the saints of old would have looked to a "heavenly city," considering themselves to be strangers and pilgrims in regard to this fallen earthly realm. Instead, they would have looked to those mundane temporal blessings referred to in Deuteronomy and elsewhere. It should also be noted that it was only Israel that was under the Mosaic covenant, yet Jesus came to end the exile of all his people; people from every tribe and tongue; to this end, it was, therefore, imperative that he keep the original covenant of works. Wright has essentially taken the conditional promises of the old covenant and has made the blessings of the new covenant dependant on their fulfillment when the reality is they are two entirely different covenants.

So how can Jesus be said to have fulfilled the Mosaic law? He can be said to have done this because he was the one about whom that covenant spoke. He was the archetype of which the law bore witness to with its many types. For example, although the sacrificial system could not take away sin, and had no efficacy unto things spiritual, it did speak of God's wrath upon sin, and it did point to the need for blood to be shed. Jesus then fulfilled the old covenant only in so far as it typified the original covenant of works.

To sum up, what we can say is that where the Sinaitic covenant promised earthly blessings, those of the new covenant are eternal and spiritual. Where Sinai was dependent on fallen man's obedience, the new is guaranteed because of Christ's obedience. Where the Sinaitic law is written on tablets of stone, the new covenant is written on the heart of flesh, where the old covenant was a letter that kills, the new is of the Spirit, and where the old was a ministry of death the new is a ministry of righteousness and life.

One text that is employed quite forcibly by Wright in an effort to show that Jesus came to keep the Mosaic law is found in Galatians 4:4–5, where we read, "But when the fullness of time had come, God sent forth his Son, born of a woman, born under the law, to redeem those who were under the law." Although I intend to look at this verse when I look specifically at Galatians, perhaps a few words are in order here. None would argue that Jesus was born under the law, but we must ask, which law? Of course, as an Israelite he found himself under the Mosaic law, and as a faithful Israelite he would have kept this perfectly, but as touching the world's salvation he was under the same covenant that our first parents failed to keep. Again we see the type and the antitype. At best, the old covenant served as a means to an end. Unfortunately, many Jews failed to appreciate this and made the law an end in itself.

There are Reformed Baptists who hold to the idea that the Mosaic covenant promised eternal life should one keep its statutes and commandments. For example, Reformed Baptist Jeffrey Johnson writes, "according to the terms of the Mosaic covenant, eternal life was dependent upon the establishment of perfect righteousness."[21] Whilst this is, of course, correct, the passage he uses to justify this is Christ's encounter with the lawyer in Luke 10:27. The lawyer approached Christ and asked what he needed to do to have eternal life. Christ told him to "love the Lord your God with all your heart and with all your soul and with all your strength and with all your mind, and your neighbor as yourself" (v27). The question is, was Jesus actually saying that if it were possible for him to do this eternal life would be his? I don't think so. This is again to mix up the covenants and their respective promises. The text does not say that Jesus told him that he would have life eternal, but that he would live. It appears to me that a possible interpretation would be that Jesus was first directing the lawyer to Leviticus 18:5, and then referring to life

21. Johnson, *The Kingdom of God*, 60.

which is "equivalent to the Deuteronomic lengthening of days . . . to an abundant life in the promised land."[22] By this Jesus was effectively showing that the lawyer could not keep the commandments to secure temporary blessings, how much less, therefore, could he, through his own obedience, secure blessings of an eternal nature. In other words, Jesus is thus alluding to eternal blessings under the types of the mundane, to emphasize the weakness of the flesh. What Meyer applies to Paul can here be applied to Jesus, where his "appropriation of the OT text relies on an eschatological extension, which takes the realities from the old age and transposes them onto their eschatological counterpart in the new age."[23] I would, however, qualify this by referring to old and new covenant instead of old and new age. It must be stressed that even perfect obedience to the Mosaic commandments could not secure spiritual life simply because the law also demands punishment for all wrongdoing. So even if fallen man were capable of keeping the law perfectly from birth, he would still find himself separated from God and subject to wrath because of original sin in Adam.

The idea of Christ obtaining a righteousness that is then available for his people is, according to Wright, nonsensical. However, the fact that Jesus was "born under the law" is itself clear evidence for his securement of this positive righteousness. He was under law in the same way that we are under it, and as it demands obedience from us, in like manner, it demanded the same from Christ. Owen states that we "were so under law, as not only to be obnoxious unto the curse, but so as to be obliged unto all the obedience that it required."[24] So, of course, if the Mosaic covenant was pattered after him, it would be unimaginable for him not to have fulfilled the type perfectly, although this is not what secures salvation

Many, even in evangelical circles, reject Christ's active obedience, failing to grasp the essential fact that in order to secure salvation for his people it was imperative that Jesus keep the law preceptively and suffer because of its penal requirements. Once again, to quote Owen, "if the Lord Christ has redeemed us only from the law's curse of it by undergoing it, leaving us in ourselves to answer its obligation unto obedience, we are not free nor delivered."[25] To maintain that Christ was only under the

---

22. Meyer, *The End of the Law*, 218.

23. Ibid., 218.

24. Owen, *Works*, 5, 272.

25. Ibid., 272.

law's curse in regard to our salvation would be tantamount to saying that his active obedience was for none other than himself.

About Christ's imputed righteousness Calvin states: "For if the observance of the law is righteousness, who can deny that Christ, by taking this burden upon himself, and reconciling us to God, as if we were the observers of the law, merited favour for us."[26]For believers, in virtue of their union with him, his obedience to the original covenant of works, becomes their obedience in the sight of God. A longer passage from Owen deserves quoting here:

> It is excepted, with more colour of sobriety, that he was made under the law only as to the curse of it. But it is plain in the text that Christ was made under the law as we are under it. He was "made under the law, to redeem them that were under the law." And if he was not made so as we are, there is no consequence from his being made under it unto our redemption from it. But we were so under the law, as not only to be obnoxious unto the curse, but so as to be obliged unto all the obedience that it required; as hath been proved. And if the Lord Christ hath redeemed us only from the curse of it by undergoing it, leaving us in ourselves to answer its obligation unto obedience, we are not freed nor delivered. And the expression of "under the law" doth in the first place, and properly, signify being under the obligation of it unto obedience, and consequentially only with a respect unto the curse. Gal. iv. 21, "Tell me, ye that desire to be "under the law." They did not desire to be under the curse of the law, but only its obligation unto obedience; which, in all usage of speech, is the first proper sense of that expression. Wherefore, the Lord Christ being made under the law for us, he yielded perfect obedience unto it for us; which is therefore imputed unto us. For that what he did was done for us, depends solely on imputation.[27]

As Turretin, succinctly puts it: "Hence it follows . . . that God cannot show favour to, nor justify anyone without a perfect righteousness. For since the judgement of God is according to truth, he cannot pronounce anyone who is not really just . . . Therefore he who is destitute of personal righteousness ought to have another's, by which to be justified."[28]

26. Calvin, *Institutes*, 2.17.5.
27. Owen, *Works*, 5, 272–273.
28. Turretin, *Elenctic Theology*, vol.2, 647.

It was not enough to say that one was of the physical stock of Abraham. To truly be a child of Abraham one needed to exhibit a similar faith in the promises of God. This is why Paul could say that "They which are the children of the flesh, these are not the children of God: but the children of the promise are counted for seed" (Rom 9:8). Let us choose one Old Testament believer to exemplify this. Jeremiah was born an Israelite, and in view of this, he was required to keep the law. However, because he believed in the promise he was also a member of the new covenant, yet even though in Christ he possessed all, he was, however, treated like a child under age. He would have known "that circumcision, which is outward in the flesh" (Rom 2:28), and exile in Babylon, but because of his faith his exile from God had ended in reconciliation, he knew that circumcision "that is of the heart, in the spirit, and not in the letter; whose praise is not of men, but of God" (Rom 2:29).

The true believer who, being part of ethnic Israel and under the old covenant, while, like Jeremiah, suffered from the temporal calamities that beset ethnic Israel. However, in his heart, because he belonged to the one promised, could declare with Habakkuk:

> Though the fig tree should not produce blossom,
>
> Nor fruit be on the vines, the produce of the olive fail and the fields yield food, and the flock be cut from the fold
>
> And there be not herd in the stalls,
>
> Yet I will rejoice in the LORD; I will take joy in the God of my salvation. (Habakkuk 3:17–18)

Although it might seem somewhat strange, but it was quite possible that a believing Israelite born under the Mosaic law was put to death for transgressing the old covenant, who, yet because of his faith in God's promise, possessed a circumcised heart, and was ushered into heaven upon death.

As we have seen, the paedobaptist and the new perspective paradigm tends to lump all of Israel together as the children of God. This is their explanation for infant baptism, for, clearly, if the circumcised Jewish child was counted among God's people under the old covenant, should not the baptized child be similarly considered under the new covenant? To them, it is simply a logical crossover from circumcision in the old covenant to baptism in the new, and because of this erroneous logic, they have no qualms in pronouncing the baptized child to be in Christ and a child of God.

In his letter to the Galatians (4:22–31) the apostle spells out the differences between the old and new covenants in the form of an allegory. Coxe aptly explains this:

> Hagar was a type of Mount Sinai and the legal covenant established there. Ishmael was a type of the carnal seed of Abraham under that covenant. Sarah was a type of the new Jerusalem, the gospel church founded on the covenant of grace. Isaac was a type of a true member of that church who are born of the Spirit being converted by the power of the Holy Spirit for the fulfilling of the promise of the Father to Jesus Christ the mediator. And the ejection of Hagar and Ishmael was to prefigure the abrogation of the Sinaitic covenant of the dissolving of the Jewish church-state so that the inheritance of spiritual blessings might be clearly passed down to the children of God by faith in Jesus Christ.[29]

By the "Jewish church-state," he does not mean the true church of God, but rather the typical role Israel performed under the old covenant. The covenant represented by Hagar and her son Ishmael is the conditional covenant made with Abraham in Genesis 17, while that represented by Sarah and Isaac is the covenant promised, the new covenant which is alluded to in Genesis 15. The former, although having Abraham has a physical father, were born into bondage, "this means that it is not the children of the flesh who are the children of God" (Rom 9:8). Whereas, those that exercised faith in the promised Christ of the new covenant are like Sarah and her son who looked forward to the heavenly Jerusalem; these are the children of the promise, and are counted as Abraham's true offspring (Rom 9:8). Abraham's natural offspring only knew circumcision in the flesh, but those of faith experienced the spiritual circumcision of the heart. Hagar and her son Ishmael, and all Abraham's fleshly seed who were without faith, knew only the Sinaitic covenant, a covenant that spoke only of earthly Jerusalem and temporal blessings that were entirely dependent on an obedience which the people could not provide. Commenting on this passage Johnson states:

> The physical seed are the *natural* children of Abraham; the *spiritual* seed are the supernatural children of Abraham. The physical seed were circumcised in their *flesh*; the spiritual seed have been circumcised in *heart*. The physical seed inherited and earthly land; the spiritual seed are heirs to a heavenly city whose

29. Coxe, "A Discourse of the Covenants", 130–31.

builder and maker is God. The physical seed became a geopoliti-
cal nation, and *earthly kingdom*; the spiritual seed have birthed
into the *kingdom of God*.[30]

Even though physical Israel had been given the land by God's grace alone,
it would because of disobedience be like Hagar who lived in slavery and
was cast out (Gal 4:30). They would not inherit those things reserved for
the children of promise, the spiritual Israel, in the Jerusalem that is above.

Wright depicts Israel as having miserably failed because it did not
provide the necessary covenantal obedience, consequently, the gospel was
prevented from going to the whole world. He sees Christ as the "faithful
Israelite, through whom the single plan can proceed after all."[31] Jesus'
work is viewed as some kind of contingency measure. Israel had let God
down on account of its disobedience. God wanted to usher in his new
creation but was prevented from doing so. It was, therefore, left to Jesus to
step in and fix things. Jesus becomes a kind of an afterthought when the
initial plan failed to materialize. It's a picture in which God's plan A, that
involved Israel's fulfilling its vocation, had failed, it was then necessary
for God to come up with plan B, where Jesus had to step in to do what the
nation had failed to do itself. Such an interpretation is, to say the least, an
imposition on what the Scriptures teach, and it also undermines Christ's
person and work. God's salvation in Christ has never been dependent on
a sinful individual or nation, but entirely on the work of Christ. He is the
Alpha and Omega, the beginning and the end of our salvation. While Jesus is seen by Wright as fulfilling the covenant, he does not determine the
nature of it. The covenant, and not Christ, then becomes the controlling
factor. The work of Jesus as the faithful Israelite could have been achieved
by the nation if it were not for its disobedience. Such a position misses the
essential fact that far from being an afterthought, he is the one in whom
salvation for his people was predestined before the beginning of time.
The truth is God's plan had not failed, and this is exactly what the apostle
explains in Romans 9–11. Throughout the Old Testament God was working out his single plan of salvation, and men and women were, through
the various types and shadows, coming to faith in the promised Messiah.
So although physical Israel failed, spiritual Israel was very much on track.

The nation stumbled because it associated possession with doing,
and the law became a stumbling block (Rom 9:32–33). The true spiritual

---

30. Johnson, *The Kingdom of God*, 58.
31. Ibid., 83.

Israelite, on the other hand, can be said to have performed the requirements of the law because of his being in Christ, having looked not to any efficacy in the various animal sacrifices, but, in faith, to that which would take place on Calvary's tree.

THE SPIRIT OF THE LAW

The New Testament provides us with sufficient evidence of Judaism's misunderstanding of the law. We see this in a number of texts, for example, The Sermon on the Mount in Matthew chapter 5; The rich young ruler in Matthew 19:15–23, Mark 10:17-22, Luke 18:18–23, and in the story of the Pharisee and the tax collector in Luke 18:9-14. In his Sermon on the Mount, Jesus explains the difference between the letter and the spirit of the law. He exposes the error of the scribes and Pharisees, to quote Lloyd-Jones, "what our Lord is really doing here is showing the true teaching of the law over against the false representations of the scribes and Pharisees."[32] There was something very defective in what these teachers of the law considered to be righteous, as Jesus reminded them, "For unless your righteousness surpasses that of the Pharisees and the teachers of the law, you will certainly not enter the kingdom of heaven" (Matt 5:20). These so-called teachers exercised great care in copying and keeping the law, at least in so far as they understood it. Clearly then, if one were to ask the Pharisees and scribes about the law and its purpose one would have received an answer very different from that presented to us in the pages of Scripture.

Jesus tells us why the teachers of the law were wrong when he provides us with the true spiritual nature of the law. From Matthew 5:21–48 Jesus sets the law's spiritual nature against the erroneous views of the scribes and Pharisees. For example, in regard to murder, Jesus said, "You have heard that it was said of those of old, 'You shall not murder, and whoever murders will be liable to judgment.' But I say to you that every one who is angry with his brother will be liable to judgment" (v. 21). Until Jesus explained the spirit of the law one can well imagine these teachers nodding their heads in agreement, for clearly, they had not murdered. Agreement, however, would have been followed by anger when Jesus effectively said that all are murderers. They thought that because they had not committed the physical act they were innocent. Jesus shows, however,

---

32. Lloyd-Jones, *Sermon on the Mount*, 186.

that the law goes much deeper than this. It applies not only to that which a man does with his body but also to what goes on in his mind.

By "those of old" Jesus is not referring to the teachings of Moses, but to the way his teachings were added to and changed; taking on a somewhat superficial meaning, thereby escaping the full force of the law. The teachers of the law had added many external regulations on top of the Mosaic law, and these they scrupulously kept, for example, the law required fasting but once a year, the Pharisees changed this to twice a week. They, however, in reality, were simply undermining the law's function. They kept the law externally and considered themselves righteous as a consequence, they entirely missed the fact that the law was given to show up their unrighteousness.

When the Pharisees and scribes considered themselves righteous, they were thinking of themselves, not just as covenant members, as Wright would have us believe, but as having kept the law. One must be careful here because although they failed to see the law's spiritual dimension, they did not consider it necessary to provide a perfect obedience, this was because, as with covenantal nomism, they saw forgiveness for any wrongdoing as being provided through the sacrificial system. By keeping the law, they had in mind the practice of all that it required, for example, being circumcised, eating the right foods, trying to keep the moral law and falling short, then performing sacrifices to atone for these sins etc. In their superficial understanding, they saw the Mosaic covenantal stipulations, when taken as a whole, as something that they could keep, yet all the while failing to grasp the essential point that the covenant's purpose was to show that they stood condemned, and needed to look to another covenant to find true salvation. Salvation lay not in Moses through whom the law came but in Christ and his covenant, through which God provides grace upon grace.

It was because of first century Judaism's misunderstanding of the law that the rich young man, could say, when told to keep the commandments, "All these have I kept. What do I still lack?" (Matt 19:20). Yes, he may have believed that there were times when he fell short, but, again, he took it for granted that all had been forgiven because keeping the law entailed offering sacrifices for any sin. Hence he considered himself to have kept the law. However, the sacrifices for sin provided him with a Christ-less forgiveness. He was making the Mosaic law an end in itself, not seeing that it served to facilitate the promise. Like Paul prior to his conversion, he then wrongly considered himself blameless and justified, failing to appreciate the law's spiritual dimension.

PART TWO

Galatians and Romans

IN THIS SECTION I want to examine Wright's new perspective in the context of a number of biblical passages, concentrating on Galatians and Romans 1-8. This will not be a verse by verse examination, but one that focuses on those verses pertinent to the new perspective. In regard to Galatians, I will critically comment on Wright's position as I go, while, in dealing with Romans 1–8, I seek to give Wright's position before I attempt to refute it from a Reformed Baptist position. In examining these two epistles it will occasionally be necessary to explicate a passage from one epistle when examining the other, for example, when looking at the role of the law in Galatians I make reference to Romans 7, consequently, I avoid this text when examining Romans itself.

I am aware that the view I'm putting forward here is somewhat different from other critiques of the NPP, especially those written by paedobaptists. As already said, the Reformed Baptist position distinguishes between the conditional Abrahamic and Mosaic covenant (covenant in the singular because they are essentially the same covenant) and the covenant of grace[1] which is nothing other than the new covenant. The old and new covenants are not mere different administration of the one covenant of grace, but are radically different, with each being based on different mediators and different promises.

WRIGHT AND GALATIANS

The apostle knows that his opponents at Galatia will raise questions about his authority. He, therefore, provides a number of reasons for his trustworthiness and the truthfulness of his gospel. He tells the Galatians

---

1. Covenant of grace is an expression not found in the Scriptures, the only covenant in which there is salvation is the new covenant.

that it is not something he had fabricated, neither did he receive it from any man, rather, it is the result of a direct revelation of Jesus Christ himself (Gal 1:12). It is the same gospel as that preached by the apostles who had given Paul the right hand of fellowship (Gal 2:9). Paul leaves one in no doubt about what he thinks of anyone preaching another gospel, twice he says that such a person is to be "accursed" (Gal 1:7–8). Arguably, Paul believes the Judaizers to be preaching such a gospel, one that is really no gospel at all.

The apostle was having to deal with the challenges caused by certain Jewish agitators who had come from Jerusalem. They were telling the Gentile Christians that to be truly saved it was necessary for them to submit to the rite of circumcision. According to Wright, the problem has to do with "who is to be reckoned by God to be a true family, and hence with the right to share table fellowship."[2] He believes that Paul's reference to "not being justified by works of the law" is concerned "with the question of ethnic taboos about eating together across ethnic boundaries."[3] So, for Wright, "the real problem is not 'legalism' as usually conceived within traditional Protestant theology, but the question of whether one has to become a Jew to belong to the people of God."[4] The badges or identity markers, "ethnic boundaries," i.e., food laws, holy days, and, circumcision were no longer required, and now one could become a covenantal member, or justified, by faith alone. With the barriers gone, the Gentiles too can sit at the same table as Jews. It is this membership that is, according to Wright, the essence of justification.

PETER'S WEAKNESS AND PAUL'S CONCERN

About Peter, Paul tells us that "before certain men came from James, he was eating with the Gentiles: but when they came he drew back and separated himself, fearing the circumcision party" (Gal 2:12). The question we need to ask is why was Paul so annoyed with Peter's actions when he did this? Was it because Peter erroneously thought the rite of circumcision should be incorporated into the New Testament church? Or did it amount to something deeper, where the Christian Jews were effectively

---

2. Wright, *Justification*, 96.

3. Ibid., 96.

4. Wright, *The Climax of the Covenant*, 173.

putting themselves under the wrong covenant, and encouraging the Gentiles to do likewise?

Peter would have found it difficult to let go of those Jewish traditions that had determined so much of his life. We see this with Cornelius in Acts 10. Prior to Peter visiting Cornelius's house, God had revealed to him in a vision that nothing the Lord has made is to be regarded as unclean (Acts 10:11–16). Through this vision God was telling Peter that the gospel was for Gentiles as well as Jews. When Peter arrived at Cornelius's, in spite of the vision, he was still harboring doubts about his mission, and was reluctant to accept that the gospel was for the Gentiles; this was until he saw that the gift of the Spirit was given to Cornelius and his household, enabling them to speak in tongues (Acts 10:45). Again, in his first letter to the Corinthians Paul says that "tongues are a sign not for believers but for unbelievers (1 Cor 14:22). By unbeliever Paul, no doubt, had in mind not those who did not believe the gospel, but those Christians like Peter, who tended to doubt that the gospel was for the Gentiles, for people of other tongues. At Galatia, therefore, Peter, no doubt, felt a degree of fear in the presence of the Judaizers, and this, coupled with his own doubts, consequently caused him to withdraw from the Gentile Christians.

According to Wright, Paul's annoyance at Peter's actions came from the fact that Peter was using circumcision as a reason for separating from and discriminating against the Gentiles. Peter was, by his behavior, resurrecting circumcision as a badge of membership. Obviously, it included this, but, I would argue, Paul's concern went considerably deeper than merely dealing with identity markers like circumcision. He saw Peter's actions as undermining the gospel by reverting back to another covenant. The Judaizers were demanding that the Gentiles embrace what, to all intents and purposes, was another faith, one which Paul has elsewhere labeled a "ministry of death, carved in letters on stone" (2 Cor 3:6). Why one might ask, would the Gentile Christians benefit from having the law on external tablets when they already had it written on tablets of flesh? Why would they benefit from performing old rites that merely foreshadowed what was now consummated in the death of Christ? Why would they want to belong to the old when they were members of the new covenant? Paul's concern is not that these Jews were advocating the application of certain aspects of the old covenant that marked their exclusivity, but that they were effectively putting these Gentile believers under a conditional covenant from which there is no salvation to be found, one that had served its purpose and had actually ceased to exist.

COVENANT CONFUSION

Peter's action was tantamount to the abandonment of the unconditional salvation that is in Christ. It equated to a contradiction and even a denial of Christ's completed work. It resulted from a failure to grasp the fact that under the law or, old covenant, there could be no justification, "We know that a person is not justified by the works of the law, but through faith in Jesus Christ, so we also have believed in Christ Jesus, in order to be justified by faith in Christ and not by works of the law, because by works of the law no one will be justified" (Gal 2:16). It was the muddle over the covenants that explains Paul's savaging indictment in Gal 1:6–7. The law or old covenant was being viewed as part of the gospel, when, in reality, it served only to condemn.

Nowhere in this epistle is the law spoken of piecemeal, e.g., one cannot do, as Wright, Dunn, and Sanders have done, namely, take circumcision and divorce it from the rest of the law. Paul is not only demonstrating the fact that none can be justified by the law of Moses, but also that if one accepts part of the law then one must accept it in its entirety, "if you accept circumcision, Christ will be of no advantage to you. I testify again to every man who accepts circumcision that he is obligated to keep the whole law" (Gal 5:3). This was because the old covenant consisted of the entire package, namely, the moral law, the sacrifices, and the civil law.

I would agree with Wright in that these Jews were not attempting to be justified purely by a works righteousness in the sense that they believed it possible to offer unto God perfect obedience. As we have already seen, they believed that their many acts of disobedience could be atoned for through the elaborate sacrificial system. They saw themselves as having been specially chosen by God and given a law in which they wrongly believed true salvation could be found. They boasted of such a possession. Their great mistake was that they mistook the type for the antitype. They failed to see that the old covenant, even with its bloody sacrifices, could not take away sin and secure eternal spiritual blessings. The sin offering was only effective for those sins committed in ignorance (Lev 5:17–18), and then, unless accompanied with faith, it was efficacious only in regard to an Israelite's theocratic position within the nation. They were, to quote Wright, "a sign of penance for accidental sins: acts you committed without realizing they were sinful."[5] For those sins committed knowingly, there was no sacrifice, only punishment. This clearly shows

5. Wright, *Revolution*, 329.

the limitations of the sacrificial system. The death of the animal could cover for the sins of ignorance but not for sins wilfully committed. There was in the region of thirty-six capital offenses, these included blasphemy, murder, and idolatry etc. For such as these the sacrificial system, and the rest of the law could only serve to exacerbate one's awareness of sin. The only sacrifice that could provide forgiveness for sin was that made by Christ, and all those who believed the promises concerning him were safe in Christ in regard to their eternal salvation.

Paul was not then dealing with those who said that to be saved one would have to do merit-based works, i.e., keep the law. He was rather concerned that the Judaizers were misleading the Gentile Christians by confusing the covenants. The Jewish Christians at Galatia obviously did not reject faith, but they, nevertheless, found difficulty in letting go of the law, so for them, it became a necessary adjunct to faith. They were insisting that Gentiles be circumcised but were not forthcoming about the full implications of this. Circumcision marked initiation into the old covenant, and by accepting the rite Jewish Christians were essentially putting themselves under the entire old covenant, one that promised earthly, transient blessings conditional upon an impossible obedience. They were failing to appreciate the fact that they had been given heavenly and eternal blessings because of Christ's obedience. Why should anyone want to go back to the type when the antitype has been revealed? It reminds one of the Israelites after they had been freed from bondage in Egypt, in spite of this, they all too often yearned to be back under the tyranny from which God had liberated them.

Wright, no doubt, would consider Old Testament Jews as justified because of their membership in the old covenant. However, when Paul says that "by works of the law no one will be justified" (2:16) he is not just saying that what justified one in times past can no longer do so. There was never a time when the law justified one before God, and, therefore, the Israelite, unless he, like his father Abraham, exercised faith, was never justified.

The Reformed Baptists believe that there were two-covenants, one promised, the other made with Israel, one unconditional, the other conditional. This is, however, far removed from another two-covenant view that has grown in popularity. The two-covenant view maintains that ethnic Israel will be saved through their own covenant, namely, the old covenant, while the church will be saved through its own covenant, namely, the new covenant." Wright's position appears similar. He confuses the old covenant with the new and this results in applying to spiritual Israel promises that essentially belonged to carnal Israel. He states that "Israel will be vindicated, will inherit the age to come–but it will be the Israel that has kept Torah, or that, through penitence and amendments of life (as in Daniel 9, looking back to Deuteronomy 30), has shown its heartfelt desire to follow God's ways and be loyal to to his covenant."[6] A few lines on he says "the way to tell in the present, who would thus be vindicated in the future was to see who was keeping the Torah."[7] Not only does this deny covenantal consistency, but it poses more questions than it answers. No amount of obedience to the Torah could vindicate Israel, and as for being loyal to the covenant, Wright presumably means the old covenant. However, since the old covenant is essentially the law, he appears to be saying that Israel's vindication was through the law. Furthermore, even if Wright is not looking to perfect conformity, he fails to mention faith. In this letter, Paul could not emphasize more plainly than he has done, namely, that one receives God's Spirit, not by works, but by faith (3:2), and it is only "those of faith who are the sons of Abraham" (v.7). In the Old Testament, those Israelites who exercised faith were saved on account of believing in Christ, and, in him, they were made partakers of the new covenant. Throughout this letter faith is compared with works to show the impossibility of salvation by the law; it is extremely doubtful then that Paul would have considered ethnic Israel as having been saved by works. It is a truism for both Jews and Gentiles "that no one is justified before God by the law" (v.11).

The law's function was to show Israel its need for justification, and this could only be attained by exercising faith in the promise. Another point to bear in mind is the way Paul contrasts the "works of the law" with faith. If "works of the law" was a reference to "boundary markers" it would be difficult to see how these would be opposed to faith. Whereas, if Paul is thinking about the Jewish misunderstanding of the law, their belief that salvation comes through the law, such a contrast becomes meaningful. To paraphrase, Paul is essentially saying: "You have got it wrong, you are looking to the old covenant for salvation when it has always been by way of the promise, the new covenant."

As I commented above, Wright embraces much of what Sanders had to say. Points 6 to 8 of Sanders eight points of covenant nomism state:

---

6. Wright, *Justification*, 57.

7. Ibid.

(6) The law provides the means of atonement and atonement results in (7) the maintenance or re-establishment of the covenantal relationship. (8) All those who are maintained in the covenant by obedience, atonement and God's mercy belong to the group which will be saved. An important interpretation of the first and last points is that election and ultimately salvation are considered to be by God's mercy rather than human achievement.

He further states that "the all-pervasive view is this: all Israelites share in the world to come unless they renounce it by renouncing God and his covenant."[8] When he speaks of the atoning efficacy of the law one is left wondering what atonement he is alluding to. Is it true atonement that corresponds to that available under the new covenant? Does it correspond to being "in Christ"? One comes away with the understanding that Sanders believes all Israel to have been in a saving relationship with God. He also seems to be saying that the performance of the rigmarole of the law would have served to ensure the Israelites' in this saved relationship. However, not only was this not true, but, as said earlier, it was not the law's purpose, and, indeed, it was this erroneous thinking that the apostle was alluding to when he said that "no one is justified before God by the law" (Gal 3:11).

In point 8 Sanders speaks of salvation for those Jews who were obedient to the old covenant, believing these Jews would be counted among the saved. But here again, he links salvation to the old covenant, missing the fact that salvation only came through the promise and not through the old covenant. This is what results when one fails to distinguish between spiritual salvation in the antitype and that typical earthly redemption that the nation experienced when it was redeemed from bondage in Egypt and placed into the land of Canaan.

When Sanders and Wright ascribe forgiveness to the sacrificial system they appear to confuse Abraham's physical seed, ethnic Israel, with the spiritual Israel that constitutes Abraham's spiritual seed. There was no true forgiveness, namely, that forgiveness that cleanses the conscience, through the sacrificial system. The old covenant made with Abraham's physical seeds expressed in earthly categories what the new covenant, made with its spiritual seed, achieves for those in Christ. Physical Israel was redeemed from Egyptian bondage, but God's true people are redeemed from spiritual bondage. Physical Israel was led into the promised

8. Sanders, *Paul and Palestinian Judaism*, 75.

land, whereas true Israel is placed into the very kingdom of God. Physical Israel was to keep one day in seven, whereas true Israel has entered into God's perpetual rest. Physical Israel was to perform sacrifices that cleansed the body, whereas spiritual Israel, benefitting from Christ's sacrifice, knows a cleansing of the conscience. Physical Israel has the law written on tablets of stone, while spiritual Israel had it written upon the heart.

UNION WITH CHRIST

In v.19 of chapter 2, Paul states, "For through the law I am dead to the law, that I might live unto God." Paul again speaks of being dead to the law in chapters 6 and 7 of his letter to the Romans. He reminds the Christians there that they have "died to the law through the body of Christ, so that you should belong to another, to him who has been raised from the dead, in order that we may bear fruit for God" (Rom 7:4). Regarding his own salvation, Paul tells the Galatians: "I have been crucified with Christ. It is no longer I who live, but Christ who lives in me yet nevertheless I live; yet not I, but Christ lives in me: and the life I now live in the flesh I live by faith in the Son of God, who loved me and gave himself for me" (Gal 2:20). So what exactly do these verses mean?

In this text (Gal 2:19) Paul has become dead to all of the old covenant rigmarole because now the Christ, the one typified by the law has come. There is no longer any need for types and shadows. Moreover, and this lies at the heart of the verse, the apostle has in mind the Ten Commandments, the law that served to condemn; the same natural law that is written on the consciences of all men. He knew that Christ alone was the sacrifice by which he has truly been forgiven. Because believers are now united with him the law cannot touch them, it has already done its worst in the death of Christ. Believers are, as it were, now on the other side of the law. They are viewed by God, "in him", and as such are themselves viewed as having kept the law perfectly, and suffered the law's penal demands. In the words of Murray, "Before the law of God, Christ and those for whom he died stand as one single person, therefore, the believer shares fully in all that Christ did for him."[9] The law does not need to be kept twice, and sin needs to be punished once. The curse and the obedience demanded by the original covenant of works are no longer applicable. As the apostle

9. Murray, *The Old Evangelicalism*, 83.

tells us, "For Christ *is* the end of the law for righteousness to every one that believeth" (Rom 10:4). It is because of this union with Christ that Paul can say he had "been crucified with Christ." Christ underwent crucifixion, was raised on the third day, and later went to sit at his Father's right hand. In virtue of union with him, of becoming flesh of his flesh, the believer can be said to have undergone all that Christ underwent. He is now a new man, the old man has gone forever. The new creation which he has become has entirely different motives. Where the old man considered only himself and willingly rebelled against God, the new man seeks just the opposite, namely, to please God in all he says and does. He knows that his body is now the temple of the Holy Spirit, and it is this body he brings into submission and makes living sacrifices unto God.

To be justified is to be legally pronounced righteous, it is a declaration from God declaring the believer's obedience, death, and resurrection in Christ. Being justified believers are no longer accountable to the law, whereas previously if we broke the law in one point we would have been accountable for all of it (James 2:10). The believer can say on account of his being married to Christ, being one flesh with him, that the law cannot touch him because he has kept it all perfectly. Believers are now blameless before God's holy law. This is why Paul could say, "The sting of death is sin, and the power of sin is the law. But thanks be to God, who gives the victory through Jesus Christ our Lord" (1 Cor 15:56–57). Sin is the transgression of God's law, and it is the breaking of this law that results in God's wrath; this is where sin secures its power. But for all those "in Christ" this power has been broken forever.

Peter's folly lies in his apparent willingness to undermine his union with Christ in his desire to go back to the Mosaic covenant. Having been made a participant in Christ, in a union that is indissoluble, having been justified, he was effectively denying all of this by putting himself under a law that could only pronounce the sentence of death. Yes, he might have started with circumcision, but Paul shows that he has effectively placed himself under the law in its entirety, and not simply, as Wright seems to think, boundary markers, to distance himself from the Gentile world. The bottom line for Paul is that by accrediting the law with any degree of saving efficacy, Peter was essentially saying that "Christ died for no purpose" (Gal 2:22).

JESUS' CURSE BEARING DEATH

Galatians 3:6–14 is one of the pivotal passages for understanding Wright's new perspective:

> 6 Just as Abraham believed God, and it was counted to him as righteousness.
>
> 7 Know then that it is those of faith who are the sons of Abraham.
>
> 8 And the Scripture foreseeing that God would justify the Gentiles by faith preached the gospel beforehand to Abraham, saying, "In you shall all the nations be blessed."
>
> 9 So then, those who are of faith are blessed along with Abraham, the man of faith.
>
> 10 For all who rely on the works of the law are under a curse; for it is written, "cursed be everyone who does not abide by all things written in the Book of the Law, and do them."
>
> 11 Now it is evident that no one is justified before God by the law, for "The righteous shall Live by faith."
>
> 12 But the law is not of faith, rather "the one who does them shall live by them."
>
> 13 Christ redeemed us from the curse of the law by becoming a curse for us-for it is written, "Cursed is everyone who is hanged on a tree"-
>
> 14 so that in Jesus Christ the blessing of Abraham might come to the Gentiles, so that we might receive the promised Spirit through faith.

According to Wright, "Paul is working . . . on the basis of the single plan-of-God-through-Israel-for-the-world," believing that "this alone makes sense of the larger unit and the smaller details."[10] He says that "The problem is that the law gets in the way of the promise to Abraham."[11] It is not difficult to see that a major bone of contention lies in Wright's understanding of why Jesus became a curse and the consequences of this. Wright asks the question, "'Why did the Messiah become a curse for us?" the normal answer is something like, 'so that we might be freed from sin and share fellowship with God to all eternity.'"[12] He tells us that the apostle's answer is very different from this, it was rather, "So that the blessings of Abraham might come upon the Gentiles, and so that we (presumably Jews who

---

10. Wright, *Justification*, 101-102.

11. Ibid., 102.

12. Ibid., 103.

believe in Jesus) might receive the promise of the Spirit through faith."[13] It is most certainly not, as he keeps saying in his latest book,[14] about how the believer can go to heaven when he dies. He sees verse 14 as the logical conclusion of Paul's argument from verses 6–13: "What then, is the curse-bearing death of the Messiah the answer? The problem is that the law looked as if it would prevent the single-plan-of-Israel-for-the-world coming to pass."[15] Israel had failed in its mission to take the gospel to the Gentiles; it had fallen victim to idolatry and was, consequently, under God's curse. The curse was getting in the way and preventing the gospel going out to the nations. Wright states that "The death of Jesus launched a revolution, it got rid of the roadblock between the divine promises and the nations to whom they were intended."[16] He believes that Jesus' death ushered in a revolution, eliminating the hindrance caused by Israel's disobedience so that now the promises of God might achieve their desired ends. It was necessary then for Jesus to complete the mission Israel had been given, but in order to do this, he had to get rid of the curse that was upon Israel. Jesus then took the curse upon himself in order that the gospel might be preached unto the Gentiles.

"If Israel were to stay under that curse forever–as appeared inevitable, granted that nobody in Israel did, in fact, abide by everything written in the Torah-then the promises would never be released into the wider world."[17] Again, he tells us that "The Messiah became a curse for us by hanging on a tree, coming himself in place of the curse as indicated in Deuteronomy—and thereby making a way through the *curse and out the other side*, into the time of renewal when the Gentiles would at last come into Abraham's family, while the Jews could have the possibility of covenant renewal."[18] In other words, the Messiah, as the faithful Israelite, would need to fulfil the Mosaic covenant as a necessary condition for the gospel to be made available to the Gentiles, "God's promises to Abraham were stuck in the Deuteronomic curse, and could not go forward in history to their fulfilment; the Messiah came and bore the covenantal curse

13. Ibid., 103.

14. *The Day the Revolution Began.*

15. Wright, *Justification*, 103.

16. Ibid., 83

17. Ibid., 104.

18. Ibid., 104.

in himself, so that the new covenant blessings might flow out at last to the world."[19]

Jesus' curse-bearing death seems to concern the Gentiles only indirectly, because without it they would not have received the gospel. I emphasize this because according to Wright it has nothing to do with the idea that Jesus took upon himself the sins of all his people, both Jews and Gentiles, so that they could be forgiven. Wright has effectively taken one of the New Testament's most important messages relating to our salvation and has restricted it to the Jews alone. Jesus was not made a curse to rescue us from the curse of the original covenant of works, but solely for Israel, because it found itself under the Deuteronomic curse, a curse which was preventing Israel from carrying out her mission to be a light to the Gentiles.

Wright believes the traditional Reformation or old perspective reading of this text has failed to follow the true flow of the apostle's argument, for example, Paul tells us in v.14 why the Messiah was made a curse, that it's not " 'so that we might be freed from sin and go to heaven' or anything like it."[20] Rather, it is "so that the blessings of Abraham could flow through the nations in King Jesus-and so that we might receive the promise of the spirit[21] through faith."[22] What Wright has effectively produced is an interpretation which, in the words of Eveson, "leaves us with the impression that in Paul's theology the Messiah does not directly become a curse for the sins of the Gentiles. It becomes a secondary issue out of the Messiah's concern to exhaust the curse on Israel."[23]

So is Wright correct? To understand what Paul is getting at it is necessary to bear in mind that before the Abrahamic covenant the gospel promise was already universal, and although the new covenant was only revealed in the form of a promise, its blessings were even then available to all who believed. The universal promise did not go away after God chose Israel. One can easily envisage this promise, first revealed in Genesis 3:15, being communicated orally among the Gentiles unto the salvation of many. The fact is, the promise never changed, the way of salvation never

---

19. Ibid., 114.

20. Wright, *Revolution*, 83. Italics in the original.

21. Spirit in lower case in the original.

22. Ibid., 83.

23. Eveson, *The Great Exchange*, 141.

changed, and the coming of the law served only to elevate and promote the promise to a particular nation until the arrival of the Messiah.

There is no New Testament evidence to suggest that Israel was frustrating God's plan for the Gentile world. The idea has been conjured up by Wright to fit his novel paradigm. Particularization only started with Abraham and was further reinforced under Moses. The purpose of this was to channel the promise. If Wright's interpretation of this text is correct one would have to say that it was necessary for Christ to become a curse so that the gospel message should regain something of the status it had before the formation of the Jewish nation; when men such as Abel, Enoch, and Noah were saved by faith alone, irrespective of what nation they belonged to. It, however, seems highly unlikely that God would have taken his gospel promise and straightjacketed it by making its fulfillment dependent on the obedience of a sinful nation whose purpose was merely to serve as a cradle for the Messiah. Not only this, but it again sounds implausible that God would then make his gospel dependent on punishing his Son simply because this nation was somehow getting in the way of the gospel.

To maintain that circumcision, food laws, and, observing certain holy days were badges of membership of the old covenant, but have now, with the arrival Christ, been replaced by the badge of faith is to entirely miss the point of Paul's argument. Wright tells us that this passage is not concerned with the notion of earning one's salvation, but with the:

> question of how you define the people of God: are they to be defined by the badges of Jewish race, or in some other way? Circumcision is not a "moral" issue, it does not have to do with moral effort, or earning salvation by good deeds. Nor can we simply treat it as a religious ritual, then designate ritual as crypto-Pelagian good works, and so smuggle Pelagius into Galatia as the arch-opponent after all.[24]

The problem with Wright's position here is that he places too much faith in the supposed saving efficacy of the law. He has completely reversed what the apostle is saying. No amount of keeping the law could merit salvation, this is because the promises associated with the old covenant concerned only temporal matters. The badges of membership may have served to identify those who belonged to the old covenant, but this was not the covenant through which true salvation is to be found. It was only

---

24. Wright, *WSPRS*, 120–21.

those who saw beyond the rites and exercised faith in the Messiah who knew true salvation. Before Abraham, faith was the only badge, and it continued to be for the Israelite who saw past the old covenant types to the Christ of the new covenant. As the writer to the Hebrews put it, "Now faith is the assurance of things hoped for, the conviction of things now seen" (Heb 11:1). Indeed, the whole point of Hebrews chapter 11 is to magnify the faith exhibited by God's people through time. The apostle is demonstrating to the Galatians that all the old covenant could success-fully do was condemn. The Jews may have been in possession of the law, but it was not the path to salvation because it is not the possession that counts, but obedience; the very thing the people could not provide. As we have seen, Paul is not thinking about the obedience of going through the motions, i.e., in the performance of the sacrifices, these were entirely impotent to provide forgiveness for sins like murder and blasphemy etc. Paul says "the law is not of faith" (v.12), it was never meant to be. As Abraham was saved by faith before the old covenant, so too were those in Israel who believed, for "the righteous shall live by faith" (v.11).

While Wright rightly sees the nation as being under God's curse, he goes astray in maintaining that it is this that prevented the wider proclamation of the gospel. He is effectively looking for the fulfillment of the type as a necessary condition for the outworking of the antitype. The Sinaitic law served to remind sinners that they have fallen short of God's standards and are under his curse. In this passage, Paul specifically speaks of the law in a Deuteronomic context because he is dealing with Jews who appealed to the law and wanted to be back under its stipulations. The law served to facilitate the promise and, as we will see in v.8, the gospel that was revealed to Abraham beforehand; the gospel he had believed and by which he was accounted righteousness, was actually given to him before God had established any formal covenant with him. The promise and its fruition cannot then be said to be dependent on the law or any curse that resulted from disobedience to the old covenant. Before the law was revealed at Sinai mankind was already under the curse. It is this curse Paul is referring to in Galatians and not some kind of separate curse that applied only to the Jews. Yes, he may have drawn the attention of the Judaizers to Deuteronomy, but that was only to emphasize that they too are under the law's curse. The curse and punishment in exile Israel experienced was typical of humanity's spiritual exile from the presence of God, and, unlike the latter, this typical exile from the geographical mundane land was such that no one was going to vicariously stand in

Israel's place to meet the necessary conditions. The law given to Israel served to encourage the people to realize their true spiritual exile. Israel did not come under the antitypical law, which is the universal law of God that is written on the consciences of all men, after the law was given at Sinai, but disobedience to the Sinaitic law, and the subsequent temporal curse served, to remind Israel of a significantly more important curse that the people were already under in Adam. Paul, therefore, makes use of the Sinaitic law and the curse, which he sees as being a type, to all the more bring out the significance of the universal natural law and the curse we are all under from birth. There was no roadblock that thwarted the message going to the Gentile world. One also needs to bear in mind that the only spiritual redemption revealed in Scripture concerned not the Israelite nation's liberation from Egypt under Moses' mediation, but the liberation from sin under the mediation of Christ.

Wright fails to duly separate Deuteronomy and its particular conditional blessings, from those secured by Jesus in the new covenant. Israel was promised, on the condition of obedience, what we read of in chapters 27–30, and these are exactly what the nation would have merited for itself if it had been faithful. Being faithful to these conditions could never, however, secure spiritual and eternal blessings because these belonged to another separate covenant. This is the very understanding reached by Paul, where he came to see that even with all his so-called good works (Phil 3:3–6), he could not lay claim to God's salvation because he was looking to the wrong covenant. Wright then draws the wrong conclusions because he views new covenant blessings flowing out of Jesus' faithfulness /obedience to the old covenant, making spiritual new covenant blessings dependent upon Jesus becoming the Deuteronomic curse.

The blessings of Abraham referred to in verse 14 refer to the fact that Abraham had a righteousness imputed to him solely on the basis of his faith in the promise. Israel was chosen by God because through this nation he was going to bring the Messiah into the world. To this end, to protect the promise, Israel was hedged about with the law until the promise came to fruition in the Christ. The one who came forth from Abraham's loins, the seed, to attain salvation for his people, kept the original covenant of works. The proclamation of the gospel to the Gentile world had to wait, not for the Mosaic covenant to be fulfilled, or for the curse upon carnal Israel to be lifted, but for Christ to come in the flesh. After this, there was no longer any need to safeguard the nation and to have a covenant that spoke of conditional temporal blessings.

Wright seems fixated on the plight of carnal Israel and its so-called exile when he should be thinking of that exile that resulted from the first Adam's sin. Wright again confuses the old covenant with the new, stating: "The problem is that God made a promise not only to Abraham, but through Abraham to the world, and if the promise bearing people fall under the Deuteronomic curse, as Deuteronomy itself insists that they will, the promise cannot get out to the wider world."[25] As we have seen, the problem is the Deuteronomic curse belongs to the conditional old covenant, whereas the promises made to Abraham belong to the new covenant. Even in the conditional old covenant that spoke of earthly blessings, the punishment which denoted death by hanging on a tree was a type which prefigured Christ's death on a cross. The death of Christ, the antitype, however, spoke of blessings far exceeding those of the old covenant. Christ had become a curse for his people not in order to allow physical Israel to secure those temporal blessings, but to secure eternal life for all those that his Father had given him (John 6:44). He became a curse not to save the Jewish nation from any exile it might have suffered under the Mosaic covenant, but to free his people who were exiled in Adam; a people from all tribes and nations. Because of this, the writer to the Hebrews speaks of "better promises" (Heb 8:6). Wright misses the essential point, namely, that the promise and the law had different trajectories and were two entirely different entities. By making Christ's curse bearing work efficacious unto Israel's so-called called exile, rather than humanity's exile, Wright has essentially reversed the nature of things. He has effectively taken the promises that concerned temporal Israel and applied these to spiritual Israel, failing to acknowledge the all-important fact that each covenant had its own promises that were independent of each other.

SPIRIT AND GOSPEL

With the law having served its purpose, Paul can say, "so that in Christ Jesus the blessings of Abraham might come to the Gentiles, so that we might receive the promised Spirit through faith" (v.14). The flow of Wright's thought takes this text to be the consequence of Jesus' curse-bearing death that had cleared the roadblock. Israel's sin could no longer prevent the Spirit being received by the Gentile world. Any barrier that

25. Wright, *Revolution*, 241.

existed between the Jewish and Gentile world had effectively come to an end because there was no longer any need to hedge the nation in, as the apostle tells us: "For he himself is our peace, who has made us both one and has broken down in his flesh the dividing wall of hostility by abolishing the law of commandments expressed in ordinances, that he might create in himself one new man in place of the two, so making peace, and might reconcile us both to God in one body through the cross, thereby killing the hostility" (Eph 2:14–16).

Paul is, however, not considering a supposed roadblock, but is simply dealing with the consequences of the promise's fulfillment. He is effectively declaring that the reason for Israel's exclusivity had been achieved, there was no longer any need for it, therefore, the gospel is to go to the Gentile world. As for unbelieving Israel after the flesh, all are, like the rest of humanity, still under the exile with the curse of the original covenant of works remaining upon them.

Wright is a paedobaptist and believes the old covenant to be an earlier administration of the one covenant of grace. The old and new covenants are deemed to be one and the same, with the new covenant being an extension of the old covenant with its substance remaining the same. This, no doubt, partly explains the emphasis that Wright places on the old covenant. Children of believing parents are believed to become members of the church as a result of their baptism in the same way that the Israelites became God's people when circumcised. Because of this association, the Deuteronomic curse is viewed within the covenant of grace, and this gives the curse greater significance where ethnic Israel is concerned.[26]

The Spirit is here referred to (v.14) because it was only after the Messiah had completed his redemptive work in the ratification of the new covenant that the people of God could enter into the liberty of the sons of God. And, as I've said above, even before Christ's first advent, all who believed the promise were God's true and special people, only they were treated as children under age; they lacked that subjective Spirit of adoption that New Testament Christians received at Pentecost. However, following the dissolution of the old covenant, from Pentecost onward, God had, because they are true sons, sent the Holy Spirit of his Son, in a new dimension, into the hearts of his people, "crying, 'Abba! Father!' So you are no longer a slave, but a son, and if a son, then an heir through God" (Gal 4:6-7).

26. See my book *Covenant Theology: A Reformed Baptist Perspective*. Be sure to get the 2018 edition.

The Pentecostal baptism, or baptism by the Spirit, lies at the heart of the difference between Old and New Testament believers. It is a blessing that is subjective, almost visceral, in nature, in other words, it lies not in the believer's union with Christ, but in the believer's experiential realization of this union. It was only following the Spirit's arrival in this new dimension at Pentecost that the believer was granted a new level of assurance and a greater subjective understanding of what he is in Christ. Prior to this time, all true believers were united to Christ and were heirs to the entire estate, yet they were treated like children, "I mean that the heir, as long as he is a child, is no different from a slave, though he is owner of everything, he is under guardians and managers until the date set by his father" (Gal 4:1–2).

In reference to the Gentiles Paul simply seeks to point out that this Spirit-filled blessing is for all that believe. Let me repeat the essential, namely, that Paul is not saying, as Wright would have it, that the reason for Christ's becoming a curse was that blessings might be given to the Gentiles as if it were dependent on Israel's relationship to the Deuteronomic requirements. The apostle was, rather, stating that now Israel's function was at an end because the promise had been fulfilled, with Christ himself being faithful to the original covenant. There was then no longer any need for ethnic Israel, now the gospel, in all its fullness, was to be preached to other nations.

Again, Wright's interpretation leaves one somewhat confused as to what covenant he is referring to. Is he speaking of the original covenant of works, the Abrahamic covenant or the Mosaic covenant? He quite simply doesn't tell us. He seems to adopt a kind of covenantal monism, failing to differentiate between the various covenants. By implying that Christ, the faithful Israelite, kept the Mosaic covenant, and in so doing brought to an end Israel's exile, one could reasonably conclude that Israel is thereby entitled to inherit those blessings referred to in Deuteronomy and elsewhere. For, clearly, these are the promises peculiar to that covenant. History, however, has shown us that this is not the case. Wright, as already mentioned, essentially tries to get around this by changing the old covenant's conditional promises, and in so doing confuses the old and new covenants.

GOD'S PROMISE

The apostle continues in vv.15–29 of chapter three to highlight the difference between the promise that was revealed to Abraham and the covenant made with him:

> 15 To give a human example, brothers: even with a man-made covenant, no one annuls it or adds to it once it has been ratified.
>
> 16 Now the promises were made to Abraham and to his offspring. It does not say, "And to offsprings," referring to many, but referring to one. "And to your offspring," who Tis Christ.
>
> 17 This is what I mean: the law which came 430 years afterward does not annul the covenant previously ratified by God, so as to make the promise void.
>
> 18 For if the inheritance comes by the law, it no longer comes by promise; but God gave it to Abraham by promise.
>
> 19 Why then the law? It was added because of transgressions until the offspring should come to whom the promise had been made, and it was put in place through angels by an intermediary.
>
> 20 Now an intermediary implies more than one, but God is one.
>
> 21 Is the law then contrary to the promises of God? Certainly not! For if a law had been given that could give life, then righteousness would indeed be by the law.
>
> 22 But the Scripture imprisoned everything under sin, so that the promise by faith in Jesus Christ might be given to those who believe.
>
> 23Now before faith came, we were held captive under the law, imprisoned until the coming of the faith would be revealed.
>
> 24 So then, the law was our guardian until Christ came in order that we might be justified through faith.
>
> 25 But now that faith has come, we are no longer under a guardian.
>
> 26 For in Christ Jesus you are all sons of God, through faith.
>
> 27 For as many of you were baptized into Christ have put on Christ.
>
> 28 There is neither Jew nor Greek, there is neither slave nor free, there is no male and female, for you are all one in Christ Jesus.
>
> 29 And if you are Christ's, then you are Abraham's offspring, heirs according to promise.

One cannot overstate the importance of this passage for understanding the Reformed Baptist paradigm and its critique of Wright's new perspective. In vv.16–18 Paul is referring back to the promise God made to

Abraham, namely, the promised "offspring" in Genesis 3:15, a promise that was given to him prior to the establishment of any covenant.

There are at least two possible ways of looking at Genesis 15. First, one could take Genesis 15 to be a reference to the future new covenant, distinguishing between this and the later covenant of circumcision made with Abraham in Genesis 17. In chapter 15 God credited Abraham with righteousness (v.6) because he believed. Later, in the same chapter, we are told that the covenantal promise was presently ratified by God. The covenant in chapter 15 was unconditional, and although we know that any conditions were later fulfilled by Christ, no conditions are listed in regard to Israel. The entire chapter is about that which will occur in the future irrespective of Israel's obedience. This includes those blessings given to Abraham's natural seeds or "offsprings," for example, the land of Canaan, and, of course, the promise concerning the "offspring," who is the Messiah. Israel after the flesh, Abraham's natural seed, failed to appreciate that although the initial giving of the land was unconditional, the same did not apply to its continuance in the land. Because of disobedience it would never have the security accorded to Abraham's spiritual seed, and would know only calamity. Those, however, who laid claim to the promised seed could look forward to realizable spiritual blessings on account of the seed's obedience. For these there awaits an imperishable and undefiled inheritance.

The guarantee of the covenant, where God confirmed the future realization of the promise, is what we read of in v.6, "When the sun had gone down and it was dark, behold, a smoking fire pot and a flaming torch passed between these pieces." This was the Lord himself passing between the dismembered sacrifice. So essentially, while the new covenant is revealed and guaranteed, the work entailed for its establishment will be in the future work of Christ. In the actual covenant (v.17) God was essentially saying to Abraham, to paraphrase, "I make a covenant with you which will presently consist of a promise. I myself am passing between the cut animal to guarantee the promise to you. I myself shall meet all of the covenant's requirements." It was to this promise (Gen 15:4–6) Paul was referring in Galatians 3:18. So although this is called a covenant, it is essentially a covenant of guarantee or a promissory covenant because it concerns God's promise and not fallen man's obedience.

In chapter 17 of Genesis the conditional covenant was made with Israel, it was dependant on Israel obeying the stipulation to circumcision every male child. This covenant was itself but a type of the new covenant that was promised in chapter 15, and as with the Mosaic covenant that appeared 430 years later, it did not change or in any way interfere with the promise. It was essentially the old covenant that came in alongside and ran concurrently with the promise made in chapter 15. From an earlier illustration, the old covenant is the companion who walks beside the man throwing bread to the hungry. He did not change the nature of the one feeding the hungry, but pointed them toward him.

The second position, and perhaps the most prevalent, concerning the covenants in Genesis 15 and 17 is to regard both as referring to the same covenant. This is the view of, as far as I know, the overwhelming number of paedobaptists and not a few Reformed Baptists.[27] As we saw earlier, it maintains that the covenant in Genesis 17 is one of grace rather than works. It is essentially an earlier administration of the one covenant of grace with the new covenant being the last manifestation of this. This position maintains that the promises about the Messiah and those relating to the nation are intertwined, with great care being required to separate the one from the other.

I am growing increasingly sympathetic toward the first position that views the covenant in Genesis 15 as being of grace and an entirely separate covenant from that made in chapter 17. Paul refers to the earlier covenant being "ratified by God" (Gal 3:18) and this is, I believe, what we see in Genesis 15, with the Lord himself passing between the dismembered sacrifice constituting what Paul calls the covenant's ratification (v.15). While this covenant was ratified by way of promise, its fulfillment or consummation had to wait until the appearance of the "offspring" in the singular, which is the Christ.

There are, of course, those who believe the two covenant interpretation is untenable because when other texts refer to Abraham they speak of one covenant.[28] The mistake with this arises from a failure to appreciate that the covenant of promise referred to in Gen 15 is borne witness to in the promise itself. It is essentially nothing less than the new covenant. In chapter 15 we have essentially a unilateral covenant. I say this because its fruition or fulfillment is based on God's faithfulness. This is why throughout this chapter we are presented with what will come about irrespective of sinful man's obedience. In chapter 17 we read of a covenant that is dependent on fallen man's obedience. This is the same covenant

27. It is also viewed in this way by Jeffrey Johnson, a Reformed Baptist, in his book *The Fatal Flaw*.

28. See Gentry's and Wellum's *God's Kingdom Through God's Covenants*, 118.

that was later made at Sinai. So in chapter 15 we have a covenant whose formal legal establishment will occur at the time of Christ, and in chapter 17 a covenant that was established with Abraham. The former concerned the promise that was guaranteed because of Christ's righteousness, while the latter's promises were contingent on the obedience of sinners. The purpose of the latter was to serve the former. It did this by making man aware of his inability and pointing him to the obedience of Christ.

In Galatians Paul emphasizes the Mosaic covenant because it represents the covenant of works, the same covenant that was made with Abraham in Genesis 17. The apostle wants to highlight the fact that the Mosaic covenant has in no way changed the promise made to Abraham. To paraphrase, the apostle is essentially saying, "look, God made his promise to Abraham and credited righteousness to him before any covenant was made. The covenant that was made with him did not alter the promise, and neither did the covenant made with Moses. Salvation has always been by way of the promise." This is the very thing the Jews at Galatia failed to see; they had incorporated the promise into the law, thereby making it dependant on keeping the law. The Jews placed their faith in the old covenant, instead of looking to the promise made to Abraham. They had confused these two things and wrongly believed salvation to be by the law. This is the mistake made by "covenantal nomism," where, although the old covenant is entered through grace, staying in was dependent on keeping the law. Israel, however, was not a saved people, and to expect the people to keep the law on account of having been saved is something of a contradiction in terms.

Wright has something of a novel understanding of Galatians 3:16. He does not believe the "seed" in the singular to be a reference to Christ, but, rather, to Abraham's one family, "The singularity of the seed in v.16 is not the singularity of an individual person contrasted with the plurality of many human beings, but the singularity of one family contrasted with the plurality of families which would result if the Torah were to be regarded the way Paul's opponents apparently regard it."[29] He believes, as in Romans 7, that referring to seed in the singular is a peculiar Pauline trait, where he is really talking about a collective body of people. Such an interpretation is, however, something of an oddity, especially in light of what Paul says in the same verse, "'And to your offspring,' who is Christ." Again, in v.19 Paul clearly identifies the "offspring, "Why then the law? It

29. Wright, *The Climax of the covenant*, 163.

was added because of transgressions, until the offspring should come to whom the promise had been made." Furthermore, since the establishment of what is promised still lay in the future, it seems that to believe the promised "seed" spoke of the single family of Christ is to assume that the family only came into existence with the fulfillment of the promise. The family of Christ, however, has been in existence since the first person believed the promise. The promise itself was the singular seed who would be the ransom and surety who would guarantee the family's existence. From Genesis 3:15 the expectation throughout the Old Testament was for a singular figure. In v.29 we are told that all who belong to Christ are considered as Abraham's offspring. This is not, however, to be taken as the interpretative key for understanding v.16.This appears to be what Wright has done. In vv.27–28, the apostle is speaking of the believer's union with Christ. He is one who has been baptized into Christ, indeed, all those who have been spiritually baptized by God's Spirit into Christ's body are one in him. Believers are Abraham's offspring because they are one with him (v.29). What we then have is Christ, the singular seed, and those who are counted as Abraham's seed in virtue of their being in Christ.

Deductively, one can say:

- Jesus is Abraham's seed in the singular.

- we are in the seed, at one with him.

- therefore, we are Abraham's seed.

In Galatians 3:17 the apostle again speaks of a covenant ratified. Again, this is a reference to the covenant in Genesis 15, where he distinguishes this unconditional covenant from the conditional in Genesis 17. Although it would take in the region of 1800 years for the promise to come to fruition in the "offspring," Paul wants to emphasize that this covenant of promise was not annulled, either by the covenant of circumcision or by that covenant made at Sinai.

THE LAW'S PURPOSE

In 3:18 the apostle refers to the impossibility of the law to save. He tells us that this did not change at Sinai. If it did it would have involved a contradiction because the promise was given to Abraham through faith alone. Not only would the law undermine the grace given to Abraham, but it would make the inheritance an impossibility because none can keep the law. Verse 19 tells us about the law's purpose. It "was added because of transgressions until the offspring was come to whom the promise had been made." Paul is not suggesting that those commandments that represent God's holy character came to an end with the demise of the old covenant, but their particular function as part of that covenant had ended. The covenant itself, with all its paraphernalia, functioned to reveal the sinfulness of sin, and in so doing, highlight the people's need to seek salvation from another source, i.e., the promise.

The traditional interpretation that sees the law driving people to despair in order that they might look to the promise is rejected by Wright, "Paul is not saying, as traditional readings have had it, that 'the law was a hard taskmaster, driving us to despair of ever accomplishing its demands, so that we would be forced to flee to Christ." Such an interpretation is believed to be inadequate, even a caricature, one which implies that:

> God has an initial plan about saving people (the law), but finds that nobody can make it that way, so devises an easier one (faith) instead. That is not only bad theology, it is manifestly bad exegesis, not least of the present chapter in which the whole point is the single plan, the covenant promise to Abraham, and the strange but vital role of Torah within that.[30]

Wright does not tell us to whom this "traditional reading" is addressed. If its target is those of the Reformed school, it is itself a caricature. Both Reformed Baptists, and Reformed paedobaptists, completely reject the idea that God had more than one plan, or that it was necessary for him to change the way of salvation from that of law to faith. Faith has always been the badge of membership for God's true people. Wright's description is more in keeping with the teachings of Dispensationalism, something Reformed Baptists reject. We, therefore, wholeheartedly agree with Wright that this chapter is about God's single plan to save his people through the promise, we, however, differ from him in our understanding of the nature of this single plan.

The law's function and the way it affects an individual is highlighted in Romans chapter 7. Paul alludes to his own experience, "But sin, taking occasion by the commandment, wrought in me all manner of concupiscence, for without the law sin is dead" (Rom 7:8). He goes on to describe in verses 7–12 how the law enabled him to see his own complete inability to keep it:

30. Wright, *Justification*, 107-8.

> What shall we say then? That the law is sin? By no means! Yet
> if I had not known the law I would not have known sin. For I
> would not have known what it is to covet if the law had not said,
> "You shall not covet." But sin, seizing an opportunity through
> the commandment produced in me all kinds of covetousness.
> For apart from the law sin lies dead. I was once alive apart from
> the law, but when the commandment came, sin came alive and
> I died. The very commandment that produced life proved to be
> death to me. For sin, seizing the opportunity through the com-
> mandment deceived me and through it killed me. So the law is
> holy, and the commandment is holy and righteous and good.

When Paul was a Pharisee, he believed himself able to keep God's law.
He describes himself as being "alive." He does the same in his letter to
the Philippians: "If anyone else thinks he has reason for confidence in the
flesh, I have more: circumcised on the eighth day, of the people of Israel,
of the tribe of Benjamin, a Hebrew of Hebrews: as to the law a Pharisee,
as to zeal, a persecutor of the church: as to righteousness under the law,
blameless" (Phil 3:4–6). Those of the new perspective allude to this passage as proof that Paul was keeping the law. This, however, could not be
further from the truth. The apostle is simply speaking of the way he saw
himself before he came to understand the spiritual significance of the law.
He was like the rich young ruler who saw himself as keeping all of God's
commandment or the Pharisees who thought that because they had not
had physical sexual intercourse they could not be accused of adultery.
Paul is not here, as Wright would have us believe, actually saying that he
kept the law; but is speaking with the benefit of hindsight, showing that
he completely misunderstood the law in its spiritual demands. He came
to see that the sacrificial system was powerless to provide true forgiveness, no matter how meticulously one performed it. Paul was effectively
"without the law" in the sense that he lacked a true understanding of its
requirements. When God opened his eyes and applied the commandment to him, "thou shalt not covet," he truly saw sin for what it is, and he
realized that he was completely unable to keep it. Far from being "alive,"
he saw himself dead in trespasses and sins, dead in the eyes of God. He
shows that this is not the fault of the law. The law is "holy, just, and good,"
and it was once "ordained unto life," however, since sin entered in, it
could now only pronounce death.

Wright would entirely disagree with this, claiming that in Romans
7 the apostle is not actually referring to himself, "It is not intended as

an exact description of Paul's or anyone else's actual experience."[31] It is instead descriptive of the time when the law was given to the nation through Moses at Sinai, and Israel's experience under it. He believes the passage speaks of a corporate rather than an individual application. He tells us that Paul is describing "the actual situation (as opposed to felt experience) of Israel living under the law."[32] I would argue that, while this is, no doubt, the case for those within the nation who truly came to faith, it is certainly not the case for the nation as a whole, for the majority of Israelites considered themselves anything but dead in the eyes of God. To apply this blanket fashion to Israel would be to assume that the nation not only came to a true understanding of sin but also truly embraced the promise as the only remedy. I say this because it is not possible to have been brought under such conviction of sin in the way Paul describes without turning to Christ for remedy. Again, if the "I" referred to by Paul is ethnic Israel one would have to conclude that this Israel delighted in God's law in its "inner being" (v.22), and sought to keep God's law with its mind (v.25). We are then presented with a sinful people who are dead in their sins and trespasses seeking to honor God in their "inner being." Such a portrait is very wide of the mark. The truth is something very different. Only a remnant within the nation saw sin for what it is and turned to the Lord in faith, "Even so then at this present time also there is a remnant according to the election of grace" (Rom 11:5). Only believers in the promise were counted as the true Israel, and knew the law "inwardly; and circumcision is that of the heart, in the spirit, and not in the letter; whose praise is not of men, but of God" (Rom 2:28–29), for clearly, "they are not all Israel which are of Israel" (Rom 9:6). The vast majority sought only those things that accorded with their sinful Adamic natures; not only were they not able to seek the things of God, but they were not willing to do so.

In Romans 7 it seems clear that Paul is talking about the man in chapter 6, and the plight of his mortal body. The spirit of such a man, having been made alive, delights in God's law, and the spirit, being a slave unto righteousness, seeks to keep the law. The mortal body, however, being still unredeemed, seeks to do the very opposite. The apostle is aware of the internal battle and the dichotomy this engenders. The spiritual side of him was telling him to do one thing, while the unredeemed side, the

31. Wright, *Everyone Romans*, 127.
32. Ibid.

flesh, was telling him to do something else. As for Israel, the vast majority within ethnic Israel would not have encountered this inner conflict Paul is describing. This kind of warfare does not take place in the unbeliever because both his spirit and body are dead in sin. Such a person lives according to the flesh, and this is what they set their minds upon (8:5). It was only those from within the nation who had been made partakers of the new covenant who experienced this inner warfare. Paul is then essentially describing the believer's sanctification. He knows that ultimately, even his sinful mortal body will be rendered perfect because of Christ's work (v.25). Until that time, his glorified spirit, with the aid of the Holy Spirit working within him, is allowing him to progressively bring his body into conformity with his spirit.

In chapter 3:28 of Galatians the apostle speaks of baptism, "For as many of you were baptized into Christ have put on Christ." Wright again seems to go askew in that he associates this text with the rite water baptism. The problem with this, as in Romans 6, is that it makes putting on Christ dependent on an outward rite, when, in truth, the reverse is the case, where the rite serves as an outward expression of the believer's already existing union with Christ. Restricting baptism to the rite of baptism also excludes all who have not been baptized in water. Paul does not have in mind here that which is done with water, but that which is performed by the Holy Spirit; where the Spirit of God engrafts the believer into the body of Christ; where one is by the Spirit dipped, or better still, immersed into him and all that he has accomplished. It is the same thing we read about in 1 Corinthians 12:13 where the believer is baptized by the Spirit into the body of Christ, in other words, united with him, becoming a benefactor of all that his work achieved. To say that this refers to water baptism is tantamount to saying that one cannot belong to the body of Christ unless one submits to the outward rite. We will return to this when examining Romans 6. The believer(s) can be said to "have put on Christ." This is essentially speaking of the new man as opposed to the old man he once was in Adam.

I have already touched upon Galatians 4, so here I will briefly examine chapter 5. In v.1 where the apostle tells the Galatians that they are now freed from the law, and are no longer under that covenant, "Stand fast therefore in the liberty, wherewith Christ has made us free, and be not entangled again with the yoke of bondage" (Gal 5:1). Should the Galatians submit to the rite of circumcision they will be effectively denying the finished work of Christ, embracing the redundant type whilst rejecting the reality, "Behold, I Paul say unto you, that if ye be circumcised, Christ shall profit you nothing" (Gal 5:2). What they were doing made no sense, and was tantamount to putting themselves under that which spoke of unattainable mundane blessings when they were in actual fact, in Christ and in possession of eternal and heavenly blessings. In going back to the old covenant they were denying the fact that Christ has fulfilled all that is necessary for salvation. To accept circumcision is to accept the whole law, or as Paul puts it, to become "a debtor to do the whole law" (Gal 5:3). The "problem confronting Paul's opponents is not simply that they have chosen a way of justification other than that of faith in Christ; *it is also that they have chosen a way of justification that is beyond the realms of human possibility*."[33] To have liberty in Christ and then want to put oneself back under bondage, where temporal blessings are dependent on doing the impossible, is the height of folly. One sees in this the very opposite of that which Wright argues, where to maintain Jewish exclusivism only certain aspects of the law are obeyed to signify separation from Gentiles.

At the heart of this epistle is the promise alluded to in Genesis 15:5–6. The apostle has sought to untangle the mess the Jews had apparently got themselves into, where they have got the law or old covenant mixed up with the promise. It is only through the promise that one can, like Abraham, be justified by faith. The promise, being made prior to any covenant, finds its *telos* in the coming of Christ. Although the conditional aspects of the covenant made in Genesis 17, that spoke of earthly blessings, could never come to fruition because of man's inability, the promise itself was guaranteed because it depended for its fulfillment on the Son of God. So from the perspective of sinful man, the conditional covenant, for those with eyes to see and ears to hear, through its many types, spoke of the unconditional new covenant that was revealed in the promise. Although he was a paedobaptist, Berkhof states:

> On the one hand it had reference to temporal blessings, such as the land of Canaan, a numerous offspring. Protection against and victory over the enemies; and on the other, it referred to spiritual blessings. It should be borne in mind, however, that the former were not co-ordinate with, but subordinate to, the latter. These temporal blessings did not constitute an end in themselves, but served to symbolize and typify spiritual and heavenly things. The spiritual promises were not realized in the

---

33. Vanema, *Free Acceptance of the Gospel*, 186. Italics in original.

natural descendants of Abraham as such, but only in those who followed in the footsteps of Abraham.[34]

34. Berkhof, *Systematic Theology*, 296.

Wright and Romans

ONE OF THE REASONS for Paul writing this epistle was to spell out his gospel message in anticipation of his intended visit to the city. In it, he has provided the church with the most systematic presentation of theology found anywhere in Scripture.

In this section, I will seek to give a brief description of Wright's understanding of the text before I put forward the Reformed Baptist position, where I will seek to explain why I believe Wright's exposition to be erroneous. When reading Wright, it is not difficult to understand why some see his presentation as being somewhat arrogant. This is simply the result of the faith he has in his own position. He is anything but hesitant in criticising his forebears and contemporaries, believing them to have been wrong about the true meaning of Romans since the time of Augustine. He denies that the message of Romans is about how one is saved, with justification by faith being central in this. He tells us that "this way of reading Romans has systematically done violence to the text for hundreds of years, and that it is time for the text itself to be heard again."[1] The chief purpose of the letter, he maintains, is not soteriological, but ecumenical. He tells us that this letter should not be seen as a "detached statement of how people get saved, how they enter a relationship with God as individuals, but as an exposition of the covenant purposes of the creator God."[2] It is to exhibit the fact that God has been faithful to his covenantal promises. He appears to believe that his is the only correct understanding of the epistle. He does not pause to consider the possibility that it is his interpretation of the text that is effectively obscuring the apostle's intentions. One can but repeat the words of Oliver Cromwell to

---

1. Wright, *WSPRS*, 117.
2. Wright, *WSPRS*, 131.

the Roman Catholics in Ireland, "I beseech you in the bowels of Christ, think it possible you may be mistaken."[3]

In chapter 1:16 the apostle provides us with the essential ingredients of his message:

> For I am not ashamed of the gospel, for it is the power of God for salvation to everyone who believes, to the Jew first and also to the Greek. For in it the righteousness of God is revealed from faith to faith, "as it is written, "the righteous shall live by faith.

Wright rejects the standard Protestant reading of this verse, insisting that it is not about a righteousness that God imputes to the believer, but about God's own covenant faithfulness, "nobody would have supposed that 'God's righteousness' was anything other than his faithfulness to the covenant, to Israel, and beyond that again to the whole of creation."[4] Again he argues that Romans 1:16–17 "are not statements about the gospel",[5] and the verse does not "mean 'the gospel reveals justification by faith as the true scheme of salvation, as opposed to Jewish self-help moralism.'"[6] Rather, by gospel here, the apostle means "announcing Jesus as Lord of the world."[7] It is not specifically about the work of Christ in obtaining salvation for his people, but a declaration that Jesus is Lord. Wright also takes umbrage with the Reformed view concerning the wrath of God in v.18, where he distances himself from penal substitution in relation to God's wrath. As we will see, he replaces penal substitution, where Christ propitiates God for our sin, with the *Christus Victor* model.

Chapter 2:1–16 is, according to Wright, a dramatic picture of the last judgment. It presents a picture that is "rooted in Jewish thinking about the final assize."[8] From v.13, he informs us that "When Paul speaks of 'doing the law' in 2:13, he is thereby "setting up a long chain of thought which will run through several passages until, in 8:5–8, he explains, and even then obliquely, that it is the mind of the flesh that does not and cannot submit to God's law, so by implication the mind of the spirit can and does make that submission."[9] Concerning v.13 we are told that the apos-

---

3. https://en.wikiquote.org/wiki/Oliver_Cromwel

4. Wright, *Justification*, 154.

5. Ibid., 156.

6. *WSPRS*, 126.

7. Ibid., 154.

8. Wright, *Justification*, 158.

9. Ibid., 165.

tle's referent to the doers of the law being justified, is not to be taken as a hypothetical example, but is speaking of those who actually, in reality, do the law, "These will not be the people who only hear the Torah but do not perform it; they will be those who 'do the law.'"[10] These "doers of the law" are Gentile believers who, because the law is written upon their hearts by the Spirit of God, even though they are physically uncircumcised, are faithful to God's commandments. About these, the verdict of God at the end of time will be based on their good works. Wright believes the church has been reluctant to acknowledge this, stating that there has been:

> A massive conspiracy of silence about something that was quite clear for Paul (as indeed for Jesus). Paul, in company with mainstream second Temple Judaism affirms that God's final judgement will be in accordance with the entirety of a life led-in accordance, in other words, with works. He says this clearly and unambiguously in Romans 14:10-12 and 1 Corinthians 5:10. He affirms it in that terrifying passage about church builders in 1 Corinthians 3. But the main passage in question is of course Romans 2:1-16.[11]

Wright appears to be paralleling the Christian's experience with Sanders understanding of Israel. The Christian is initially justified by God's grace, but to stay in the covenant, to be declared justified in the last judgment will be dependent on the believer's works. God will, on that day, "render to each person according to their works."[12]

Referring to the old perspective's view of this Wright states "to most Christian theologians, the idea that Paul would insist on such a judgement at which the criterion will be, in some sense, 'works', 'deeds', or even 'works of the law', has naturally been an anathema to those who have taught that the sole word about judgement and justification is that, since justification is by faith, there simply cannot be a final 'judgement according to works.' "[13] He then goes on to comment on a number of verses that speak of the last judgment, for example, 1 Corinthians 6:9, Romans 14:10–12, along with texts that speak of the Christian's duty to please God, Romans 12:1, 14:18, Colossians 1:10 etc. Essentially, for Wright, "Paul is talking about the final justification . . . point is: who will be vin-

---

10. Ibid., 159.

11. Wright, "New Perspectives on Paul," 253.

12. Ibid, 159.

13. Ibid, 160.

dicated, resurrected, shown to be the covenant people of God, on the last day?"[14]

It seems that Wright is saying that the believer is provisionally justified now but the final justification will be based on the works he has done; on the life he has lived. He is saved unto good works, and it is these works that are considered for his ultimate justification. In other words, one is, at least partially, saved by works. I don't think it is an exaggeration to say that such a semi-Pelagian view would not be out of context in Roman Catholicism. So what we find in Wright's understanding is two justifications, one based on faith, the other, and last, based on works.

Israel was chosen by God to be faithful as the covenant people of God and it had failed miserably. What was lacking was "*faithfulness* on the part of Israel, not some kind of meritorious behaviour through which Israel would rescue itself, but a faithfulness to God and his covenant purposes that would enable Israel to live up to its calling as the light to a dark world."[15] Where Israel had failed God himself was going to do "*through the faithfulness of the Messiah.*"[16]

The revelation of the "righteousness of God" in 3:21 has again nothing to do with God providing a righteousness that can then be imputed to sinners. The "righteousness of God" is "God's faithfulness to the single-plan-through-Israel-for-the-world."[17] He links this in with v.26, "It was to show his righteousness at the present time, so that he might be both just and the justifier of the one who has faith in Jesus Christ." Wright tells us that:

> It is not only surprising, it is actually quite shocking, that people who claim 'the authority of Scripture', and often mean that by that the authority of Paul', 'the authority of Romans', and even 'the authority of Romans 2:21-26', have so often simply failed to read what this all important section says.[18]

Wright believes that God's "*single plan began with the promises made to Abraham*, and if Paul is to show what, in 3:4ff., he promised that he would show that, despite the failure of Israel, God was going to be true to his

14. Wright, *WSPRS*, 126.
15. Wright, *Justification*, 177.
16. Ibid., 178.
17. Ibid., 177.
18. Ibid., 176.

single plan."[19] However, as we will see, he goes awry by failing to draw the correct deductions in distinguishing between the covenant that was promised to Abraham and that covenant that was established with him. One must also remember that God's plan, in its application, goes back further than Abraham, all the way back to Genesis 3:15.

The "righteousness of God through faith in Jesus Christ for all who believe" (3:22) again should be taken as referring to God's faithfulness to his covenantal promises. It is not through our faith, but Jesus' faith as the faithful representative Israelite. This, according to Wright, does not touch upon the idea of the sinner receiving a righteousness, "what has not happened within the law court scene. The judge has not clothed the defendant with his own 'righteousness'. That does not come into it. Nor has he given the defendant something called 'the righteousness of the Messiah.'"[20] He maintains that, "what the judge has done is to pass judicial sentence on sin, in the faithful death of the Messiah, so that those who belong to the Messiah, though in themselves 'ungodly' and without virtue or merit, now find themselves hearing the law court verdict, 'in the right.'"[21] He further states:

> God does indeed "reckon righteousness" to those who believe. But this is not, for Paul, the righteousness either of God or of Christ . . . This is not God's own righteousness, or Christ's own righteousness, that is reckoned to God's redeemed people, but rather the fresh status of "covenant member," and/or "justified sinner," which is accredited to those who are in Christ, who have heard the gospel and responded with "obedience of faith."[22]

Faith then becomes "the badge of covenant membership, not something someone 'performs' as a kind of initiation test."[23]

Wright believes that chapter 3:24-26 "means that those who believe in Jesus Christ are declared to be members of the true covenant people of God; which of course means that their sins are forgiven, since that was the purpose of the covenant."[24] It is that justification "affirmed on the

---

19. Ibid., 177.
20. Ibid., 180.
21. Ibid., 180-81.
22. Wright, *"New Perspectives on Paul."*
23. Wright, *What St Paul Really Said*, 12.
24. Ibid., 129.

basis of faith, what future justification will affirm publicly."[25] Wright even tells us that "it was not so much that 'God needed a sinless victim', though in sacrificial terms that is no doubt true as well, as that 'God needed a faithful Israelite', to take upon himself the burden of rescuing the world from sin and death."[26] In this rescue of the world he does not draw attention to Jesus becoming a curse for the sins of the world, but, it is apparent that he is again thinking along the lines of Jesus taking upon himself the Deuteronomic curse; not for the world, but for Israel. The world is believed to benefit from this because sin came to a head in Israel and any punishment it suffered had a collateral dimension for other nations.

Romans 3:28, "For we maintain that a man is justified by faith apart from the works of the law," is seen by Wright not to be a re-cap on what that apostle has said previously from 3:21. Instead of looking back to what was said in chapters 2 and 3 regarding the position of both Jews and Gentiles under the law, Wright restricts this verse to Jews alone, showing that covenant membership does not come by keeping the law (badges of membership) but by faith. So the apostle is saying "that all who attempted to legitimate their covenant status by appealing to possession of Torah would find that the Torah itself accused them of sin."[27]

What then of boasting? The Jews were given to boasting, not because they believed they kept the law and merited God's favor, but because they considered the mere possession of it to be a sign that they already had his favor; they were already the exclusive people of God. From verse 3:27 to the end of this chapter God is, according to Wright, essentially telling the Jews that this is far from being the case. "The Jewish claims that possession of the Torah was sufficient to establish him or her as part of God's people, those through whom God is bringing light to the world, is confronted with an apparently different 'Torah', which says, 'No, not so fast: this faith-fulfilment is what I had in mind all along, and it eliminates your boasting as surely as if it was drowned in the depths of the sea."[28]

Chapter 4 picks up a further subject: "the one family, Abraham as its father, and the God who, by being the life giver and creator, has been true to his promise."[29] He rightly sees the emphasis being placed on Genesis

25. Ibid.

26. Wright, *Justification*, 178.

27. Wright, *Romans*, 461.

28. Wright, *Justification*, 186.

29. Ibid., 192.

15. His conclusions are, however, somewhat different from the Reformed Protestant understanding, instead of seeing the chapter to be principally about justification by faith, especially in the example of Abraham, it is instead about God's faithfulness to what he promised Abraham in providing him with a family whose badge of membership is faith.

He takes the events of the exodus, the old exodus, and uses these as a template for the new exodus. Chapters 3-5 signifies the Passover and its consequences, and in chapter 6 we essentially have the crossing of the Red Sea with its reference to baptism, so as Israel was saved by passing through the waters, so too are believers saved by water baptism. Again, when Paul speaks of the law in chapter 7 in the first person he is not referring to himself, but to the giving of the law at Sinai and the Jewish experience under this law. Essentially then, Paul is using the exodus as a template, a kind of mirror image, for that which occurs in new covenant salvation. Chapter 8 shows how the Christian has obtained the victory, and this is paralleled with how the Jews should have lived in Canaan, but did not.

There is much more one could say about Wright's position. The above should, however, suffice in order for one to show how a Reformed Baptist paradigm will provide a 'better fit' for these chapters.

Refutation of Wright's understanding of Romans

LET US REMIND OURSELVES of the main themes of this letter as seen from the Reformed Baptist perspective. In contrast to Wright's understanding, we believe the primary purpose of the letter to be soteriological, i.e., concerned with salvation. In chapter 1:16 Paul introduces his gospel, and then from 1:18 to chapter 3:29, he shows why humanity needs the gospel by demonstrating that all are under the wrath of God. We essentially have a diagnosis of man's sinful position, demonstrating that, without exception, both Jew and Gentile are under God's condemnation, "There is no one righteous, not even one" (3:10), for "all have sinned and come short of the glory of God" (3:23). Having shown that all stand condemned Paul introduces the gospel 3:21, a gospel that is the antidote to God's wrath; a declaration of what God has done in Christ to save his people from his wrath and reconcile them to himself.

From 3:21, to the end of the chapter Paul spells out the nature of his gospel showing the only remedy for sin is God's own righteousness. Paul then tells us exactly what the gospel saves us from, namely, "the wrath of God that is being revealed from heaven against the ungodliness and unrighteousness of fallen humanity."

He then, to the end of chapter 4 shows that one can only access what Christ's work achieved on the basis of faith, Using Abraham and David as examples, he shows that this has always been the case. Chapter 5 moves on to examine the believer's assurance that results from justification. From questions that he envisaged being asked as a result of what he said at the end of chapter 5, the apostle digresses in chapters 6 and 7, to deal with these questions. These chapters are then essentially a parenthesis, a diversion from his main theme. In chapter 6 the apostle shows why the Christian will not continue to sin, namely, because he has, in Christ, become dead to sin. Chapter 7 explains the role of the law and why this can no longer condemn the believer on account of his being married to Christ. In chapter 8 the apostle then picks up from where he left off in chapter 5 and continues with the theme of assurance. In chapters 9–11 the apostle deals specifically with Israel, where he shows that God has not abandoned his true people. These three chapters can also be seen as a parenthesis where Paul finds himself compelled to address important questions people might have about God's faithfulness to his people. Paul seeks to demonstrate that God has not abandoned his true people. He then in chapter 12 to 15 takes up where he left off at the end of chapter 8. These three chapters are concerned with the Christian life; with the practical application of the truths he has been dealing with. The last chapter is concerned with greetings and exhortations.

PAUL'S GOSPEL

The key to the epistle is found in chapter 1:16–18.

> For I am not ashamed of the gospel, for it is the power of God for salvation to everyone who believes, to the Jew first and also to the Greek. For in it the righteousness of God is revealed from faith to faith, as it is written, "the righteous shall live by faith." For the wrath of God is revealed from heaven against all ungodliness and unrighteousness of men, who by their unrighteousness suppress the truth.

Paul uses a figure of speech called litotes. This is where one employs a negative to emphasize a positive. Therefore, when Paul tells us that he is "not ashamed of the gospel" he is actually saying that he is extremely proud of it. This is because "the gospel is the power of God unto salvation to all that believe."

As we shall see, one cannot do what Wright has done, namely, speak of the gospel without God's wrath. By examining what we have been saved from we can all the more appreciate God's work. Lloyd-Jones, speaking of God's love and wrath reminds us that "The two things always go together and you cannot separate them. It is only as you have some conception of the depth of His wrath that you will understand the depth of his love. It was God Himself who found the way whereby His own wrath could express itself against sin, and yet the sinner not be destroyed but rather justified, because His own Son had borne the punishment."[1]

Wright's understanding of what constitutes the gospel is very different from that of the Reformers who believed it to be about Jesus' death and resurrection; the fact that something happened to him in order that we might be saved. He tells us that "Paul's gospel to the pagans was not a philosophy of life. Nor was it, even a doctrine about how to get saved."[2] Again, "the gospel is not an account of how people get saved. It is . . . the proclamation of the lordship of Jesus Christ."[3] The gospel is essentially "the announcement that Jesus is Lord–the Lord of the world, Lord of the cosmos, Lord of the earth, of the ozone layer, of whales and waterfalls, of trees and tortoises."[4] The gospel is, "at its very heart, *an announcement about the true God as opposed to false gods.*'" Jesus is the one who has "defeated principalities and powers."[5]

Wright is correct to state that the cross and resurrection stand at the center of Paul's theology, however, when he speaks here of things we have been liberated from, things that Christ has triumphed over, God's wrath, which the old perspective places at the very centre of its theology of the cross, is noticeable by its absence. On those occasions when he does speak about wrath, it is an impersonal force, something entirely separate from any notion of an angry God punishing his Son. One gets the impression that he is doing some kind of theological gymnastics, presenting us with a cross that sanitizes the awful nature of what occurred at Calvary.

Wright seems to suggest that the specific knowledge concerning the work of Christ in providing forgiveness of sins somehow just arises from knowing that Jesus is Lord:

> Paul discovered, at the heart of his missionary practice, that when he announced the lordship of Jesus Christ, the sovereignty of King Jesus, the very announcement was the means by which the living God reached out with love and changed the hearts and lives of men and women, forming them into a community of love across traditional barriers, liberating them from paganism

1. Lloyd-Jones, Romans 1, 349.
2. Ibid., 90.
3. Ibid., 133.
4. Ibid., 154.
5. Ibid., 59.

which had held them captive, enabling them to become, for the
first time, the truly human beings they were meant to be.[6]

For one who is under the wrath of God, to be told that Christ is Lord
hardly constitutes good news. To be told that Jesus has "defeated principalities and powers" does not get to the heart of the gospel message. One
might be told that Elizabeth ll is queen, yet this knowledge does not mean
that one has to be in subjection to her. Every soul suffering the miseries
of hell is fully aware that Jesus is Lord. This knowledge does not deliver
them from their sins. When Martin Luther was battling against sin he already knew that Christ is Lord. This knowledge only drove him to greater
despair. He needed to know that God would forgive him and pronounce
him righteousness on the basis of faith alone. When Luther read Romans
1:17 he initially thought that the "righteousness" referred to was nothing
less than God's character, which, because it is righteous, would condemn
all sin. It was only when he saw that it spoke of a righteousness procured
by Christ, a righteousness that would become his by faith alone, that he
knew himself liberated from God's wrath.

The sinner wants to know how the gospel affects him personally; he
wants to know that the awful righteous anger of God has been removed
from his head and that for him the impossible is now made possible. The
gospel is the very thing that Wright claims it is not, namely, the fact that
Jesus came to save his people from their sins by suffering his Father's
wrath in his own body. The gospel is good news and proclaims that "God
so loved the world that he gave his only Son that whoever believes in him
should not perish but have eternal life" (John 3:16), and that Christ came
to offer his life a ransom for many (Mark 10:45).

Christ becomes Lord and King in the sinner's heart not before but as
a consequence of believing and confessing his sins. The very act of God's
giving of his Son implies something of Christ's redemptive life and death.
To believe that Christ is Lord is not a gift in the same category as to be
told that in Christ God has provided the hell-bound sinner with complete
forgiveness of sins and life eternal. John tells us that his gospel was written "so that you may believe that Jesus is the Christ, the Son of God, and
that by believing you may have life in his name" (John 20:31). To believe
that Jesus is the Christ, the Son of God, means for John, believing certain
things about him. John clearly had in mind here all that he had written
about in his gospel, for example, that Jesus had come to do the works of

6. Ibid., 61.

his Father (John 10:37), and die for the sins of his people. Luke plainly tells us what his gospel message included, namely "that through this man forgiveness of sins is proclaimed to you" (Acts 13:38). It is the gospel Paul is referring to when he tells the Galatians about "the Lord Jesus Christ, who gave himself for our sins to deliver us from the present evil" (Gal 1:3–4). While at Corinth, Paul decided to know nothing except "Jesus Christ and him crucified" (1 Cor 2:2). He later spells out the essence of his gospel, "For I delivered to you as of first importance what I also received, that Christ died for our sins in accordance with the scriptures, that he was buried, that he was raised on the third day in accordance with the scriptures" (1 Cor 15:3–4). This was the message that Paul was entrusted with. It was the *raison d'être* of his missionary journeys. He strove to communicate to all the fact that "there is one God, and there is one mediator between God and men, the man Jesus Christ, who gave himself as a ransom for all, which is the testimony given at the proper time. For this, I was appointed a preacher and an apostle . . . a teacher of the Gentiles in faith and truth" (1 Tim 2:5–7).

People in Paul's day were, of course, concerned about eternal matters and how eternal life may be attained. Eternal life is part of the Christian's hope, as Paul tells us in his letter to Titus, "Paul, a servant of God and an apostle of Jesus Christ, for the sake of the faith of God's elect and their knowledge of the truth, which accords with godliness, in the hope of eternal life through the preaching with which I have been entrusted by the command of God our Savior" (1:1–3). We see this again in the case of the rich young man (Mark 10:17; Matt 19:16; Luke 18:18) who asked Jesus about eternal life. The gospel is good news because it speaks of deliverance from wrath, peace with God, and life eternal with him. The message was not then simply about declaring Jesus to be Lord and King, but, rather, the declaration to sinners that Jesus died and rose again in order that their sins might be forgiven.

DOERS OF THE LAW

Paul returns to what he said in chapter 1:16–17 in chapter 3:21. In the interim he spells out the reason for God's intervention in Christ. The apostle seeks to show that God's wrath is not something arbitrary, but something that is earned because of sin. In 1:21:32 he describes sin as it affects all men, especially the Gentiles. The Jews are dealt with next, from

2:1–29. Here Paul demonstrates that they are, in terms of sin, no different from the Gentiles, both equally deserve God's wrath. From what he has said it may appear that there are no advantages in being a Jew, but this would be a mistake, so from 3:1–8 Paul alludes to the benefits that have been conferred on the Jews. Then from 3:9–20 he rounds off what he has said from 1:21–3:8, by emphasizing that all are guilty and without excuse.

The Gentile world did not have those privileges that belonged to Israel, they did, nevertheless, have some knowledge of God, as Paul puts it: "For what can be known about God is plain to them. For his invisible attributes, namely, his eternal power and divine nature, have been clearly perceived, ever since the creation of the world, in the things that have been made" (1:20). Having said this, the Gentile world, in some shape or form, still possessed the first promise (Gen 3:15), and there was still the possibility, of faith in this. The Gentiles had, however, turned away from God and worshipped created things instead (v.25). As a result of their sins, God "gave them up to dishonourable passions" (v.24). Continuing to the end of chapter 1 Paul draws attention to their various sins.

Concerning the Jews, the apostle emphasizes the point that although they have the law they fail to keep it. They considered themselves to know what was excellent (v.18), to be a "guide to the blind, a light to those who are in darkness" (v.19), and "an instructor of the foolish . . ." (v.20). They preach against stealing (v.21) and adultery (v.22), yet they were themselves guilty of these very things. They were Jews in the external sense only, failing to appreciate that the true Jew "is one inwardly, and circumcision is a matter of the heart, by the Spirit, not by the letter. His praise is not from man but from God" (v.29). This might appear that the law was given in vain, however, this was not the case. Whilst the law did benefit Israel (vv.1–4), the Jews, or most of them, failed to glean its essential purpose. Far from being a light to the nations in the proper performance of the Mosaic ordinances, the Jews, in their misunderstanding of the law's purpose, made it something it was never meant to be, namely, a covenant unto salvation, instead of a signpost to Christ and the new covenant. From v.9 to the introduction of God's remedy in 3:21, Paul brings both the Jew and Gentiles together, showing that both are under the law and fully deserving of his wrath.

In chapter 2:6–11, Paul emphasizes the fact that God will only reward those who do what he requires, whether they have the Mosaic law or not. All who do evil will face God's wrath, whilst all those that do good will be blessed. God will "render to each according to his works: to those who by patience in well-doing seek for glory and honor and immortality, he will give eternal life; but for those who are self-seeking and do not obey the truth, but obey unrighteousness, there will be wrath and fury" (vv.6–8). Paul is not here suggesting a salvation by works. Neither is he saying that Jews and Gentiles can obtain immortality by good works. He is, rather, expressing a general truth that if one does good works one will be rewarded with eternal life, whereas, if one does unrighteous works one will face God's wrath. It's like one saying, "if you have wings you will be able to fly, whereas, if you don't have wings you will not be able to fly. It is just a matter of cause and effect. The Christian has eternal life because of his identification with Christ, where Jesus' good works become the Christian's good works. It is a salvation which Christ himself earned by his life, death, and resurrection.

Wright makes much of 2:13, "it is not the hearers of the law, but the doers of the law who will be justified." (v.13). He maintains that "There is, then, for Paul, a final judgment, and it will be 'according to works.'" Paul in this verse, so he claims, is speaking about a future justification where, at the final assize, people will be judged according to their works. He states that "the verdict on the last day will truly reflect what people have actually done."[7] He believes these works to be valid in regard to the final justification because they are the result of God's Spirit working within, "They are the things which show, rather, that one is in Christ; the things which are produced in one's life as a result of the Spirit's indwelling and operation. In this way, Romans 8.1–17 provides the real answer to Romans 2.1–16."[8] He again states:

> And we now discover that this declaration, this vindication, occurs twice. It occurs in the future, as we have seen, on the basis of the entire life a person has led in the power of the Spirit–that is, it occurs on the basis of 'works' in Paul's redefinition sense. And near the heart of Paul's theology, it occurs in the present as an anticipation of that future verdict, when someone is responding in believing obedience to the 'call' of the gospel.[9]

Such an interpretation would, however, go against everything the apostle is saying from 1:18 to 3:20. It simply fails to fit the context, where the apostle's intention is to show that both the Jews and Gentiles stand

---

7. Ibid., 167.

8. Wright, ntwrightpage.com/2016/07/12/new-perspectives-on-paul/

9. Wright, "The New Perspective on Paul," 287.

condemned and in need of the gospel message which he reveals from 3:21. Why would he, in the middle of showing all to be lawbreakers, suddenly make reference to the possibility of keeping the law to be justified on the last day? Indeed, Paul has nothing to commend the Gentiles and Jews for, the entire passage is an indictment. At the end of this section, he sums up his whole argument by declaring, "Now we know that whatever the law says it speaks to those under the law, so that every mouth may be stopped, and the whole world may be held accountable to God" (Rom 3:19). Murray's commenting on verse 13 is undoubtedly correct:

> It is quite unnecessary to find in this verse any doctrine of justification by works in conflict with the teaching of this epistle in later chapters. Whether any will be actually justified by works either in this life or in the final judgment is beside the apostle's interest and desire at this juncture. The burden of this verse is that not the hearers or mere possessors of the law will be justified before God but that in terms of the law the criterion is *doing*, not hearing.[10]

What can be said to occur on the last day is what might be called declarative justification. When persons are presently justified they know it in their hearts, the guilt of sin has been removed, but there is not the declaration to others that they have been justified. Fesko, commenting on John Owen, tells us that:

> Owen distinguishes between the nature and essence of justification and the manifestation or declaration of it. The former occurs in this life, the latter on the day of judgment. In this life when a person is justified, they know of it in their heart, but there is no formal external evidence of it before the church and the world. At the final judgment, the believer's justification will be publicly declared and made manifest before the church and world.[11]

So on the last day, whilst there shall be no justification, there will be a public declaration, or public pronouncement, by God concerning those who have been justified. As John Owen puts it: "Yet is it not a second justification: for it depends wholly on the visible effects of that faith whereby we are justified, as the apostle James instructs us; yet is it only one single justification before God, evidenced and declared, unto his

10. *Murray*, John, *The Epistle to the Romans*, 71.

11. Fesko, "John Owen," 15.

glory, the benefit of others, and increase of our own reward."[12]By his insistence on a second justification based on the life lived subsequent to the first justification, Wright confuses justification with sanctification. The former entails a declaration by God that one is accepted as righteous, and that one's sins have been forgiven. The latter concerns the impartation of righteousness, whereby the person is intrinsically being made righteous, although it will remain incomplete in this life. Essentially then, justification is forensic while sanctification is transformative. God does not base justification on anything but the perfect righteousness of Christ. The Christian's righteousness this side of heaven is always imperfect, to then say that God will base a supposed second justification based on this is to call God's holiness into question.

In the King James Bible, vv.13–15 of chapter 2 are placed in brackets. These are useful because this section is essentially a parenthesis. Verse 16 should be seen as a continuation of where Paul broke off in v.12. In v.12 he makes a universal statement, "For all who have sinned without the law will also perish without the law," and in vv. 12–15 he is, in the words of Lloyd-Jones, "dealing with the possibility that someone might say, 'All right, I understand that about the Jew, but then, what about the Gentile? Is it right that a man should be condemned by a law he has never heard?'"[13] Paul's intention is to show that Gentiles cannot plead an ignorance of the law to excuse themselves. The Jews, on the other hand, considered themselves to be the true people of God simply because they had received the law. Paul, however, tells them that this means nothing unless the law is obeyed. To paraphrase the apostle, he is essentially saying to the Jews, "Okay, great, you boast, thinking yourself something special because you have the law, but the law is of little value to you because you fail to keep it. Indeed, the law itself tells us that only those who keep it will be considered righteous in God's eyes." The emphasis is on the impossibility of doing what the law commands.

Paul was also conscious of the fact that the Jews might think that God is showing some partiality, for why should they be judged on the basis of their having the law when the Gentiles have not even heard of the law? Paul has said that "God shows no partiality" (v.11), and when he comes to dealing with the Gentiles he explains why. The Gentiles, who although not possessing the law in the explicit manner in which was given

12. Owen, *Works* 5, 139.
13. Lloyd-Jones, Martyn, *Romans* 2: 116.

to the Jews, "do not have the law by nature, do what the law requires, they are a law to themselves, even though they do not have the law" (2:14). By the Gentiles "not possessing the law" the apostle means they did not receive the explicit revelation which the Jews were provided with at Sinai. By the "doers of the law", Paul simply means that some of the things done by the Gentiles show they have an innate knowledge of right and wrong. For example, they shun murder and stealing etc. In other words, they possessed natural law. All pagan societies display the fact that they possess a moral consciousness or compass. When someone does that which is wrong, e.g., murder, his conscience bears witness and accuses him. The conflicting thoughts that even those without the law have concerning right and wrong is the result of the work of the law that God has written on their hearts (v.15), and borne witness to by their conscience.

Wright seems unable to reconcile v.12, about the Gentiles without the law, with v.15 that speaks of the requirements of the law being written upon their hearts. He states that "If those who are a 'law to themselves', because 'the law' (presumably the Jewish law) is written on their hearts, are non-Christians, then Paul has been talking nonsense."[14] He calls it nonsense because he believes it leads to a contradiction. How can they be without the law and at the same time have the works of the law written on their hearts? These two texts are, however, both referring to non-Christians and they are certainly not contradictory. When Paul speaks of these Gentiles who "by nature do what the law what the law requires" (v.13) he is speaking about their natural state in which they were born, and not, as Wright believes, their new natures in the light of Jeremiah 31. Far from talking nonsense, the apostle is speaking of the law in two different contexts. In v.12 he is referring not to Gentiles who are completely unaware of God's moral law, but to all who are outside the law made with Israel. To paraphrase, "the Jews have the law and will perish by the law since they fail to keep it, the Gentiles, although not possessing the explicit revelation of the law that was given to Israel, nevertheless, still have the law in their hearts, and they too will perish by the law." It is about the latter that Paul is speaking in v.15, the law that is written on the consciences of all humanity.

Wright maintains that "there is one class of Gentiles who in a sense will be judged with reference to Torah. This class consists of Gentile Christians; though by birth they do not possess the Torah, they are now

14. Wright, "The Law in Romans 2" 142.

in the strange position of 'doing the law', since the Spirit has written the 'work of the Torah' on their hearts."[15]

The Gentiles, however, will not be judged by the Torah and the Torah will never be written on their hearts, neither will it be written on the hearts of the Jews. If Wright has Jeremiah 31:33 in mind he is essentially looking at two different covenants and laws. Jeremiah was not speaking of the Torah, but the law of God of which the Torah was but a reflection. This law is "God's basic moral demand available to all people."[16] Any reference to the Torah must be limited to the entire Sinaitic package. In Romans 2 Paul uses the "law" (*nomos*) in two different contexts. When he refers to those who do not possess the law (v.14) it is the Torah he has in mind. When he then refers to the Gentiles who are a law unto themselves, he is speaking of the universal law.

According to Wright, this text is about Gentile Christians who are experiencing the blessings of the new covenant as referred to in Jeremiah 31:33. There are, however, a number of reasons why this is not the case.[17] First, if they were Gentile Christians Paul's comments that "they are a law to themselves" (v.14) would be superfluous. It only makes sense if he is referring to a people who have never heard of the special revelation of law as given to Israel. For clearly, if they had received God's special revelation why would they be "a law to themselves"?

Secondly, there is a big difference between those who have "the work of the law written on their hearts" (2:15) and what Jeremiah says, namely, "having the law written on their hearts." The former is suggestive of an awareness of the law's demands, while the latter concerns conformity to the law in the believer's sanctification. The apostle is simply saying that these Gentiles, although they do not have the explicit revelation of the law as do the Jews, nevertheless, know what the law requires because they have the necessary awareness in their hearts. This is just what we would expect, bearing in mind that man was made in the image and after the likeness of God. While the image and likeness of God may have been partially expunged by the Fall, an innate knowledge of what God required is still there.

Thirdly, Schreiner shows how Wright's understanding is undermined by v.15, where Paul says that the Gentiles "show that the work

15. Wright, http://ntwrightpage.com/2016/05/09the- law-in-romans-2/
16. Moo, *Romans*, 88.
17. Argument taken for Schreiner's *Romans*.

of the law is written on their hearts, while their conscience also bears witness and their conflicting thoughts accuse or even excuse them." To quote Schreiner:

> Any notion that this is saving obedience is ruled out by this clause, for the text emphasizes that 'accusing' thoughts predominate . . . Indeed, the words . . . ("or even") that precede . . . ("defending") intimate that the defending thoughts are relatively rare, or at least the exception rather than the rule. Therefore, the doing of the law described in verse 14 should not be understood as a consistent and regular observance of the law.[18]

The apostle speaks of a day approaching when judgment will take place, "on that day when, according to my gospel, God judges the secrets of men by Christ Jesus" (2:16) Paul says nothing about another eschatological justification that will be based on the believer's works. This verse is simply showing that the final arbiter will be God, who will on the day of judgment judge the deeds of sinful humanity. So, even should anyone say that he is without the law, and therefore not bound to keep it, he will be shown to be wrong on the day of judgment. Also, many Jews rejected what Paul was saying because they mistakenly believed themselves to have kept the law. Paul is simply saying that in the end they too will be proven to be wrong. For clearly, God shows no preference between Jew and Gentile in his judgments. So all will be without excuse. Paul is showing that in spite of what people may say they do, or do not do, nothing is hidden from God, he knows the hearts of all men, and in the end he will judge righteously.

What can be said about those texts like v.16, which Wright informs us speak of God's judgment in the future in relation to the justification of believers? For example, 2 Corinthians 5:10, where Paul states that "we must all appear before the judgment seat of Christ, that each one may receive what is due for what he has done in the body, whether good or bad." According to Wright Paul is speaking about a future trial in the court of God, where God will take one's works into consideration before announcing a final justification.

Let me first say that these texts have nothing to do with a second justification for those who are in Christ. One of the key passages for understanding the judgment of God regarding Christians is found in 1 Corinthians 3:13–15:

18. Schreiner, *Romans*, 124.

each one's work will become manifest, for the Day will disclose it, because it will be revealed by fire, and the fire will test what sort of work each one has done. If the work that anyone has built on the foundation survives, he will receive a reward. If anyone's work is burned up, he will suffer loss, though he himself will be saved, but only as through fire.

There will, no doubt, be a judgment of the saints concerning their works, however, it will not be in regard to their justification and their position in Christ. Yes, believers who have fallen into sin will be answerable to their Father, and their works will be judged, but as for their position as those justified, this will never be brought into question. They were justified once and for all when they came to faith in Christ. The believer's union with Christ is indissoluble and he is now part of Christ's body, to suggest that he will have to undergo another justification, if applicable to the believer, must likewise be applicable to Christ. Yet we know that Christ is already at the right hand of God, and the believer is where he is. Another justification would then tend to contradict one's position in Christ.

Although some of the believer's works may be rejected, the believer's status in the kingdom as one justified by faith will remain the same. Let me use a simple illustration. Imagine a father who has a number of children. He may give the children certain tasks that each is to complete. Some may do this well, while others may fall short of what is required. The father may reward those who have done well, and provide some form of punishment for the others. However, the father will never call into question the status of the children within the family. So it is with justification. This will never be called into question. Any judgment will occur within the family and not affect the believer's filial relationship with his Father. The 1689 Baptist Confession states:

> God continues to forgive the sins of those who are justified, and although they can never fall from the state of justification, yet they may because of their sins, fall under God's fatherly displeasure. In that condition they will not usually have the light of God's countenance restored to them until they humble themselves, confess their sins, ask for pardon, and renew their [consistent walk of] faith and repentance.[19]

Jesus said, "O Truly, truly, I say to you, whoever hears my word and believes him who sent me has eternal life. *He does not come into judgment,*

---

19. The Baptist Confession of Faith 1689. 11.4.

but has passed from death to life" (John 5:24).[20] Since all true believers have, in the new birth "passed from death to life" there can be no judgment that will call this life into question. This text alone should be sufficient to dispel any idea of there being a second justification, for if such a justification is to be based on God judging one's works, then Christ's words are contradicted.

Texts like 2 Corinthians 5:10 are not speaking of the judgment that will befall unbelievers where they shall appear before a wrathful God. They are, rather, speaking of a judgment for believers, not as to justification, but as to whether they have utilized their mortal bodies as slaves unto righteousness. Notice the text does not speak of the judgment seat of God, but of Christ. This is a judgment that will be for Christians alone. We are here talking about rewards and punishments for those who are already in the family and kingdom of God; who are already partakers of the new covenant. The bottom line for Wright's reading of this passage is well expressed by Macleod:

> For all its labored originality, this theory completely fails to escape the gravitational pull of the religion of self-justification. Wright's basic thrust is that justification is no legal fiction: the believer *is* righteous. This righteousness may be the result of grace and the Spirit's work within us, but when all is said and done it is our own personal righteousness. It is inherent, not imputed. We are asked to stand on the rock of our own covenant-keeping. Could that have given Martin Luther peace? Could it give any of us peace? On the contrary, our hope would ebb and flow with every rise and fall in the tide of our personal spirituality.[21]

KEEPERS OF THE LAW

Wright believes that 2:17 is not referring to a "works contract" but the vocation to which God had called Israel: "The Jew against whom he is arguing were saying, 'Yes, the world is indeed in a mess; but we Jewish people, armed with the Torah, are God's chosen solution to this problem. We have been given the divine vocation or sorting out this mess, of putting the world right.'"[22] Paul is, however, not suggesting this, and neither is

---

20. Italics added.
21. Macleod, *A Faith to Live By*, 166–7.
22. Wright, *Revolution*, 309.

he suggesting that the Jews believed in a legalistic righteousness. Instead, he is saying that the Jews were wrong in their belief that salvation could come through the Mosaic covenant. Wright states that "Paul's concern is that the Creator's whole plan is put in Jeopardy by the failure of humans to *worship him alone*."[23] However, to suggest that Israel had a work to do, failed to do that work and that it was then left to Jesus to complete appears to undermine God single plan and, furthermore, fails to account for salvation prior to the giving of the law. As I have said a number of times, if salvation was available prior to the Mosaic law, why would God then change his method of saving sinners by making salvation in some sense dependent on the law? If Israel was important, if it had a vital job to do, it consisted in carrying out the ordinance of the law, so that they might typify the work of him who was to come, in other words, as well as exposing sin, it also declared the gospel through its various rites and sacrifices. It was because Israel possessed the types that spoke of Christ that it was a light to the nations. They were to keep themselves from being contaminated by surrounding nations because through them the Messiah was to come forth.

Romans 2:26–29 is another text from which Wright deduces what is an aberrant teaching. According to Wright, these verses are clearly an allusion to Gentiles who, although uncircumcised, obey God's commandments, thereby fulfilling the law (2:27).[24] One obvious problem with this understanding is that it would compel one to say that these Gentiles could keep the moral law. I say moral law because the Gentiles were not given the threefold Mosaic law. They knew nothing about the civil and sacrificial laws which were revealed specifically to Israel. Wright cannot then get around this by suggesting they were somehow observing "boundary" or "identity markers." To suggest that they were keeping God's moral law is to effectively undermine the apostle's teaching on humanity's sinfulness and need for justification. One may ask, if it were possible that these Gentiles could already keep the law, why then did Christ have to come to keep it for them? The impossible would be possible in that the promise would be attainable by works. Wright's view contradicts the apostle's main summing up of the law: "Now we know that whatever the law says it speaks to those who are under the law, so that the whole world may be held accountable to God. For by the works of the law no

23. Ibid., 85.
24. Wright, *Justification*, 166.

human being will be justified in his sight, since through the law comes knowledge of sin" (Rom 3:19–20). By "world" the apostle means both Jews and Gentiles.

In Romans 2:26–29 Paul uses a hypothetical argument to teach the Jews about the true meaning of circumcision. The apostle knew how important circumcision was to the Jews, and he anticipated their saying, "we are clearly God's special people because we alone have circumcision." It is, as Lloyd-Jones tells us, the Jews "final line of defence."[25] The Jews were effectively saying, "we will go back beyond Moses and the law, we will go back to the fountain, to the beginning, to Abraham our father–the one man out of whom the whole race has come; to whom God gave this sign and this seal of circumcision, which surely is indissoluble."[26]Paul is simply demonstrating, quite logically, that if a Gentile, one who is uncircumcised, were to keep the law, the fact that he is uncircumcised will make no difference. His obedience to the law would condemn the Jews because they do not keep the law. In chapter 4 he goes further because even Abraham himself was justified by God before he was circumcised. True circumcision is not that which is performed on the flesh, rather, it is that of the heart, the very thing so many Jews were ignorant of.

In vv.28–29 Paul pinpoints the error of the Jews. They had been guilty of viewing the externals of the law or old covenant, thinking that adherence was acceptable to God. They failed to go beyond the letter, putting their faith in the covenant that was established with Abraham instead of the promised new covenant by which he was reckoned righteous. God's true people are not like those who merely participated in the externals, the outward motions, e.g., circumcision in the flesh, but, rather, those who had experienced circumcision of the heart, and thereby, by God's Spirit saw the law of God for what it truly is. These inwardly circumcised Jews (and Gentiles) walked in the footsteps of Abraham by believing in the Messiah God himself had provided.

Again, Wright understands "works of the law" in 3:20 to be a reference to those "boundary markers" which the Jews were using to exclude Gentiles from the covenant. Here, again, such a view makes little sense. The law here means the entire law; a law that condemns because of sin. Following this Paul introduces justification, "For by the works of the law no human being will be justified in his sight since through the law comes

25. Lloyd-Jones, *Romans 2*, 152.
26. Ibid., 152.

knowledge of sin" (v.20). The apostle is obviously not speaking to Jews alone, but to every human being who is under the covenant of works. No one can save themselves; none can appear just in the eyes of God. It is against this backdrop of human sinfulness and inability that the righteousness of another is alluded to.

Both the Jews and the Gentiles are under the law and all, without exception, are guilty of not keeping it. No special requirements were imposed by God on the Gentiles, they had no special food requirements, no Sabbaths, and no circumcision, yet they are in the same guilty position as the Jews. It would, therefore, make no sense to restrict the "works of the law" to anything less than that law which the Gentiles had upon their hearts, and the Jews also had written on the two tablets of stone. The problem with the Jews then had nothing to do with "boundary markers". Rather, it was that they, like the Gentiles, had failed to live up to God's standards. They, like the rest of humanity, had broken God's law.

JESUS' RIGHTEOUSNESS

One must not forget that the law as given to the Jews was a revival or reiteration of the covenant made with Adam, only now there was no possibility of life, it was, essentially, a covenant only unto condemnation. However, the original covenant by which all stand condemned must be kept if there is to be any salvation. Having finished his depiction of humanity's sin, Paul introduces the answer that God himself has provided in his own Son Jesus Christ: "But now the righteousness of God has been manifested apart from the law, although the prophets and the law bear witness to it –the righteousness of God through faith in Jesus Christ for all who believe" (3:21–22). So what exactly are these verses saying? Are they, as Wright maintains, speaking of Jesus' faithfulness to the covenant or are they speaking of a righteousness that God gives to his people? Wright believes that "through faith in Jesus Christ for all who believe" applies not to the faith of the believer because this would result in needless repetition. This is because to write "all who believe" would be saying the same thing as "through faith." He, therefore, believes that "through faith in Jesus Christ" is a reference to Jesus' faithfulness to the covenant. One should, therefore, read the verse as "through the faith of Jesus".

Wright's reading of this verse does, however, seem out of step with the way Paul expresses his theology, both in this and other epistles. One should also consider carefully Cranfield's words, "I would also suggest that we should be wise to hesitate about trying to construct a theology in which Jesus Christ's faith has an important place."[27] As Fitzmyer points out:

> While this interpretation might seem plausible, it runs counter to the main thrust of Paul's theology. Consequently, many commentators continue to understand the gen. as objective, "through faith in Jesus Christ," as in 3:26; Gal 2:16, 20; 3:22; Phil 3:9; cf. Eph 3:12 . . . Indeed, as Dunn rightly notes (*Romans*, 166), Paul does not draw attention to Christ's faithfulness elsewhere in the extended exposition of Romans, even where it would have been highly appropriate, especially in chapter 4, where Abraham's pistis (faith) is the model for the believer. Paul is not thinking of Christ's fidelity to the Father; nor does he propose it as a pattern for Christian conduct. Rather, Christ himself is the concrete manifestation of God's uprightness, and human beings appropriate to themselves the effects of that manifested uprightness through faith.[28]

A good understanding of this passage is provided by James R. White:

> It would appear that the clue to the interpretation is provided by Paul himself in a passage that furnishes the closest parallel, namely, 3:22 (cf Gal. 3:22). There he speaks of "the righteousness of God through faith of Jesus Christ unto all who believe". It might seem that the expression "unto all who believe" is superfluous in this instance because all that it sets forth has been already stated in the expression which immediately precedes it, "through faith of Jesus Christ." But the apostle must have some purpose in what seems to us repetition. And the purpose is to accent the fact that not only does the righteousness of God bear savingly upon us *through faith* but also that it bears savingly upon *every one* who believes. It is not superfluous to stress both. For the mere fact that the righteousness of God is through faith does not of itself as a proposition guarantee that faith always carries with it this effect.[29]

It seems to me that it is possible that both the Reformed view and that put forward by Wright can be applied to this passage, although I would be more sympathetic to the former. These verses can be read in the light

27. Cranfield, *On Romans*, 97.
28. Fitzmyer, Romans, 345.
29. White, *The God Who Justifies*, 149.

of Jesus' faithfulness to the covenant, as, Wright emphasizes, without losing that righteousness that is made available for all those that believe. It
is because of the former that we have the latter. "Through faith in Jesus
Christ" could possibly mean the faithfulness exercised by Jesus Christ
in his keeping the requirements of the covenant. This prevents needless
repetition that occurs when one assumes the verse to be speaking of the
faith of the believer. To paraphrase these two verses, I would suggest: "the
righteousness of Jesus Christ, that righteousness achieved because of his
faithfulness in keeping the covenant as the second Adam, is available to
all who believe in him." Of course, this speaks of covenant faithfulness
because without this there can be no salvation. Jesus had to keep that
covenant that the first Adam broke. It was by his faithfulness in doing this
that he was able to achieve a righteousness for his people. By believing in
Jesus this righteousness is then reckoned to the sinner.

PROPITIATION AND THE LOVE OF GOD

In 3:25 Paul, for the first and last time in this letter, uses the word propitiation, "whom God put forward as a propitiation by his blood, to be
received by faith." The following quote by Wright clearly shows that he
once held a view that no Reformed believer would disagree with:[30]

> The idea of punishment as part of the atonement is itself deeply
> controversial; horrified rejection of the mere suggestion has led
> on the part of some to an unwillingness to discern any reference
> to Isaiah 40-55 in Paul. But it is exactly that idea that Paul states,
> clearly and unambiguously, in [Romans] 8:3, when he says that
> God "*condemned sin in the flesh*"—i.e., in the flesh.
>
> Dealing with wrath or punishment is *propitiation*, with sin,
> *expiation*. You propitiate a person who is angry, you expiate a
> sin, crime or stain on your character. Vehement rejection of the
> former idea in many quarters has led some to insist that on "*ex-
> piation*" is in view here. But the fact remains that in [Romans]
> 1:18-3:20 Paul has declared that the wrath of God is revealed
> against all ungodliness and wickedness and that despite God's
> forbearance this will finally be meted out; that in 5:8, and in the

30. In his most recent book, *The Day the Revolution Began* (2017) Wright appears
to have rejected propitiation, that God the Father vented his wrath against his own
Son at Calvary.

whole promise of 8:1-30, *those who are Christ's are rescued from wrath.*[31]

Yet having said this, he writes a glowing endorsement of Steve Chalke's book *The Lost Message of Jesus*, in which Chalke does not mince his words in his denial of what the above quote suggests.

One must ask why, having read Chalke's book, Wright could write such a positive commendation? Chalke tells us that: "punishing the Son for an offence he has not even committed" is tantamount to "cosmic child abuse . . . If the cross is a personal act of violence perpetrated by God towards humankind but borne by his Son, then it makes a mockery of Jesus' own teaching to love your enemies and refuse to repay evil with evil."[32] In explaining his reasons Wright says that he understood Chalke to be essentially saying:

> on the cross, as an expression of God's love. Jesus took into and upon himself the full force of all the evil around him, in the knowledge that if he bore it we would not have to; but this, which amounts to a penal substitution, is quite different from other forms of penal substitution, such as the mediaeval model of a vengeful father being placated by an act of gratuitous violence against his innocent son. In other words, there are many models of penal substitution, and the vengeful-father-and –innocent-son story is at best a caricature of the true one.[33]

This, however, presents one with a problem because both these depictions are a "caricature." The kind of penal substitution, Wright tells us, he thought Chalke was advocating is itself very wide of the mark. Instead of saying that Jesus took upon himself the wrath of God, he suffered "the full force of evil around him." One does not have to look too far to see what Wright's now believes. He believes that we have "paganized our soteriology." His views are not too far removed from those of Chalk:

> thousands of young people really do believe that the creator God was very angry and wanted to lash out and kill us all because we'd offended him, but that somebody else happened to stand in the way, it happened to be his own innocent Son so that somehow makes it all right, and that the angry creator exhausted wrath on his Son so that everyone else could go free.

31. Wright, "The Cross and the Caricature."
32. Chalke, *The Lost Message of Jesus*, 182-3.
33. Wright, "The Cross and the Caricature."

"This is thoroughly pagan soteriology and it is not taught in the New Testament.[34]

He tells us that such a view is a "major failure of the Western tradition" one that presents us with a "thoroughly paganized soteriology and it is not found in the New Testament."[35]

This so-called medieval view that he seems so determined to reject is closer to the biblical portrayal than the view he claims to embrace. The Reformed view believes that the innocent Son was the one punished by his Father, and it is on the basis of this that the Father's wrath is placated. This is the very thing conveyed by the idea of propitiation. Concerning generalities, one might ask what exactly does Wright mean when he says "Jesus took into and upon himself the full force of all the evil around him"? To say that somehow Jesus took upon himself all the world's evil forces and exhausted them will simply not do because it amounts to the depersonalization and sanitization of God's wrath. One feels that those who subscribe to such a view do so because it has become unfashionable to believe in penal substitution and the very notion of wrath.

The God of Scripture is a vengeful God, and not only can he not look upon sin, but he demands that it be punished. Grudem tells us:

> If we ask, "Who required Christ to pay the penalty for our sins?" the answer given by Scripture is that the penalty was inflicted by God the Father as he represented the interests of the Trinity in redemption. It was God's justice that required that sin be paid for, and, among the members of the Trinity, it was God the Father whose role was to require payment. God the Son voluntarily took upon himself the role of bearing the penalty for sin.[36]

Christians must be specific and not be hesitant to say that it was the Father's wrath that was vented against his own Son, Jesus Christ; "that God the Father, the mighty Creator, the Lord of the universe, poured out on Jesus the fury of his wrath: Jesus became the object of the intense hatred of sin and vengeance against sin which God has patiently stored up since the beginning of the world."[37]

---

34. Wright, The Cross, Youtube.
35. Ibid.
36. Grudem, Systematic Theology, 577.
37. Ibid., 575

The word propitiation means: "a sacrifice that bears God's wrath to the end and in so doing changes God's wrath toward us into favour."[38] Lloyd-Jones provides us with a Scriptural view of Jesus' suffering:

> How exactly did He do this? Let me answer that question; and as I do so you will see why I was at such great pains to defend the word 'propitiation' and to hold on to it at all costs because it was so vital. How has God done this on Calvary? How has He vindicated His character? How has He given us an explanation of His 'passing over' of those sins in past times in His self-restraint and tolerance? There is only one way in which He could do it. God has stated that He hates sin, that He will punish it, that He will pour out His wrath upon sin, and upon those guilty of sin. Therefore, unless God can prove that He has done that, He is no longer just. He has shown that. What the Apostle is saying is that on Calvary He has done just that. He has shown that He still hates sin, that He is going to punish it, that He must punish it, that He will pour out His wrath upon it. How did He show that on Calvary? By doing that very thing. What God did on Calvary was to pour out upon His only begotten and beloved Son His wrath upon sin. The wrath of God that should have come upon you and me because our sins fell upon Him[39]

One cannot speak of salvation apart from God's wrath because this is the very thing the sinner has been saved from, as Don Carson reminds us:

> When the biblical writers say that Christ's death saves us, from what does it save us? We could say it saves us from death, from the consequences of our sin, from our lostness, but centrally it saves us from the wrath to come. Death, the consequences of our sin, and lostness are nothing other than preliminary manifestations of the wrath of God. It is, of course, true that the Bible depicts God as working to rescue his people from sin. Yet it is no less true that the most central consequence of sin from which they must be rescued is the wrath of God: it is impossible to read the Old Testament narrative without tripping over this theme in countless chapters. This dynamic tension lies at the heart of what the New Testament writers insist that the cross achieves, and Wright misses it almost entirely.[40]

---

38. Ibid.

39. Lloyd-Jones, *Romans: Exposition of chapters 3:20–4:25*. 103–104.

40. Carson, review of N.T. Wright's "Evil and the Justice of God."

Such a position is according to Wright "thoroughly pagan soteriology and it is not taught in the New Testament."[41] The fact of the matter is somewhat different. In the Scriptures there are more references to the wrath of God than there are to his love. The following quote from the prophet Nahum 1:2–8 gives a flavor of what we read in the Old Testament:

> The Lord is a jealous and avenging God;
> the Lord is avenging and wrathful;
> the Lord takes vengeance on his adversaries
> and keeps wrath for his enemies.
> The Lord is slow to anger and great in power,
> and the Lord will by no means clear the guilty.
> His way is in whirlwind and storm,
> and the clouds are the dust of his feet.
> He rebukes the sea and makes it dry;
> he dries up all the rivers;
> Bashan and Carmel wither;
> the bloom of Lebanon withers.
> The mountains quake before him;
> the hills melt;
> the earth heaves before him,
> the world and all who dwell in it.
> Who can stand before his indignation?
> Who can endure the heat of his anger?
> His wrath is poured out like fire,
> and the rocks are broken into pieces by him.
> The Lord is good,
> a stronghold in the day of trouble;
> he knows those who take refuge in him.
> But with an overflowing flood
> he will make a complete end of the adversaries,
> and will pursue his enemies into darkness.

We find the same thing in the New Testament, "Since, therefore, we have now been justified by his blood, much more shall we be saved from the wrath of God" (Rom 5:9). John the Baptist warned the Scribes and Pharisees "to flee from the wrath to come (Matt 3:7). It is this wrath which rests

41. Wright, The Cross. Youtube.

upon all who do not believe, "Whoever does not obey the Son shall not see life, but the wrath of God remains on him" (John 3:36). It is in this context that one must view justification. Those who are in Christ have been saved from this wrath, and have been declared righteous because of what the Messiah has done on their behalf.

Wright appears to espouse a view of the cross that by-passes God's wrath in connection with his Son. The following quote clearly shows that the wrath of God plays no part in his understanding of the atonement:

> The cross is for Paul the symbol, as it was the means, of the liberating victory of the one true God, the creator of the world, over all the enslaving powers that have usurped his authority . . . For this reason, we give priority-a priority among equals, perhaps, but still a priority-to those Pauline expressions of the crucifixion of Jesus which describe it as the decisive victory over the 'principalities and powers.' Nothing in the many expressions of the meaning of the cross is lost if we put this in the centre . . . The death of Jesus had the effect of liberating both Jew and Gentile from the enslaving force of the 'elements of the world' (Gal 4:1-11). And towering over almost everything else, the death of Jesus, seen as the culmination of his great act of obedience, is the means whereby the reign of sin and death is replaced with the reign of grace and righteousness.[42]

About the Reformed understanding of propitiation, Wright states: "It is confusing, it is ambiguous, it is contradictory, it is obfuscating of the highest level, an academic sleight of hand."[43] He tells us, the idea "that Christ died in the place of sinners is closer to the pagan idea of an angry deity being pacified by a human death than it is to anything in either Israel's scriptures or the New Testament."[44] In his recent book, *The Day the Revolution Began*, any equivocation there may have been in his previous works concerning penal atonement has gone, now he is willing to completely deny this doctrine. He is fond of expressing the Reformed doctrine in caricature:

> a. All humans sinned, causing God to be angry and to want to kill them, to burn them forever in "hell."

---

42. Wright, *WSPRS*, 47.
43. MacArthur, John MacArthur on N. T. Wright, Youtube.
44. Ibid.

b. Jesus somehow got in the way and took the punishment instead (it helped, it seems, that he was innocent-oh, and that he was God's own son too).

c. We are in the clear after all, heading for "heaven" instead (provided, of course, we believe it).[45]

Even when it is presented "more subtly than this," it gives a picture of a God who is abhorrent, who is "a bloodthirsty tyrant." Further into the book Wright alludes to a video he had been sent from an evangelical which put forth the idea of penal substitution. His reaction to this speaks volumes, showing unambiguously, the stance he takes:

Intrigued, I watched it. It was well put together, with clever sequences and plenty of hi-tech touches. But at the centre of the message was a line that made my blood run cold. The video had described how we all mess up our lives, how we all do things that spoil God's world, and so on. Then said the narrator, "Someone has to die." And it turned out, of course, to be Jesus. That sums up the problem. What kind of "good news" is that? What kind of God are we talking about once we say that sort of thing? If God wants to forgive us, why can't he just forgive us? . . . Why does "someone have to die?"[46]

He says that such an "idea belongs not in the biblical picture of God, but with pagan beliefs."[47] Wright is clearly providing the reader with one part of what was shown in the video. One wonders why he appears so uncomfortable at the fact that for there to be any reconciliation with God someone does have to die, and, yes, it is something that only Christ can accomplish. Wright correctly states that "what happens in the death of Jesus happens because of the *love* of God,"[48] yet he fails to see how the death of Jesus at the hands of his Father can be in any way reconciled with verses like John 3:16. He is essentially ridiculing the notion of propitiation; the idea of God's wrath being displayed in this manner seems to offend Wright. Indeed, one gets the impression that salvation could be possible without the death of Christ, without someone having to die.

Propitiation has perhaps been more caricatured than any other doctrine, in the words of Murray:

45. Wright, *Revolution*, 38.

46. Ibid., 42-43.

47. Ibid., 43.

48. Ibid.

it has been assailed as involving a mythological conception of God, as supposing internal conflict in the mind of God and between the persons of the Godhead. It has been charged that this doctrine represents the Son winning over the incensed Father to clemency and love . . . When the doctrine of propitiation is presented in this light it can be very effectively criticized and can be exposed as a revolting caricature of the Christian gospel.[49]

Why Wright deliberately seeks to caricature the old perspective is rather puzzling. Unfortunately, many who read *TDTRB may* come away believing in his distorted portrayal. One can only assume that he does so to bolster his own position and make it appear more authentic.

When we examine propitiation in the Scriptures we discover something very different from those paganized notions that have been attributed to it. Rejection of propitiation is often the result of projecting onto God our sinful dispositions and inclinations, e.g., when we think of anger we associate it with what we see in ourselves and others, which usually involves a loss of self-control. We then eschew any notion of anger in regard to God, and find it a more attractive proposition to believe that Jesus suffered the consequences of our sins, but not their penalty. Wright, like others before him, appears sympathetic to the notion that "wrath" has more to do with impersonal forces rather than with the wrath of a personal God. If we depict God as being angry with sin and punishing it in his own innocent son, according to Wright, we should then read John 3:16 as, "God so hated the world that he killed his own Son."[50] He accuses us of neglecting God's love, with merely, inserting the word love onto the end of that story to legitimize what God did.

Those who reject God's anger as unbefitting to a God of love fail to draw the necessary distinction between righteous anger and the impetuous tantrums and hurts we associate with human anger. This is clearly stated by W. F. Lofthouse: "To be angry simply because I have been injured, to wreak my vengeance like a spoiled child on the person or thing that has thwarted me, - there is no morality in that . . . But anger may be the highest form of altruism. When the mind is irradiated with the flame of anger against tyranny or meanness, high-handed violence or slavish cunning, anger is then simply virtue in operation."[51] The holy anger of God displayed in Christ's suffering is nothing less than the outwork-

49. Murray, *Redemption Accomplished and Applied*, 24.

50. Wright, *The Cross*, YouTube.

51. Lofthouse W. F. *Ethics and Atonement*, 161.

ing of God's love. In Jesus' death, we see the full extent of God's love, in the words of Thomas Watson, "The cross was a pulpit in which Christ preached his love to the world."[52]

Those who reject propitiation tend to speak of expiation instead.[53] The two must, however, go together, as MacLeod states:

> Unless our sins are remitted, God's anger is inevitable, but before they can be remitted they must be expiated. Christ, by his blood, is that expiation, the place where sin is atoned for, and where God meets with us and speaks to us. Justifying those who put their faith in Jesus Christ (Rom 3:26). This is how the divine anger is averted, and this is why the *hilasterion* was provided. The speak of an expiation which does not propitiate is meaningless.[54]

Most of our illustrations, if not all, are inadequate for what occurred on the cross at Calvary some two thousand years ago. We must remember that Christ, being the Son of God, does not equate with my being the son of my earthly father. Humans are both sinful and capricious. All that we do is imperfect. The persons of the Trinity, however, are on another plane. All that they do is perfect, and, of course, this applies to God's wrath.

What then does Scripture mean when it speaks of God being angry or wrathful? John Stott tells us that "to speak of God's anger is a legitimate anthropomorphism, provided that we recognize it is no more than a rough and ready parallel, since God's anger is absolutely pure and uncontaminated by those elements which render human anger sinful."[55] His wrath is not what God is in the way that love, light, and holiness are. Had there been no sin there would have been no wrath. Love, light, and holiness, however, are attributes that will always apply because they are part of God's essential nature, whereas wrath is the consequence of offending God's holiness. God cannot but demand the punishment of sin, to do otherwise would be to contradict his nature. If one gets too close to the sun one will be burnt, it will occur as a consequence of what the sun is, likewise, sin leads to punishment because of who God is.[56] The

---

52. Watson, *A Body of Divinity*, 175.

53. See C. H. Dodd's *The Epistle of Paul to the Romans*. Fontana 1970.

54. MacLeod, *Christ Crucified*, 147.

55. Stott, *The Cross of Christ*, 105–6.

56. All comparisons are limited in what they do. This one fails to get across the fact that unlike the sun, God's anger is personal. Also, where the sun is always hot and likely to burn, God's anger is only displayed when sin is present.

wrath of God is "his steady, unrelenting, unremitting, uncompromising antagonism to evil in all its forms and manifestations,"[57] and propitiation lies at the very heart of our salvation, as Murray put it:

> The essence of the judgment of God against sin is his wrath, his holy recoil against what is the contradiction of himself (see Rom.1:18). If Christ vicariously bore God's judgment upon sin, and to deny this is to make nonsense of his sufferings and death and particularly of the abandonment on Calvary, then to eliminate from this judgment that which belongs to its essence is to undermine the idea of vicarious sin-bearing and its consequences. So the doctrine of propitiation is not to be denied or its sharpness in any way toned down.[58]

The pagan notion of a God whose mind toward his people needs to be changed through sacrifice is entirely alien to Scripture. The cross is a demonstration of God's love. It was Christ who suffered, but it was the love of God that provided the sacrifice:

> It cannot be emphasized too strongly that God's love is the source, not the consequence, of the atonement . . . God does not love us because Christ died for us; Christ died for us because God loved us. If it is God's wrath which needed to be propitiated, it is God's love which did the propitiating. If it may be said that the propitiation "change" God, or that by it he changed himself, let us be clear he did not change from wrath to love, or from enmity to grace, since his character is unchanging. What propitiation changed was his dealings with us.[59]

Again, to quote Murray:

> The propitiation which God made his own Son is the provision of the Father's love, to the ned that holiness may be vindicated and its demands satisfied. Thus, and only thus, could the purpose and the urge of his love be realized in a way compatible with, and to the glory of the manifold perfections of his character . . . And so we must say that this love of the Father was at no point more intensely in exercise than when the Son was actively drinking the cup of unrelieved damnation, then when he was enduring as substitute the full toll of his Father's wrath . . . What

57. Stott, *The Cross*, 173.

58. Murray, "The Atonement," in *Collected Writings of John Murray*, Edinburgh, Banner of Truth, 1974, 429–33.

59. Stott, *The Cross*, 174.

love for men that the Father should execute upon his own Son
the full toll of his holy wrath, so that we should never taste it![60]

God's wrath demands propitiation and it is God himself who does the
propitiating. Propitiation does not represent "the Son winning over the
incensed Father to clemency and love . . . When the doctrine of propitiation is presented in this light it can be very effectively criticized and can
be exposed as a revolting caricature of the Christian gospel."[61] It should
not be seen as that which constrains the Father's love, and neither is it
"turning the wrath of God into love." Nothing could be further from the
truth, for "The atonement did not procure grace, it flowed from grace."[62]

At Calvary, "in the cross of Christ, God's justice and love are simultaneously revealed."[63] It is God himself who is propitiation's fountain and
initiator. What we see in Christ is God himself suffering for us, where
God is appeasing his own wrath through the sacrifice of his own Son. As
Barth put it: "It was the Son of God, i.e. God himself . . . the fact that it
was God's Son, that it was God himself who took our place on Golgotha
and thereby freed us from the divine anger and judgment, reveals first the
full implication of the wrath of God, of his condemning and punishing
justice,"[64] It is because "it was the Son of God, i.e., God himself, who took
our place on Good Friday, the substitution could be effectual and procure
our reconciliation with the righteous God . . . Only God, our Lord and
Creator, could stand surety for us, could take our place, could suffer eternal death in our stead as the consequence of our sin in such a way that it
was finally suffered and overcome."[65]

Scripture makes it clear that anyone who dies outside of Christ will
face punishment, the divine displeasure. It is only those united to Christ
who will avoid this punishment because God has propitiated his wrath in
Christ. This is simply another way of saying that Christ by his death has
satisfied divine justice. In Christ, we see God himself paying the ransom
price to himself by suffering himself the wrath that was meant for us.
With men, the greatest exhibition of love is to lay down one's own life for

60. Murray, *Collected Writings*, 2:146-7.

61. Murray, *Redemption Accomplished*, 24.

62. Reymond, *Systematic Theology*, 640.

63. Stott, *The Cross*, 131.

64. Barth, *Church Dogmatics* II:I, 398.

65. Stott, *The Cross*, 174-75.

one's friends (John 15:13), yet how much more love do we see expressed by God in Christ, who laid down his life for those who were his enemies.

It is important to bear in mind that propitiation is not, first and foremost, directed toward man, but toward God. It is his wrath that needs to be appeased. It is never directed to the one who has committed the offense, but to the one who is offended. Propitiation, to quote R. W. Dale:

> denotes that by which a change is produced in the disposition of a person who has committed an offence; it always refers to that which changes the disposition of the person who has been offended; and when used in relation to offences against the Divine law, it always describes the means by which the sin was supposed to be covered in order that the Divine forgiveness might be restored."[66]

PROPITIATION AND SECOND TEMPLE JUDAISM

Following Sanders, Wright places much emphasis on the need to understand Second Temple Judaism as a prerequisite for understanding the message of Paul. He stresses that the message should be understood in its original setting, or at least as close to it as we can get. One would have to agree with him here. The contemporary usage of a word needs to be understood, as Wright points out, "To understand any event in history, you must put it firmly *into* that history and not rest content with what later generations have said about it."[67] By "later generations" he is clearly thinking of the Lutheran position, where Paul was interpreted against the backcloth of Roman Catholicism.

However, when one examines some of the extra-biblical sources from the time, one finds that Wright appears not to have heeded his own advice in his understanding of *hilaskomai* and its cognates. In classical Greek, the word always denoted the pacification of an angry deity. As George Smeaton said, "The uniform acceptation of the word in classical Greek, when applied to the Deity, is the means of appeasing God, or of averting His anger; and not a single instance to the contrary occurs in the whole Greek literature."[68] Morris[69] is of the same opinion,

---

66. Dale, *The Atonement*, 162ff.

67. Ibid., 51.

68. Smeaton, *The Apostles Doctrine of the Atonement*, Edinburgh, 455.

69. It is interesting that after writing *The Cross* and *The Apostolic Preaching of the*

"Throughout Greek literature, biblical and non-biblical alike, *hilasmos* means 'propitiation'.[70] In spite of this, Wright has seen fit to apply to the New Testament a meaning to the word that would have been foreign to its hearers.

The church fathers certainly made reference to it. One of the first letters written to Christians after the inspired New Testament writings, was *First Epistle of Clement*, and in this *hilaskomai* denotes the placation or appeasement of an offended Deity, "Jonah preached destruction to the people of Nineveh, but they, repenting of their sins, propitiated God by their supplications and received salvation." The same is found in the early 2nd century *Shepherd of Hermas*, "Then I said within myself, 'if this sin is recorded against me, how shall I be saved? Or how shall I propitiate God for my sins which are full blown?'" We find the same in the writings of the Jewish historians Josephus and Philo:[71]

> Eusebius of Emesa (c. 300–360)
> Thus the Lamb of God, that taketh away the sins of the world, became a curse on our behalf." He then stated, "And the Lamb of God not only did this, but was chastised on our behalf, and suffered a penalty He did not owe, but which we owed because of the multitude of our sins; and so He became the cause of the forgiveness of our sins, because He received death for us, and transferred to Himself the scourging, the insults, and the dishonour, which were due to us, and drew down upon Himself the appointed curse, being made a curse for us.[72]

Athanasius' Letter to Macellinus.

> Speaking in the Saviour's own person, describes the manner of his own death. Thou has brought me into the dust of death, for many dogs have compassed me, the assembly of the wicked have laid siege to me. They pierced my hands and my feet, they numbered all my bones, they gazed and stared at me, they parted my garments among them and cast lots for my vesture. They pierced my hands and my feet-what else can that mean except

---

Cross, Morris drew close to Wright's understanding before moving back to his earlier position.

70. Morris, The Cross, 349.

71. Full examination of the wrath of God, see, Roger R. Nichol's piece entitled: "C. H. Dodd and the Doctrine of Propitiation" in *Westminster Theological Journal*, xvii.2, 1955, pp.117-157.

72. Eusebius, *Demonstio Evanglica* 10:1, Trans. W. J. Ferrar, http://www.early-christian writings.com/fathers/eusebius_de_12_book10.html (accessed 27/03/17.

the cross? And Psalms 88 and 69. Again speaking in the Lord's own person, tell us further that He suffered these things, not for His own sake but for others. Thou has made Thy wrath to rest upon me, says the one; and the other adds; I paid them things I never took. *For He did not die as being Himself liable to death: He suffered for us, and bore in Himself the wrath that was the penalty for our transgression.*[73]

To "draw down" is to make oneself the object of God's wrath, and in the first of the above quotes, we are told that Christ "drew down upon himself" the punishment that should have fallen on us. In Athanasius' letter, we have the explicit reference to the penal nature of the atonement, "thou has made thy wrath to rest upon me." The above makes it clear that one cannot speak of Christ's sacrificial death without factoring in the Father's wrath; it is the essential component, without which atonement becomes impossible.

Although it is true that there was not a worked out exposition of penal substitution in the early church, the incidental references show that it was something readily believed, as Ovey and Sach state, "[if] a writer makes a passing, but nonetheless explicit, reference to the doctrine of penal substitution in a work largely devoted to another subject, this probably indicates that penal substitution was both widely understood and fairly uncontroversial among his contemporaries."[74] Furthermore, as Morris points out, quoting from Dale, "If the LXX translators and the New Testament writers did not mean propitiation, why did they choose to use words which signify propitiation and are saturated with propitiatory associations?"[75]

In the Old Testament the display of God's wrath[76] is not seen as being simply the natural consequence of sin, but of a personal God's reaction to sin. Wright completely overlooks the propitiatory significance of Passover, even maintaining that it has nothing to do with the concept. However, contrary to what Wright believes, Passover, as recorded in Exodus 12, provides an excellent example propitiation. When in Egypt the Israelites had sinned against the Lord, "But they rebelled against me and

---

73. www.Athanasius.com/psalms/aletter.htm#22

74. Jeffrey, et al, Steve, Ovey, *Pierced for our Transgressions: Rediscovering the Glory of Penal Substitution* (Wheaton, Ill.: Crossway, 2007) 163.

75. Leon Morris's *The Apostolic Preaching of the Cross*, 148.

76. See Leon Morris's *The Apostolic Preaching of the Cross*, London, Tyndale Press, 1972, pp. 148–154.

were not willing to listen to me. None of them cast away the detestable things their eyes feasted on, nor did they forsake the idols of Egypt" (Ezek 20:9). It was on account of this, before they could enter the promised land, their sins would need to be atoned for. God's wrath would have to be placated. The death of the Egyptian firstborn was a direct result of God making his wrath known. The Israelites were told to take a young lamb, one without blemish, to sacrifice it and to daub the blood on the posts and lintel of their doors. That night God sent his angel to smite all the firstborn in Egypt. The Angel of the Lord, however, passed over the Israelites firstborn because of the blood of the lamb. In this, we have a type of Christ, the true Passover, where those covered by his blood were spared from God's wrath. Believers are spared from the wrath of God because they have been sprinkled with the blood of Christ, the true lamb without blemish. It, therefore, strikes me as somewhat odd that Wright insists that the Passover had nothing whatsoever to do with propitiation.[77]

No doubt, Wright, and others would say that Passover is about redemption, not propitiation and atonement. There cannot, however, be redemption without propitiation. When the believer is translated from the kingdom of darkness and into the kingdom of Christ, it is a redemption made possible by Christ's propitiatory sacrifice. In a similar manner, again, as a type, God's translating Israel from Egyptian bondage into Canaan was also a redemption that demanded a sacrifice. Redemption and propitiation are bedfellows, one cannot have one without the other.[78]

God can then look favorably on his people because his wrath was vented on him in their place. What occurred in the great flood, and later the destruction of Sodom and Gomorrah was no impersonal consequence of sin, but, again, the deliberate action of a personal God punishing sin. Throughout the Old Testament, we witness God's wrath toward Israel because of its failure to keep the covenantal conditions. Speaking about the sin of the Israelites God said to Moses, "Now, therefore, leave me alone, that my wrath may burn hot against them, and I may consume them . . ." (Ex 32:10).[79] The rest of the Old Testament is a continuation of this theme, yet it is interspersed with the revelation of the promised Messiah, the only one in whom the wrath can be removed.

77. For more on this see Holland's *Tom Wright and the Search for Truth*, 265–273.

78. For more on this see Tom Holland's *Tom Wright and the Search for Truth*, 165–171.

79. For further examples see Leon Morris' *The Apostolic Preaching of the Cross* pp.147–154.

In *The Day the Revolution Began,* Wright provides a number of reasons why he believes the Reformed exegesis of Romans 3:21–27 is erroneous, stating that:

> the usual reading is that through this 'propitiation' those who trust in what Jesus did on the cross can be declared 'in the right . . . In this usual narrative of 'justification,' humans start off with no moral credit, nothing to qualify them to escape hell and go to heaven; but God's action in Christ gives them the credit, the 'righteousness,' they need.[80]

First, Wright tells us that "this understanding of 3:25–26 leaves vv. 27–31 stranded. It appears to change the subject, from how you acquire this 'righteousness,' to 'how Jews and Gentiles come together into a single faith family.'"[81] I must confess that I am a little baffled by this. It appears to me that the apostle is being entirely consistent. He, in the words of Lloyd-Jones, "was dealing with actual difficulties in the minds of many at that very time. For instance, the Jews were in real difficulties about the Gospel. It seemed to them, on the surface, to be doing away with the whole of the Old Testament."[82]

Paul had reached his climax in saying that God is the "just and justifier," showing that not only is God just and faithful, that he is the one who always deals with sin in the appropriate way, but he alone is the one who, through the work of his Son, justifies his people. Having said this the apostle then emphasizes three essential consequences. First, that there is no room for boasting (v.27). Second, Jews and Gentiles are justified in the same way (v.28), and thirdly, God's way of salvation does not involve the abolishment of the law (v.31).

Because the Jews alone possessed the explicit revelation of the law, they wrongly believed that this excluded the Gentiles. They considered themselves to be God's special people and were not slow to boast about this. Paul is showing that while the law was indeed given to them they had misunderstood it. While they exulted in the covenant, they forgot that even Abraham was justified before any covenant had been made with him. The gospel, instead of abolishing the law actually establishes it because it finds its true fulfillment in Christ's obedience. God then is

---

80. Wright, *Revolution,* 300.

81. Ibid., 301.

82. Lloyd-Jones, *Romans 3,* 112.

just because his law is honored, and he is the justifier because he imputes Christ's righteousness to his people.

Wright tells us that the traditional old perspective reading of Romans chapter 3 leads to chapter 4 becoming "seriously undervalued . . . Sometimes the chapter is simply labelled as a 'proof from scripture of the 'doctrine' that Paul has supposedly been expounding in chapter 3. But this misses the whole point."[83] We do not, however, as Wright would have his readers believe, see it as being just about Abraham as the great exemplar. Of course, this is included, but one must ask why Paul was using Abraham in this manner. It is clear from the text that he is seeking to demonstrate that Abraham was credited with righteousness before the covenant of circumcision had been made with him. As well as having the law which they later received through Moses, many Jews were boasting about the circumcision that separated them from the Gentiles. Paul points out from what had occurred in the case of Abraham that they had entirely missed the point, namely, that it is not circumcision of the flesh that makes one a true child of Abraham, but faith in the Lord Jesus Christ. When God credited righteousness to Abraham he was at the time in the same place as uncircumcised Gentiles; the covenant of circumcision was only made with him sometime later, so if one is then going to employ circumcision to exclude the Gentiles, this would mean a contradiction with regard to what happened in the case of Abraham.

Wright wrongly charges those who disagree with him of reading Scripture in the light of going to heaven when we die, "This usual reading is all about how we get 'right with God' in order to 'go to heaven'; but Paul never mentions 'going to heaven, here or elsewhere in Romans, and the idea of being 'right with God, though related to Paul's theme, is usually taken out of the specific context he intends."[84] He tells his readers nothing about the exhaustive studies that have been carried out in regard to *hilastērion*. All he says is that the orthodox view is "lexically possible" and that it "sometimes claims support from the use of the term in a Jewish book called 4 Maccabees."[85] This, obviously, encourages many readers to think that such a view is based on scant evidence.

He presents us with a number of reasons why he believes *hilasterion* should not be interpreted as propitiation. First, instead of denoting

83. Wright, *Revolution,* 301.

84. Ibid., 302.

85. Ibid., 300.

wrath it deals with "cleansing of both people and the sanctuary so that the meeting can take place."[86] Secondly, he maintains that in the sacrificial system the idea of an animal being killed in the place of the believer is a mistake. Thirdly, when the apostle "says that if we have been 'justified by his blood,' we *shall* be saved from the future wrath. He cannot, therefore, intend the phrase 'justified by his blood'–the summary of 3:24–26-to mean 'being saved from wrath,' or 5:9 would be a tautology."[87] Fourthly, he takes umbrage with the traditional reading of 3:25 "where God has passed over former sins in his forbearance" because it is "the very opposite of 'punishment.'"[88] Let us examine each of these four points.

SACRIFICE, BLOOD, AND DEATH

The Greek word translated propitiation in Romans 3:25 is *hilasterion*, which in Hebrew is *kepporeth*. Whether it is translated as mercy seat or propitiation is dependent on the context of the passage. The important point to keep in mind is that the mercy seat was where the high priest sprinkled the blood of the slain animal, not just for cleansing, as Wright maintains, but because it represented the wages of sin which is death (Rom 6:23). What we have is the washing away of sin through the shed blood.

In the Old Testament, the various animal sacrifices were types of the great archetypical sacrifice of Christ. Perhaps the most vivid type was that performed on the Day of Atonement as recorded in Leviticus 16. The high priest was to take two male goats for the sin offering (v.5). One goat was to be sacrificed while the other was to be set free and sent into the wilderness. The blood of the sacrificed goat was to be brought into the most holy place and sprinkled "over the mercy seat and in front of the mercy seat" (v.15). After this, the High Priest was to lay hands on the head of the live goat and "confess over it all the iniquities of the people of Israel, and all their transgressions, and all their sins, he shall put them on the head of the goat and send it into the wilderness" (v.21). In sending the goat away it was to "bear all their sins on itself to a remote area" (v.22).

It is important to bear in mind that no type can perfectly represent the thing typified. What occurred on the Day of Atonement was

86. Ibid., 302.
87. Ibid., 303.
88. Ibid., 303.

no exception. Two goats were used to represent what would happen in the one life, death, and resurrection of the one represented. Stott states, "Some commentators make the mistake of driving a wedge between the two goats, the sacrificed goat, and the scapegoat, overlooking the fact that the two together are described as 'a sin offering' in the singular."[89] In the words of James Packer, "this double ritual taught a single lesson: that through the sacrifice of a representative substitute God's wrath is averted and sins are borne away out of sight, never to trouble our relationship with God again."[90] Each stage of the process teaches an important lesson about the one sin offering; they show us different aspects of the same sacrifice.

The mercy seat on which the blood was sprinkled was the lid of the ark of the covenant that was overlaid with gold. The ark contained "manna and Aaron's staff that budded" (Heb 9:4), and the two tablets of the law that was given to Moses on Mount Sinai. Above the ark, facing each other, were two cherubs made of beaten gold. These represented the presence of the Lord. The whole point of the sprinkled blood was to show that God's wrath had been covered. The consequences of the broken law of God had been covered by the blood. Without this, the people, because of sin, would remain exposed and subject to divine wrath. The blood represented not life, but, rather, a life laid down in death. It was pointing to the blood of Christ, the one God himself put forth as a propitiation (Rom 3:25). The goat that was released into the wilderness signified that which the sacrifice had secured, namely, the removal of sin. On the Day of Atonement, we essentially see God's vengeance, sin covered, and the removal of God's wrath, where, in the words of Murray, "Vengeance is the reaction of the holiness of God to sin, and the covering provides for the removal of divine displeasure."[91]

Wright draws a wedge between the two sides of the one offering. He does not believe the killing of the animal to have been an important aspect of the sacrifice.[92] He further states that "Cutting the animal's throat was simply a prelude to the release of blood, symbolizing the animal's life, which was then used as the all-important agent for purging or cleansing

89. Stott, *The Cross of Christ*, 144.

90. Packer, *Knowing God*, 210.

91. Murray, *Redemption Accomplished*, 23.

92. Wright, *Revolution*, 329.

the worshippers and also the sacred place and furniture."[93] He appears to believe the sacrifice has nothing to do with punishment. One can see where he is going with this, like others before him, he, no doubt, has Genesis 9:4, Leviticus 17:11, and Deuteronomy 12:23 in mind. In Leviticus we read, "For the life of the flesh is in the blood, and I have given it for you on the altar to make atonement for your souls, for it is the blood that makes atonement by the life."

Wright does not elaborate on this. What he does say, however, suggests that he is adopting a view put forward by Westcott in his *Epistles of St John*, back in 1892, which was thoroughly refuted by Stibbs and Morris.[94] It is interesting that Wright makes no mention of their works. One feels, perhaps, that views like that put forward by Wright, are the result of trying to safeguard the fact that the one who saves is a living Saviour. This is, however, the wrong approach, Jesus is alive, not because his life was released in his blood but because he who was dead is alive, having been raised from the dead. As Denney points out, Christ "did something when He died, and that something He continues to make effective for men in His Risen Life; but there is no meaning in saying that by His death His life—as something other than His death—is 'liberated' and 'made available' for men."[95] I fear that, in Wright's case, the main reason for arguing that blood represents life is to avoid the idea of propitiation, for to equate it with death is to acknowledge that the wages of sin is death resulting from the wrath of God.

Concerning Leviticus 17:11, Morris states:

> Further, it may not be without significance that *nephesh*, which is translated 'life' in Leviticus 17:11, is not coterminous with the English 'life'. It can mean something very like 'life yielded up in death'. It occurs in passages which refer to 'taking away', 'losing', 'destroying', 'giving up' or 'devouring' life, to 'putting one's life in one's hand' and to the life 'departing'. A not uncommon way of referring to slaying is to speak of 'smiting the *nephesh* (Gn. 37:21; Num. 35:11; Je.40:14 etc.), while those who desire to murder someone are usually said to 'seek his *nephesh*', an expression which occurs thirty times (e.g. Ex.4:19; Psa.35:4) and which is reinforced by others which speak of 'lying in wait

93. Ibid.

94. See chapter 3 of Morris' *The Apostolic Preaching of the Cross* and Stibbs' *His Blood Works: the Meaning of Blood in Scripture*.

95. Denney, *"The Death of Christ"* 196-7.

for the *nephesh*, 'laying a snare for the *nephesh*', etc. (1 Sa. 28:9; Pr.1:18). Some passages speak of 'slaying the *nephesh*' or the *nephesh* 'dying' (Nu.31:19; Ezk.13:19; 18:4).[96]

In the Hebrew world there was no notion of life without the body, and far from the shed blood signifying a life released, it represents a life that is given up in death. The vital ingredient for life is poured out and the life is brought to an end.

To maintain that the death of the animal is unimportant is tantamount to saying the death of Jesus is unimportant. It also fails to understand that the death of the type was a way of displaying the nature of what would happen in Christ, the antitype. Death was one of the most important aspects of the sacrifice, as we read in Hebrews, "without the shedding of blood there is no forgiveness of sins" (Heb 9:22). The shed blood represents the just wages of sin (Rom 6:23). One might ask: Since when has a life released been the wages of sin?

There is good reason to believe that Paul in Romans 3:21–26 is referring to Passover rather than the Day of Atonement. Ezekiel here is, to quote Holland, "doing only one thing–he is emphasizing the importance of the Passover as a means of dealing with the sins of the people"[97] Commenting on Ezekiel 45:18–24, Holland states:

> It is clearly significant that these sacrifices are not made on the Day of Atonement as would be expected. In fact, Ezekiel never mentions the Day of Atonement at all. What he does say is that these sacrifices (which would normally be offered on the Day of Atonement) were to be offered instead as part of the Passover celebration. Ezekiel even says that the ritual of putting blood on the door post was to be done on the temple door.[98]

In verse 25, the apostle refers to God having "because of his divine forbearance passed over former sins." Holland tells us that here we have "a clear echo of Yahweh passing over the Jewish homes on the night of the Passover because of the presentation of the paschal lambs' blood, but visiting the Egyptian homes to strike their firstborn sons in judgment."[99]

96. Morris, *Apostolic Preaching*, 116.
97. Holland, *Tom Wright*, 268.
98. Ibid.
99. Ibid., 269.

It, therefore, strikes me as somewhat odd that Wright maintains that the Passover had nothing whatsoever to do with propitiation.[100]

We see the same thing in the New Testament. The whole point of the sprinkled blood was to signify that a death had occurred. In the record of Stephen's stoning, his shed blood does not represent his life, but, rather, his life given up by way of a violent death (Acts 22:20). In Revelation 6:10 John speaks about the souls of those who had been slain crying out saying, "O Sovereign Lord, holy and true. How long before you will avenge our blood on those who dwell on earth?" They are asking God to avenge their deaths, their blood that had been spilled. We see the same thing in Luke 11:48–50, "So you are witnesses and you consent to the deeds of your fathers, for they killed them and you rebuild their tombs. Therefore, also the Wisdom of God said, 'I will send them prophets and apostles, some of whom they will kill and persecute,' so the blood of all the prophets shed from the foundation of the world, may be charged against this generation, from the blood of Abel to the blood of Zechariah." These men of old did not have their lives released by the shedding of their blood, but their lives taken in death as represented by the blood. Blood is synonymous with death. The writer to the Hebrews speaks of Abel's blood when comparing it with that of Christ, "and to Jesus, the mediator of a new covenant, and to the sprinkled blood that speaks a better word than the blood of Abel." The "sprinkled blood" clearly points to sacrifice and death, to quote Morris:

> There can be no doubt that the blood of Abel is a metaphorical way of referring to the death of that patriarch, and it is unnatural accordingly to interpret the blood of Jesus as signifying anything other than his death. Yet the reference to sprinkling shows that the thought of sacrifice is in the writer's mind, so that for him the blood of sacrifice seems to have pointed to death.[101]

In Romans 5:9–10, we read, "Since, therefore, we have now been justified by his blood, much more shall we be saved by him from the wrath of God. For if while we were enemies we were reconciled to God by the death of his Son, much more, now that we are reconciled shall we be saved by his life." Verse 8 refers Christ's dying for sinners and vv. 9 and 10 are in parallel, where the apostle is equating "being justified by his

---

100. For more on this see Holland's *Tom Wright and the Search for Truth*, pp265–273.

101. Morris, *Apostolic Preaching*, 125.

blood" in v.9 with "while we were enemies we were reconciled to God by the death of his Son" in v.10. Blood in v.9 is replaced then by death in v.10. Paul clearly saw "death" and "blood" as interchangeable. What is also interesting about these two verses is the way Paul equates justification with reconciliation, thereby demonstrating that Wright's contention that justification has to do with covenant membership is found wanting.

What can we say in regard to what Wright sees as a needless tautology in our understanding of Romans 5:9? He argues that if "justified by his blood" means saved from God's wrath, then why does Paul immediately say that if we have been justified we "shall be saved by him from the wrath of God"? From this Wright infers that to be justified cannot have anything to do with God's wrath because it would amount to needless repetition. His position is, however, extremely weak. Future judgment was a very real possibility in people's minds, and Paul is keen to allay these fears. Paul emphasizes the fact that not only have they been saved from the wrath of God in the present, but also in regard to future wrath. He is simply saying that because we have been blessed as a result of Christ's death, then how much more so are we to be blessed as a result of our union with the living resurrected Christ. This whole chapter is about the believer's assurance, the consequences of having been justified by faith and what it means to have peace with God (Rom 5:1). Such a justification does not only concern the here and now. Believers cannot be justified today and somehow lose that status at some future time. In 1 Thessalonians Paul deals with the Day of the Lord, when "sudden destruction will come upon them as labour pains upon a pregnant woman, and they will not escape" (1 Thes 5:3). It is with this in mind that Paul can say, "you turned from idols to serve the living and true God, and to wait for his Son from heaven, whom he raised from the dead, Jesus who delivers us from the wrath to come" (1 Thess 1:9–10). They clearly have nothing to fear concerning any future display of God's wrath. These Roman Christians are no different, they need to think about what we were and what they have become in Christ. Now that believers have peace with God, how much more will he bless them, "For it while we were enemies we were reconciled to God by the death of his Son, much more, now that we have been reconciled, shall we be saved by his life" (v.10). These Christians can have the assurance that "He who did not spare his own Son but gave him up for us all, how will he not also with him graciously give us all things" (8:32).

Wright appears to believe sin to be something that God can simply choose to overlook as if it never happened. Nowhere is this more apparent than in his fourth reason, where he rejects the traditional understanding of what Paul says about sins committed before the incarnation: "This was to show God's righteousness because in his divine forbearance he had passed over former sins. It was to show his righteousness at the present time so that he might be just and the justifier of the one who has faith in Jesus." (Rom 3:25–26). Wright is of the opinion that *hilasterion* cannot mean propitiation because these "former sins" have somehow been forgotten by God, that "God has drawn a veil over the past."[102] One may ask, if God has just turned a blind eye to these sins, why should he punish any future sins? The Greek for forbearance is *anoche*, and Wright tells us that the "whole point of *anoche* is that sins are not punished."[103] So what we have in v.26 is "not a statement of how that punishment fell on Jesus, but rather a statement of how the sins that had been building up were 'passed over.'"[104]

This seems to be a cop-out of the first order. Is it possible that God can simply turn a blind eye to sin? Indeed, if this were possible then God could hardly be referred to as the "just," for a judge who allows some of the guilty to go free while others are punished can hardly be called a just judge. The prophet Nahum tells us that the "LORD will by no means clear the guilty: (Nahum 1:3), yet this is precisely what he would be doing in Wright's understanding of the passage.

What Paul is saying in this verse is the very opposite of what Wright asserts. In the past it may have looked as if God was passing over sins, allowing them to go unpunished, but this was far from being the case. Wright is correct in saying that *anoche* means that sins are not punished, but by *anoche* Paul meant that those sins committed prior to Christ's death were not punished when they were committed. The word does not mean that sins are never going to be punished. Paul's argument is to show that no sin can be allowed to go without punishment, it is because of God's impartiality in the punishment of sin that Paul can call him "just." Christ, in his sacrificial propitiatory death, died not just for present and future sins, but for all the sins of his people, both before and after his incarnation, so those who believed in the promised Messiah before the

---

102. Wright, *TDTRB*, 331.
103. Ibid., 330.
104. Ibid., 331.

completion of his work were forgiven because their sins were dealt with in the future death of Christ. The best commentary for this verse is found in Hebrews 9:15, "Therefore, he is the mediator of a new covenant, so that those who are called may receive the promised eternal inheritance since a death has occurred that redeems them from transgressions committed under the first covenant." God did not then allow those sins to go unpunished but redeemed his people from those sins in the death of Christ. In this way, God's justice is revealed. In the words of Lloyd-Jones, "On the cross on Calvary's hill God was giving a public explanation of what He had been doing throughout the centuries. By doing so, and at the same time, He vindicates His own eternal character of righteousness and holiness."[105]In the punishment of Christ God manifests his justice, and in making Christ's work available to his people through faith, God demonstrates that he alone is the one who justifies.

WHAT OF BOASTING?

Having looked at Wright's peculiar take on vv.25–26, what then are we to make of what the apostle says about boasting from vv.27 to 31 of chapter 3? According to Wright, our understanding of Romans "3:21–26 leaves vv.27–31 stranded. He appears to change the subject, from 'how you acquire this righteousness' to 'how the Jews and Gentiles come together into a single faith family.'"[106] It seems to me, however, that Paul is being entirely logical. In v.21 he has told us that God's righteousness has been made known apart from the law, having shown this from v.22–26, he then, quite naturally, from vv.27–31 demonstrates that justification leaves no room for boasting because it is through faith alone.

In v.27 Paul asks three questions before providing the answer: "Then what becomes of our boasting? It is excluded by what kind of law? By the law of works? No, but by the law of faith." Paul knew the Jews and their proclivity to boast all too well, and here he is clearly referring to their boasting on account of their possession of the law. He speaks of "our boasting" because he is himself a Jew, and was a Pharisee. He could, therefore, speak from personal experience as one who had all too readily boasted about the law. The Jews possessed the law and they tried to do 'the works of the law," however, in regard to their salvation, unless they

---

105. Lloyd-Jones, *Romans* Chapter 3, 103.

106. Wright, *Revolution*, 301.

believed in the Messiah, both the having and doing secured nothing. This allusion to the law is not a reference to the so-called "boundary markers." Rather, the apostle has the entire law or old covenant in mind; the law which the Jews placed so much confidence in. It could not save and was never designed to do so. The Jews failed to see that the primary purpose was to point to the promise of God concerning the one who would keep the original covenant of works; so that by believing in him one might be justified solely by faith.

We saw in 2:17–18 that Paul had shown the foolishness of certain Jews who boasted in what they could not keep. In chapter 3, Paul returns to this Jewish tendency because now he has demonstrated the ultimate reason as to why such boasting is out of place, namely, because of Christ's work. Furthermore, the apostle knew that even though many Jews had become Christian they still had a tendency to see themselves as special because of the law. Paul is, therefore, eager to dispel such notions, and is simply being a good teacher. In the words of Lloyd-Jones:

> This subject is so great, so important, so vital that there must be no misunderstanding whatsoever with respect to it. The Apostle was much more concerned about the mere literary form or literary style. From the literary standpoint it is always a bad thing to go on after you have reached your climax. Paul was not a literary man, he was a preacher of the Gospel, an evangelist and a teacher, an ambassador for Christ . . . What he is anxious to know is whether these people have really seen this truth, and grasped it. Are they quite clear about it? He is taking no risks at all with them. Having said the thing many times, and at the risk of producing a kind of anti-climax, he comes back to it again in order to make absolutely certain. The thing is so central and crucial that there must be no mistake about it.[107]

It's also important to grasp that by "the law of faith" (v.27), Paul is not, as Wright seems to maintain, implying that there was a time when justification was by the "law of works" but now that Christ has come it is by "the law of faith." Nothing could be further from the truth. Paul is demonstrating something that Israel after the flesh has missed. Justification has always been by faith. The Jews failed to submit to the righteousness which God had provided, a righteousness accessible by faith alone, instead, they "sought to establish their own" (Rom 10:3). If they but realized the truth boasting would have been the last thing on their minds.

107. Lloyd-Jones, *Romans 3*, 111.

ABRAHAM AND DAVID'S JUSTIFICATION

In regard to Romans chapter 4, I agree with Wright that "the main theme of the chapter is the single family, Abraham as its father, and God as the one before whom Abraham stood and in whose promises, and, ultimately, character he trusted"[108] I, however, very much disagree with his idea that the chapter is not about the justification of Abraham but, rather, about God's covenantal faithfulness, where the Gentiles are given the same faith or badge of membership as Abraham. I take issue with this because the emphasis of the chapter is to demonstrate to the Jews the fact that Abraham's justification occurred independently of those things the Jews put their faith in, namely, circumcision and the law, and that he was credited with righteousness even before a covenant was established with him. Not only did the Jews, in their failure to see that it was the spiritual children that are Abraham's true children, boast that Abraham was their fleshly father, a position the apostle deals with in chapter 9, but Paul demonstrates that they cannot use circumcision or the law as valid arguments for their claim to special status. Of course, God's faithfulness to his promises is important, but I believe this is taken as a given by Paul. It is not the main question here. The chapter continues from the end of chapter 3 and is a refutation of the misguided Jewish tendency to boast because Abraham was their father according to the flesh. Again, to see faith as being some *new* family badge is to miss the point that faith has only ever been the family badge for those who belong to the true family of Abraham.

Wright tells us that chapter 4 "is not, as is so often suggested, a detached 'proof from scripture' of an abstract doctrine."[109] Of course, by this he means the chapter must not be read as Reformed evangelicals have done, using Abraham as the great example of one justified by faith alone. He correctly states that "Genesis 15 is the backbone of the entire chapter—Genesis 15, that is, seen as the chapter in which the covenant with Abraham was established in the first place."[110] And none would take issue with his assertion, "The emphasis of the chapter is, therefore, that covenant membership is defined, not by circumcision (4:9–12), nor by race, but by faith."[111] The purpose of this chapter for Wright is not about Justification, but with answering the question, "Who are the family

108. Wright, *Justification*, 192.
109. Wright, *WSPRS*, 129.
110. Ibid., 129.
111. Ibid., 129.

of Abraham? Who are his seed"[112]This is where I take issue with him. I would maintain that Paul is first and foremost seeking to show that the Jews were wrong about using Abraham as their father to justify their position, and to this end, he uses two of the big names, namely, Abraham and David. In so doing, Paul, using what happened to these two central figures, strips the Jews of their misplaced confidence resulting from erroneous notions about circumcision and the old covenant by showing that Abraham was credited with righteousness prior to any rite, whereas David received God's righteousness after circumcision. Far from just using examples to highlight what he said in vv. 21–26 of chapter 3, he teaches a very important lesson, namely, the proper place of circumcision and the receiving of God's righteousness is independent of the physical rite. God's righteousness, as seen from Abraham's example, is for the for the uncircumcised, and, as seen in the case of David, also for the circumcised, hence, it is applicable to the uncircumcised Gentiles, but to the Jews too. The chapter is then about showing that justification is by faith alone, and is not in any way dependent on elements of the old covenant.

The Jews revered Abraham, not only was he their great ancestor, but he was also their great model of faith. If Paul can then show what was true in the case of Abraham, he will have clinched the argument. Paul envisages objections that might be brought by the Jews to his teaching, he, therefore, goes for the jugular, so to speak, by dealing with these at their source.

In doing this the apostle seeks to highlight four things. First, that faith is very different from "works" (vv.3–8). Secondly, faith is not dependent on any religious ceremony (vv. 9–12). Thirdly, one's faith is not related to the law (vv.13–17), (at least not where the sinner is concerned in relation to his works), and fourthly, faith is based on, and rests in the promise; it is not dependent on ancestry, the old covenant, or in any way things related to the flesh.[113]

At the end of chapter 3, Paul had shown that both Jews and Gentiles are justified by faith, a faith independent of circumcision. Now, in chapter 4 he uses what happened to Abraham to argue this fact. Abraham could not boast because the righteousness that was counted to him was a free gift through faith. If it had been of works Abraham would have had something to boast about, because he would have received a wage,

---

112. Wright, *Justification*, 191.

113. Moo, *Romans*, 444.

something he would have earned, "Now to the one who works, his wages are not counted as a gift but as his due. And to the one who does not work but believes in him who justifies the ungodly, his faith is counted as righteousness" (Rom 4:4–5). Paul also uses the example of David, yet another who was highly esteemed by the Jews. We see the importance of these two figures in the way Matthew begins his gospel, "The book of the genealogy of Jesus Christ, the son of David, the son of Abraham" (Matt 1:1). Like Abraham, David too received a "righteousness apart from works" (v.6). The apostle shows that any boasting by the Jews is based on an ignorance of what actually happened in both the case of Abraham and David. The Jews may have been going through the outward requirements of the Mosaic law, believing that possession of the law set them apart as God's true people, yet Paul is demonstrating the fact that they had simply misunderstood what was required to be God's true people, namely, believing in the promise. Paul shows that it can never be the result of what one does by way of works.

From verse 9 to 12 the apostle demonstrates from Abraham's experience that the blessing of righteousness occurred independently of circumcision. In doing this he again removes a cause for boasting. He is essentially stripping back the layers of everything that the Jews tended to put their faith in; leaving nothing but faith "We say that faith was counted to Abraham as righteousness. How then was it counted to him? Was it before or after he was circumcised? It was not after but before he was circumcised" (Rom 4:10). As Paul did in Galatians, so he does here, namely, show that there is a difference between the promise made to Abraham concerning a future covenant in Christ, and the covenant later established with him. This is what the Jews had missed. They assumed the covenant established with Abraham to have been of grace and that it was this that certified them as God's special people. The Jews missed it and so too has Wright, namely, righteousness was reckoned or counted unto Abraham before the covenant of circumcision that the Jews placed so much faith in. For Abraham, the route to righteousness, and what constituted the only covenant of grace, lay in that which would be legally consummated at a particular moment in history in the work of Christ.

Wright is correct to say "the promise is valid for 'all the seed,' that is, for the entire family, for the Jews and Gentiles alike, because Abraham is the father of us all."[114]He does not, however, emphasize the necessary

114. Wright, *Justification*, 191.

distinction between Abraham's two posterities. Abraham is the father of ethnic Israel in regard to the flesh, but, and more importantly, he is the father of those who believe. The Jews boasted about the former and rejected the latter because of their misunderstanding of the old covenant. Similarly, Sanders and Wright appear to confuse the two Israels'.

In this section on circumcision, the apostle is essentially saying: "Look, you may boast about your circumcision in the flesh, but you are wrong to do so. Salvation comes not through the law or through circumcision, but through the promise. A promise that was made with Abraham before any covenant was established with him." Moreover, Abraham received his circumcision as a seal of that which had already taken place, of that righteousness that had been counted unto him. The physical rite was but an outward declaration, a seal of this fact. This only applied to Abraham. For those who followed him, it was a token or type of what might be, not of what had occurred. The Jews would only be truly circumcised after they had believed, like Abraham, in the promise of a new covenant in Christ. The outward rite then only becomes meaningful where salvation is concerned when it is followed by circumcision of the heart.

The outward rite only applied to Abraham's physical posterity. Before the Jews were given the rite of circumcision, God was saving both Jews and Gentiles, and the vehicle for this was faith alone, as it would continue to be. After the establishment of the covenant in Genesis 17, although the Jews would have received the token circumcision, true salvation continued to be through faith in the promise. Paul, in using Abraham and David is essentially demonstrating that whether one is circumcised or not makes not one jot of difference for Abraham's spiritual seed. One must not allow the old covenant to obscure the fact that salvation was the same as it was prior to the old covenant, by exercising faith in the promise. What matters is that one walks "in the footsteps of faith" (v.12).

The promise runs through the Scriptures and over time it is progressively revealed, culminating in its realization in the work of Christ. The covenants that were established in the Old Testament came in beside the promise, and through various types and shadows, served to point sinners toward it. As I have already alluded to, the unconditional promised new covenant in the Old Testament was juxtaposed by the old covenant which played a subservient signpost role. So in Israel's history there was, as we saw in Galatians 4:21–31, effectively two Israel's present, one whose recipients belonged to the new covenant, the other whose members knew only the old covenant. There was the remnant, the true spiritual Israel that looked to that Jerusalem that is above, entrance into which is by faith in Christ alone, and there was Israel after the flesh that looked to earthly Jerusalem whose inheritance was dependent on good works.

In verses 13 to 17 of chapter 4, God was not saying, "I am introducing a new way of salvation. You will not need to keep my law." No, to do that would essentially make the promise useless, "For if it is the adherents of the law who are to be heirs, faith is null and the promise void" (Rom 4:14). Why is this? It is, as Paul demonstrated earlier, because none can keep the law. Again, Paul is not here referring to those identity markers, namely, circumcision etc., but to the entire law as spiritually understood. The problem with the Jews was that they failed to realize the true purpose of the law. The law is based solely on works while the promise is based solely on grace. The law was patterned after the covenant of works that Adam broke, while the promise speaks of the new covenant in the second Adam. The true children of Abraham are not those to whom the law was given at Sinai, but those who embrace the promise of him who would keep the original covenant of works.

In the remainder of the chapter, we see something of the nature of Abraham's faith. It amounted to believing the humanly impossible, "In hope he believed against hope, that he should become the father of many nations, as he had been told, 'so shall your offspring be'" (v.18). Abraham was "fully convinced that God was able to do what he had promised" (v.21). In believing the promise Abraham saw the covenant's fulfillment in Christ from afar, this is why Christ could say of him, "Your father Abraham rejoiced that he would see my day. He saw it and was glad' (John 8:56). So it was for all who, like him, believed the promise, and this is why Paul says: "But the words, 'it was counted to him' were not written for his sake alone, but for ours also. It will be counted to us who believe in him who raised the dead Jesus our Lord, who was delivered for our trespasses and raised for our justification" (vv.23-25).

From this point on I want to examine specific verses in Romans from chapters 5 to 8 to show why I believe Wright's position is untenable. Paul has shown that God's wrath is against all humanity because of sin, and he has demonstrated that both Jews and Gentiles are under God's wrath. Following this, he introduced God's remedy, namely, his own righteousness, and he has clearly shown that participating in this righteousness depends not on circumcision or the law. God's true people consists only of those that believed, who were of that Israel within Israel.

Chapter 5 is essentially dealing with the assurance that results from justification by faith. In v.1 Paul shows that justification is a past event, "Therefore, since we have been justified by faith, we have peace with God." There is no suggestion of any future justification. From vv.5–11 Paul shows why there is no possibility of this peace with God being destroyed or in any way being called into question, "for if while we were enemies we were reconciled to God by the death of his Son, much more, being reconciled, shall we be saved by his life" (Rom 5: 10). When we were ungodly, in a state of being at enmity with God, he condescended to save us, it then follows that now we have been saved, our security is safe. The Christian can rejoice in his eternal security in Christ, having received reconciliation (v.11). No longer is he in Adam, but in God's own Son, and in possession of the knowledge that there is nothing that can separate him from the love of God that is in Jesus Christ.

SIN AND DEATH

From v.5:12 to the end of the chapter, the apostle compares and contrasts humanity's two federal heads, namely the first Adam and Christ, the second Adam. Essentially, we have here a description of man's position under the covenant of works and his position under the new covenant.

Verses 12 to 14 have been the source of not a little confusion:

> Therefore, just as sin came into the world through one man, and death through sin, and so death spread to all men because all sinned—for sin indeed was in the world before the law was given, but sin is not counted where there is no law. Yet death reigned from Adam to Moses, even over those whose sinning was not like the transgression of Adam, who was a type of the one who was to come.

Many are of the opinion that before the arrival of the law at Sinai, although sin was in the world, God did not actually count it against the individual. So there was effectively no transgression since transgression is a breach of the law (1 John 3:4). Although death was present because of Adam's sin, God was overlooking the sins of individuals. This, however, is a mistake; it is to completely misunderstand what is being said. Far from saying that there was no transgression prior to the law, the apostle is saying just the opposite. "Sin is not counted when there is no Law," however, it clearly was counted because death was present. So although the explicit revelation of the law had not appeared, there was nevertheless a law present in those times. This was the law Paul referred to regarding the Gentiles in chapter 2:15, because "they show that the work of the law is written on their hearts." Before the moral law's revelation at Sinai, this same innate knowledge of the law applied to all humanity, including the Jews. All mankind had the work of the law upon their hearts, all men sinned, and this was counted against them, therefore, all men died because of both their own sins and Adam's sin. So the very fact that death was present is evidence that there was transgression and, therefore, sin. Paul is saying that this sin was taken into account, for "the wages of sin is death (Rom 6:23).

THE TWO HEADS

The sins of Adam's progeny were unlike his sin because he broke a command about not eating of a specific tree. Also, when Adam sinned he did so as humanity's federal head. It was because of his one act of disobedience that all fell into sin, becoming transgressors of God's law. And, while their transgressions are held against them as individuals, Adam's transgression concerned both himself and all his posterity.

In this passage, the apostle juxtaposes the two Adams' and the two covenants. We were once in Adam, under the covenant of works and condemned. We are now, having believed, in Christ, in the new covenant, having received the gift of righteousness. For Wright, Christ's one "act of righteousness" (5:18) is not, as the majority of Reformed Protestants believe, speaking of a righteousness secured by Christ's life in conformity to the law, but only about his obedient death. In criticising the Reformed position he tells us that Christ's work is not about the idea that "Jesus has 'fulfilled the law,' and thus amassed a treasury of law-based 'righteousness,' which we sinners, having no 'righteousness' of our own, no store of legal merit, no treasury of good works, can shelter within: this is theologically and exegetically, a blind alley."[115]

Referencing verse 18 Wright claims that to believe in a Jesus who by his active obedience fulfilled the law is to be guilty of legalism:

> The gift always preceded the obligation. That is how Israel's covenant theology worked. *It is therefore a straightforward category mistake, however venerable within some Reformed traditions*

---

115. Wright, *Justification*, 204.

*including part of my own, to suppose that Jesus 'obeyed the law'
and so obtained a 'righteousness' which could be reckoned to those
who believe in him.* To think that way is to concede, after all, that
'legalism' was true after all—with Jesus as the ultimate legalist.[116]

What can we say about this charge of legalism? First, one must say that
there can be no salvation unless the *legal* requirements of the law of God
are kept perfectly. There can be no salvation without works, and, thanks
be to God, it was Christ who fully honored the law's legal requirements
for his people. Secondly, when the Scriptures speak disparagingly about
legalism they have in mind sinful man's attempts to secure a righteousness for himself. So yes, there is legalism. Why else would Jesus be born
under law? God revealed his law to humanity and it is not a law he sets
aside. In the work of Christ, God demonstrated that he is the 'ultimate
legalist' in the true sense of the word. This is why Paul calls God the just
and the justifier (Rom 3:26).

The law is nothing less than an expression of God's very character,
be it on tablets of stone or upon the heart. Without the fulfillment of this
law no one can stand in his presence. Jesus is, therefore, the believer's
legal representative, his surety; the one who offers up to God all that is
required for salvation. Everything Christ did was for his people. This includes not only his death but the entire life lived. Jesus "humbled himself
by becoming obedient to the point of death, even to death on a cross"
(Phil 2:8). He died not for his own sin but for the sins of his people. He
was the true Lamb of God, without spot or blemish, the one to whom our
sins are imputed. It is because salvation depended on Jesus' conformity to
the law, one cannot separate his work from God's legal requirements. To
assume that "the gift preceded the obligation," that Israel was a "chosen
race, a royal priesthood, a holy nation, a people for his own possession"
solely on the basis of being in receipt of the law is to make a major category mistake, one that will lead to misunderstanding the nature of God's
purposes in both the Old and New Testaments. This appears to be what
Wright does, assuming that Israel was God's people when the Scriptures
make it clear that to become such was entirely dependent on her keeping God's commandments. For Wright, and, indeed, for paedobaptists in
general, passages like Exodus 19:5 are simply overlooked, or explained
away as if Israel would somehow fulfill the requirements because it was
expressing its gratitude for having been redeemed.

116. Ibid., 205.

Wright tells us that the Mosaic law "never was intended as a ladder of good works up which one might climb to earn the status of 'righteousness'. It was given, yes, as the way of life . . . but it was the way of life *for a people already redeemed*."[117] Israel was, however, not truly redeemed, and Wright does not tell us what this redemption amounted to. Yes, she had been released from Egypt, but this was so that she might be placed in a land where blessings were entirely conditional upon her obedience. There were, at various times, undeserved blessings bestowed on the nation in spite of its sinfulness, these were, however, a type of the grace that is available in the antitype or the new covenant in Christ. In other words, the blessings bestowed upon the nation foreshadowed what is available for God's true people. If Wright distinguishes between the redemption of the nation and the redemption that is in Christ, he certainly does not say so. He, rather, speaks of Israel as a whole, implying that Christ came to save all of it.

Concerning Romans 5:12–21 Wrights states that Paul is not:

> Suggesting that Jesus' "obedience" was somehow meritorious, so that by it he earned "righteousness" on behalf of others. That is an ingenious and far-reaching way of making Paul's language fit into a theological scheme very different from his own. Rather he is highlighting Jesus' faithful obedience, or perhaps we should say Jesus' plan by which God would save the world. On the cross Jesus accomplished what God had always intended the covenant to achieve. Where Israel as a whole had been faithless, he was faithful.[118]

The theology in these verses is essentially the same as we find in 2 Corinthians 3:3–17, where Paul is comparing and contrasting the plight of man under the law with that of the man who partakes of the benefits of the new covenant. The old covenant was external and written on stone, whilst the new is inward, written upon the heart (vv.2–7). The old could never bring life, instead, it pronounced death and killed, whilst the new covenant gives life (vv.6–7). The old was a temporary covenant whilst the new is permanent (vv.11–13). The old condemned, whilst the new is unto salvation (v.9). The old brought bondage, whilst under the new, there is liberty (vv.12–13). To view the old covenant as being of grace is a category mistake. Throughout redemptive history, the only way of salvation

117. Ibid., 204.
118. Wright, "*Romans*," In *New Interpreter's Bible*: 467

has been the same, namely through the new covenant in Christ. This is the only covenant of which Christ is the mediator. It is then a mystery why any would seek salvation through any other covenant.

How are we to understand this "one act of righteousness"? In v.17 Paul speaks of the "free gift of righteousness," and in v.18, of "one trespass" that condemned all men, and "one act of righteousness that leads to justification." This "one act of righteousness" must not be seen as referring only to Christ's death. It is a righteousness performed by the one person, and, as Murray states:

> If the question be asked how the righteousness of Christ could be defined as "one righteous act," the answer is that the righteousness of Christ is regarded in its compact unity in parallelism with the one trespass, and there is good reason for speaking of it as one righteous act because, as the one trespass is the trespass of the one, so that one righteousness is the righteousness of the one and the unity of the person and his accomplishment must always be assumed.[119]

In the words of Venema, "Christ's obedience upon the cross epitomizes his whole life of obedience."[120] Being born under law, one cannot consider Jesus' life apart from his fulfillment of the law. About Christ's active obedience Owen tells us that it:

> demonstrates that our Lord's obedience was not for Himself but for us. He writes "...the human nature of Christ, by virtue of its union with the person of the Son of God, had a right unto, and might have immediately been admitted into, the highest glory whereof it was capable, without any antecedent obedience unto the law. And this is apparent from hence, in that, from the first instant of that union, the whole person of Christ, with our nature existing therein, was the object of all divine worship from angels and men; wherein consists the highest exaltation of that nature.
>
> It is true, there was a *peculiar* glory that he was actually to be made partaker of, with respect unto his antecedent obedience and suffering, Phil. ii. 8, 9. The actual possession of this glory was, in the ordination of God, to be consequential unto his obeying and suffering, not for himself, but for us. But as unto the right and capacity of the human nature in itself, all the glory whereof it was capable was due unto it from the instant of its

119. Murray, *Romans*, Vol.1, 201–202.
120. Venema, *Gospel of Free Acceptance in Christ*, 240.

union; for it was therein exalted above the condition that any creature is capable of by mere creation. And it is but a Socinian fiction, that the first foundation of the divine glory of Christ was laid in his obedience, which was only the way of his actual possession of that part of his glory which consists in his mediatory power and authority over all. The real foundation of the whole was laid in the union of his person; whence he prays that the Father would glorify him (as unto manifestation) with that glory which he had with him before the world was.

I will grant that the Lord Christ was "viator"[121] whilst he was in this world, and not absolutely "possessor;" yet I say withal, he was so, not that any such condition was necessary unto him for himself, but he took it upon him by especial dispensation for us. And, therefore, the obedience he performed in that condition was for us, and not for himself.[122]

Again, to quote Johnson, Christ:

has fulfilled all the law's requirements, –living a true human life of holy obedience, as we were bound to do, and dying the death of pain and shame which we deserve to suffer. To all who believe the gospel, and are thus led to place their confidence in Christ, God, of His infinite mercy, imputes this perfect righteousness of the Saviour —reckons it as theirs—treats them as if they had themselves been righteous, like their Representative. This is the great doctrine of justification by faith. You see how humbling it is to man. The faith through which we obtain justification involves an acknowledgement of the reality and exceeding evil of our sin, and of our own utter helplessness. We come to God confessing that the robe of our personal character is but 'filthy rags,' in which we dare not stand in His sight; and we receive from Him the ample, stainless, fragrant robe of the Redeemer's righteousness.[123]

So essential is Christ's active obedience that to reject it is to cut his redemptive work in half and to present us with a savior whose work secures forgiveness and makes the necessary righteousness the responsibility of the believer.

---

121. Viator: an old expression which refers to man's trials in his journey through life.

122. Owen, John. *Works*, 5, 259.

123. Johnston, Robert. *Lectures on the Book of Philippians*, 246.

BAPTISM AND SIN

In chapter 6 Paul deals with a question that naturally resulted from what he said at the end of chapter 5: "Now the law came in to increase the trespass, but where sin increased, grace abounded all the more" (v.20). This might cause some to think that they should sin all the more, because the greater the sin, and the greater the grace, the greater the glory of God is displayed. This, however, would be to completely misunderstand what Paul is saying. His opening line in chapter 6 shows the impossibility of this: "What shall we say then? Are we to continue to sin that grace may abound? By no means! How can we who died to sin still live in it?" (vv.1–2). The rest of the chapter shows why this is the case, and how the Christian ought to live in light of this fact.

As previously said, in fairness to Wright, although he does not adopt the Reformed position concerning those passages that speak of justification, he does, nevertheless, believe all that Christ achieved belongs to believers because of their union with him. One can fully endorse what he says about this union, "in becoming a Christian you move from one type of humanity to the other, and you should never think of yourself in the original mode again. More particularly, in becoming a Christian you *die and rise again in the Messiah . . .* what is true of him is true of them."[124] Wright then arrives at the same conclusion, but by a different route. His mistake is that he appears to make this union dependent on the rite of baptism.

Wright maintains that the baptism referred to in this chapter has to do with water; with the external rite performed by human hands. Moreover, he appears to believe that any consequence resulting from this baptism to be applicable to New Testament believers alone. Concerning 6:1–11, he states "that what is true of the Messiah (dying to sin, rising to new life) is now to be 'reckoned' as true of all those who are baptised into him."[125] He dissociates himself from those "good Protestant readers" who see "baptism simply as an outward expression of the believer's faith, and [are] anxious about any suggestion that the act itself, or indeed any outward act, might actually change the way things are in the spiritual realm."[126] He contends "that much of post-reformation theology

---

124. Wright, *Paul for Everyone*, 101.

125. Wright, *Justification*, 202.

126. Wright, *Romans*, 533.

has tended to fight shy of taking seriously Paul's realistic theology of baptism."[127]

He makes the Christian's position in Christ dependent on what occurs at the font: "The Messiah died to sin; we are in the Messiah through baptism and faith, therefore, we have died to sin. The Messiah rose again and is now 'alive to God', we are in the Messiah through baptism and faith; therefore we have risen again and are now 'alive to God.'"[128] We are told that when "people submit to Christian baptism, they die with the Messiah and are raised with him into a new life."[129] Here he appears to be making baptism a precondition for the believer's union with Christ. He even suggests that baptism has primacy over faith, stating that Paul "never draws back from his strong view of either baptism or the eucharist, never lapses back into treating them as secondary. Indeed, in the present passage one might actually say that he is urging faith on the basis of baptism: since you have been baptized, he writes, work that out, for what is true of Christ is true of you."[130] He uses the exodus paradigm/model of baptism that the Israelites experienced when they crossed the Red Sea as a type of believers baptism in Christ. Commenting on 1 Corinthians 10:1–5 he states, "Paul has strong views of baptism and the eucharist: baptism really does bring you into the Messiah's family, and the Eucharist really does let you share in the life of the crucified and risen Jesus."[131] While he does also state that "the sacraments are not magic. They don't automatically bring you salvation,"[132] he does not explain how baptism serves to bring one into the "Messiah's family." It is through baptism that one becomes a member of God's family, "But how do people come to belong to this community of the Messiah-and-his-people? Here, as elsewhere (e.g. Romans 6.2–11; Galatians 3:27), Paul sees baptism itself as the means of entering the family." Again, commenting on Galatians 3:27, he states, "For Paul, it is a matter of belonging to a particular family, the Messiah's people; and this family is entered through baptism.[133] Baptism is, therefore, 'into the Messiah:' it is the doorway through which one passes into membership in

---

127. Wright, Paul in Different Perspectives.

128. Ibid.

129. Wright, *Paul for Everyone Romans*, 101.

130. Ibid., 535.

131. Wright, *Paul for Everyone 1 Corinthians* 10:1–5, Kindle.

132. Ibid.

133. Bold print in original.

the single family God promised to Abraham."[134] One can only conclude that Wright is teaching baptismal regeneration, a teaching which appears similar to that put forward by his forebears in the Church of England in the 1662 Book of Common Prayer. Ironically, in this respect, he is closer to Luther than to the Reformed tradition.

Wright, in wrongly asserting that the rite of water baptism provides New Testament believers with spiritual blessings in Christ, is thereby implying that these were somehow not applicable to those believers who lived prior to the rite's institution. For clearly, if it is the act of baptism through which we die to sin and become alive to God, one needs to ask about all the people of God who lived before baptism, e.g., was Abraham in God's family? Was he "in Christ? Did not he die to sin as a result of being in Christ? One must never lose sight of the fact that the believer dies to sin, not because of any water baptism, but from the work of the Holy Spirit whereby he/she is spiritually resurrected into a new realm in Christ. This takes place before any rite is performed. This was Paul's point in his allusion to Abraham receiving righteousness before circumcision. It was in virtue of the fact that Christ rose from the dead, triumphing over sin and death that all who have believed from the very beginning have been made alive to God. All spiritual blessings received by God's people, from the time of Adam's family, e.g., Abel, and even Adam himself if he believed, have been the recipients of the blessings earned by Christ's redemptive work. This is the case irrespective of whether one lived before or after Christ's work. It is, therefore, erroneous to maintain that the believer's death to sin etc., only commenced with the rite of baptism.

The rite is simply an outward declaration of the fact that one has been baptized by the Spirit of God into the body of Christ. In the case of Abraham, the rite of circumcision was a seal to what had already taken place, likewise, baptism can be viewed as an outward act, sealing that which has taken place internally. It's like the old wax seal that was used for letters. It serves as an identity marker, but it does not alter the contents of the letter.

To demonstrate that the believer will not continue in sin the apostle says: "Do you not know that all of us who have been baptized into Christ Jesus were baptized into his death? We were buried therefore with him by baptism unto death, in order that, just as Christ was raised from the dead by the glory of the father, we too might walk in newness of life" (vv. 3–4).

---

134. Wright, *Paul for Everyone Galatians*.

How are we to understand these words? We must avoid the tendency of assuming every reference to baptism has to do with water. To be baptized means to be placed into. It implies immersion or submersion. As already said, the apostle repeatedly employed the phrase "in Christ." In fact, he uses phrases like "in Christ" and "in him" no fewer than 164 times in his letters. He did so because the believer has been placed, or immersed and submerged into him, in other words, he has become united with Christ and made to share in all he achieved. Therefore, when Paul speaks of baptism in Romans 6 he has in mind a work that is performed by the Holy Spirit whereby a person is engrafted into or placed into Christ.

The word alone, however, tells us nothing about the means by which something is placed within. For example, Christ spoke of a baptism he had to undergo: "I have a baptism to be baptized with, and how great is my distress until it is accomplished!" (Luke 12:50). This baptism concerned his death, it had nothing to do with water.

We see the same thing in Colossian 2:11–14. "In him also you were circumcised with a circumcision made without hands, by putting off the body of the flesh, by the circumcision of Christ, having been buried with him in baptism, in which you were also raised with him through faith in the powerful working of God, who raised him from the dead. And you, who were dead in your trespasses and the uncircumcision of your flesh, God made alive together with him, having forgiven us all our trespasses." Here Paul alludes to inward spiritual circumcision and emphasizes "without hands" to show that it is the work of the Holy Spirit in the heart, the very thing of which the physical rite is but a type. Paul then speaks of baptism, of the believer having been "buried with him in baptism," it logically follows to say that he is again not speaking of the external rite, but the work of the Spirit, to a work performed "without hands." In Israel, it was not the rite of circumcision that made one a participator of the true church, but another circumcision, one that was not made with human hands, but by the Spirit of God. By the same token, it is not the baptism "made with hands" that counts, but the baptism whereby the Spirit engrafts one into Christ, as Sam Storms reminds us:

> The word translated "by human hands" (*cheiropoietos*) and its oppose are used in the New Testament to contrast what is made by human hands with what is made by God. It also points to the contrast between the external material aspects of the old order of Judaism under the Mosaic covenant and the internal spiritual efficacy of the new order under the new covenant (Mark 14:58;

Acts 7:48; 17:24; Heb. 9:11). Thus, to speak of something "not made by human hands" (*acheiropoietos*) is to assert that God has created (e.g., the temple that Jesus would build in three days Mark 14:58; the heavenly house [i.e., the body] which believers receive at death in 1 Cor. 5:1; and that true, spiritual circumcision of the heart which comes through the death of Christ in Col. 2:11).[135]

Wright's emphasis on the rite "made with hands," makes the spiritual inward change dependent on the external ritual, thus undermining the very point the apostle is making.

To shore up his position Wright alludes to Israel's baptism,[136] "For I do not want you to be unaware, brothers, that our fathers were all under the cloud, and all passed through the sea, and all were baptized into Moses in the cloud and in the sea, and all ate the same spiritual food, and all drank the same spiritual drink. For they drank from the spiritual Rock that followed them, and the Rock was Christ" (1 Cor 10:1–5). He disagrees with James Dunn who said that baptism is a metaphor for being plunged into the body of Christ. Wright maintains that as the Israelites were baptized into Moses crossing the sea, a baptism into freedom from Egyptian slavery, so Christian baptism is efficacious in liberating one from spiritual slavery.[137] He is, however, extracting too much from the text. While Paul is comparing like with like, there is no exact comparison. Paul is again using the old covenant type to speak of the antitype, the mundane to shed light on the spiritual. Whereas the Israelites were baptized physically into Moses, believers are baptized spiritually into Christ. The apostle is essentially saying that Israel was baptized into the old covenant whose mediator was Moses i.e., Israel entered into the realm or sphere of Moses. He is not here comparing the mundane Red Sea baptism with what takes place at the font, but with the thing it typifies, namely, being placed into the realm and sphere of Christ by God's Spirit. If one was to go along with Wright's understanding of this text, one would have to conclude that it is water baptism that brings the believer under Christ's sphere of influence. As we saw earlier, the illogicality of this becomes obvious when one considers that all the saved, not only those physically baptized, have been made recipients of Christ's work on account of their being in him. The thief on the cross in Luke 23:42–43

135. Storms, *Kingdom Come*, 182.
136. Wright, *Revolution*, 277.
137. Wright, *Paul for Everyone*, 1 Cor 10.

was as much in Christ as any Christian has ever been, yet he knew nothing of water baptism. All Wright's interpretation has succeeded is to make a false dichotomy between Old and New Testament believers, so much so, that, when looked at logically, he denies the essentials of the Faith to all who lived prior to the institution of water baptism.

The baptism made without human hands is a secret work of God in the heart. The individual is made alive spiritually, he is quite literally born again, "circumcised by putting off the body of flesh," and baptized or engrafted into the body of Christ by the Spirit of God. He is then, because of his shared identity with Christ, a recipient of all that he achieved in his redemptive work. The immediate consequence of this is faith in Christ; the outward confession made with the mouth is a demonstration of a changed heart with its new allegiances. Faith is as natural to those born again as crying is to a new born baby. It is evidence of new life.

In regard to chronology and the order of salvation, it is important to understand that although logically we can speak of one event following another, e.g., faith, justification, adoption etc., in reality, this cannot be done because one cannot be born again and not believe, and one cannot believe without being in union with Christ. And, if one is united to Christ, one immediately becomes a participant in the whole of what he achieved. In other words, all occur simultaneously. This is not to say that believers have been or are always conscious of what they have become, indeed, many do not understand much about what their position in Christ entails. All they may be aware of is the fact that they believe in Christ. In regard to justification the believer may have no knowledge of the doctrine, yet this lack of knowledge, however, does not alter the fact that he is justified. Medieval man may have believed, because of his ignorance, the earth to be flat, this did not, however, change his position. He was in reality still living on a spherical earth.

All believers throughout history have been made to share in Christ's work, and all have been participants of the new covenant. In Rom 6:3–4, Paul is essentially saying: "you have been placed into Christ, into his sphere or realm; as you were once in Adam, so now you are in Christ. All that Jesus achieved by his life, death, and resurrection belongs to you because you belong to Christ."[138] This is what Jesus was speaking about in John 6:54. To drink his blood and eat his flesh is metaphorical language to denote the believer's participation in him, and the fact that this

138. My own paraphrase.

is possible because of his broken body and shed blood. It denotes that organic union that all believers have with Christ. This is then a far cry from Wright's position, one in which water baptism, a rite performed with human hands, appears to be essential for our spiritual union with the Messiah.

Regarding 1 Corinthians 12:13, many Christians, unlike Wright, correctly understand the reference to baptism as having little or nothing to do with the rite of baptism. They do, however, make the mistake of associating it with the baptism with the Spirit that was first given to the church at Pentecost. This is an untenable position. If it is this Pentecostal Spirit baptism that makes one a member of Christ's body, and if it was not given to the church before Pentecost, the logical conclusion would be to say that all who lived prior to this were outside of Christ's body and the new covenant. This would then place them in Adam, outside of God's kingdom and separated from Christ. Such a view makes nonsense of the clear teaching of Scripture. The correct interpretation of the verse concerns the believer's spiritual union with Christ, it has to do with what we see in Romans 6, namely, one's definitive sanctification where one is engrafted by the Spirit and made to share in Christ.

MARRIAGE AND LAW

In chapter 7:1–6, Paul continues explicating the consequences of the believer's union with Christ. As chapter 6 shows the impossibility of the believer continuing to live in sin, so in chapter 7 shows the impossibility of the believer coming under the law's judgment. This is because he no longer lives in the realm in which the law operates. Here again, the apostle, speaking of the law, is thinking in terms of the old covenant type which serves to emphasize the law that all are men are under. The Jews were married to the old covenant, and it was the nation's disobedience to this covenant by which it stood condemned. All humanity, however, is married by nature to the antitype, the original covenant of works, and it too stands condemned. In 7:1–3 Paul uses an illustration to highlight the Christian's liberation from the law. Imagine that this covenant, both in terms of the old covenant type and the original antitype, to be a man to whom one is married. As long as both are living the relationship continues. What happens when the husband dies? The woman is free to remarry. When this occurs she will enter into another relationship altogether. The former relationship will be effectively dead, along with the husband, she will no longer be under the regime imposed by her dead husband. This is why Paul told the believers to realize the truth concerning their new position, "Likewise, my brothers, you also have died to the law through the body of Christ, so that you may belong to another, to him who has been raised from the dead, in order that we may bear fruit for God" (v.4). While the illustration in vv.1–3 is, of course, imperfect, because the law doesn't die, it is the old man in Adam who dies, and the new man in Christ is the one who is in the new relationship because he is now married to Christ. This new man can never come under the law's condemnation in the same way that the woman can never come under any condemnation from her first husband. The Christian will always be looked upon by God as justified before the law because of the marriage that exists between him and Christ.

In the rest of chapter 7, as we saw previously, from vv.7 to 8:4, Paul vindicates the law and demonstrates from his own experience the law's purpose before showing how the problem lay not with the law but, rather, with the weakness of the flesh, and how Jesus Christ is the answer.

I now want to briefly look at chapter 8, in particular, vv.3–8 and vv.18–25. The chapter commences with a declaration that there is no condemnation for those in Christ, and finishes with the assertion that there is nothing that can separate us from our position in him. This is hardly suggestive of a second justification that will be based on the life lived. Wright attaches particular importance to verses 3 to 8, linking these with what we read about the doers of the law in chapter 2.

> For God has done what the law, weakened by the flesh, could not do. By sending his own Son in the likeness of sinful flesh and for sin, he condemned sin in the flesh, in order that the righteous requirement of the law might be fulfilled in us, who walk not according to the flesh but according to the Spirit. For those who live according to the flesh set their minds on the things of the flesh, but those who live according to the Spirit set their minds on the things of the Spirit. For to set the mind on the flesh is death, but to set the mind on the Spirit is life and peace. For the mind that is set on the flesh is hostile to God, for it does not submit to God's law; indeed, it cannot. Those who are in the flesh cannot please God. (vv. 3–8).

The distinction Paul makes between those who "set their minds on things of the flesh" and those who "set their minds of things of the Spirit" is essentially a distinction between the non-believer and the believer. The non-believer can have no notion of those things that belong to the Spirit because he is not spiritual, as Paul says, "the natural person does not receive the things of the Spirit of God, for they are folly to him, and he is not able to understand them because they are spiritually discerned" (1 Cor 2:14). Each will live according to what they are by nature. The believer, being spiritual, cannot but set his mind on the things of the Spirit because in Christ he has himself been made spiritual. By the same token, the non-believer, being carnal, dead in trespasses and sins, cannot but set his mind on things of the flesh. Paul is not suggesting that a person can sometimes be spiritual, whilst at other times living according to the flesh. He is contrasting two different entities, and what each is in its nature.

Wright appears to be of the opinion that the Spirit, as referred to in these verses, was only made available following Christ's completed work, "the reality to which the law pointed forwards has arrived in the person and the saving death of Jesus the Messiah, and the *consequent gift of the spirit*.[139] As Paul had hinted in 2.28–29, echoing the new covenant promises of Jeremiah and Ezekiel, the spirit is the one through whose agency God's people are renewed and reconstituted as God's people."[140] However, this is again a category mistake. It is a mistake similar to the one he made concerning baptism. The Spirit did come in a new dimension following Christ's work. This is what Pentecost was all about. However, this is not what Paul is referring to in these verses. Rather, he is speaking of the consequences of the new birth. As I have kept emphasizing, this has been the case throughout all redemptive history. This was not something peculiar to the New Testament. All regenerated persons, since the first man believed, have been spiritually resurrected, and have the Holy Spirit. Should they not have the Spirit they would not belong to Christ (v.9). God's true people cannot be renewed regarding their spiritual birth. One is either born of the Spirit or one is dead in sin. There is no middle position. By the same token, God's people cannot be "reconstituted as God's people," again they are either his people or they are not. Wright is again making a false dichotomy. God's true people have always been one, born of his Spirit, constituting one church, having one savior, and one hope.

The apostle in these verses is describing the consequences of the believer's new life in Christ, explicating what he said in chapter 6. It is

---

139. Italics added for emphasis.
140. Wright, *Justification*, 209.

essentially a description of the experiences of one who has been justified by faith and united to Christ. The Christian is one whose spirit has been made alive, but whose mortal body is still awaiting its redemption, hence, he seeks to bring his mortal body under control, making it a slave unto righteousness (Rom 6:13). What we read in chapter 8 is a description of this in practice.

CHRIST'S WORK AND OURS

Paul tells us that "God has done what the law, weakened by the flesh could not do, by sending his own Son in the likeness of sinful flesh, and for sin he condemned sin in the flesh. In order that the righteous requirements of the law might be fulfilled in us, who walk not according to the flesh but according to the Spirit" (8:3–4). Wright relates these verses to what we read in 2:13–14 as if they are alluding to the same thing. From this, he is again determined to demonstrate that on the day of judgment, the believer, based on his obedience to these "righteous requirements" or his "doing the law" will face another justification.

Wright cross-references Romans 5:9 with Romans 8:3–4, where he makes what I believe to be an extraordinary comment, "When he looks ahead to the *future* day in 8:3–4, he speaks of God's condemning sin in the Messiah's flesh, so that there is 'no condemnation.'"[141] The apostle is depicted as one who is peering into the future, where he "looks ahead to the *final* day of judgment."[142] Paul is, however, not in this text speaking of a "*future* day." Wright appears to speak of a future justification here in order to bolster his argument in chapter 5:9, telling us that "Paul does not intend this passage as a statement of how the punishment deserved by sinners—the 'wrath' of God 1:18–2:16- was meted out on Jesus."[143] He seems to be saying that the blood of Christ applies not to the past or present, but to the future, "When Paul speaks in 5:9 of being 'declared to be in the right by his blood,' he is indicating the prerequisite for 'being saved from wrath,' not the idea that such a rescue has already taken place."[144] The idea then seems to be that when one comes to faith in Jesus, one is then, assisted by God's Spirit, enabled to perform good works.

141. Wright, *Revolution*, 330.
142. Ibid., 330.
143. Ibid.
144. Ibid.

These good works will then be taken into consideration on the last day, effectively becoming the criterion in our final justification. We will then be declared forgiven by Jesus' shed blood and pronounced justified by the life we have lived. This is, however, to reverse the nature of what Paul is saying. The text has nothing to do with a future justification, rather, it is what results from our past justification. For example, when Paul says that the consequence of Jesus' death was "in order that the righteous requirements of the law might be fulfilled in us, who walk not according to the flesh, but according to the Spirit" (v.4), he is alluding to progressive sanctification that results *from* our justification and union. The apostle has no need to go to justification here because he has already dealt with it in chapters 3 and 4. Following justification in chapters 3 and 4, the apostle commences chapter 5 with the words, "Therefore, having been justified by faith, we have peace with God through our Lord Jesus Christ." Following his parenthesis in chapters 6 and 7, taking up his argument from chapter 5, he commences with chapter 8, by stating that, "There is therefore now no condemnation for those who are in Christ Jesus." Both chapters 5 and 8 then examine the consequences for the believer of his being in Christ and justified. To, therefore, suggest that vv.3–4 are concerned with a future justification is the result of making the text fit one's system; it is essentially eisegesis.[145]

In comparing Romans 8:4 with "the doers of the law' in 2:13, Wright is not comparing like with like. Chapter 2 not only concerns a hypothetical case, but relates to the man still in sin and under the condemnation of the law, while chapter 8 looks to that which the justified Christian does. It links into what we saw in Romans 6 where the believer uses his body for righteousness, "Let not sin therefore reign in your mortal body, to make you obey its passions. Do not present your members to sin as instruments for unrighteousness, but present yourselves to God as those who have been brought from death to life, and your members to God as instruments for righteousness" (Rom 6:12–13). It is because of what Christ has done for us, because we are now spiritually alive and indwelt by the Holy Spirit, that we can more and more keep God's law and be transformed into the image of Christ. This is nothing less than the Christian's progressive sanctification, a process that will reach completion only when believers receive their new bodies. This must be distinguished from definitive sanctification which is a once-and-for-all action where

---

145. Eisegesis– to interpret the text according to one's presuppositions.

the believer is united with Christ, taken from his position in Adam and inserted by the Spirit of God into Christ. Christ is the only one who has kept the law, and because of this, through the grace of his Spirit, we are more and more able to do so. It is only believers who are enabled to do this because they have received reconciliation with God. It is exactly this that Paul was referring to when he appealed to the Christians at Rome, "by the mercies of God, present your bodies as a living sacrifice, holy and acceptable to God, which is your spiritual worship" (Rom 12:1).

Some go to James where he tells us that "faith without works is dead" (James 2:17) as if to prove that justification is based on works or to suggest that works at least play some role in one's justification. This is to entirely miss the point of what James is saying. There were some who claimed to be justified by faith yet who continued to live in sin as if there is no God. This is why James could say that "Even the demons believe—and shudder!" (James 2:19). The demons, by their actions, show more respect for God than many so-called believers who deny him by their behavior. True faith will always exhibit itself in works, they are the outward evidence of justification. If one does not demonstrate justification by works then it is evidence that one has not been justified. This letter is not, as Luther called it, "an epistle of straw," there is no contradiction between what Paul has said and what we read in James. All we see are different sides of the same coin; of justification viewed from different perspectives. For one who has truly been justified by faith, works must naturally follow. It cannot be otherwise for the believer because he is one who because of his new nature must walk after the Spirit and not the flesh.

JESUS' PERSON OR FLESH?

Wright again has a somewhat peculiar take on Romans 8:3, where Paul tells us that in Christ, God "sending his own Son, in the likeness of sinful flesh, and for sin, he condemned sin in the flesh." He draws an unjustifiable distinction between Jesus' person and Jesus' flesh, implying that while in his flesh he suffered the consequences of sin, namely, its punishment, the person of Jesus somehow did not. Wright states: "Paul does not say that God punished Jesus. He declares that God punished sin *in the flesh* of Jesus."[146] Again he tells us that, "The death of Jesus, seen in this

146. Wright, *Revolution*, 287.

light, is certainly *penal*. It has to do with the punishment on Sin–not, to say it again, on Jesus–but it is punishment nonetheless."[147]

The distinction that Wright makes between flesh and person is unscriptural. One cannot separate Jesus from his flesh as if to say the flesh was punished but not the person. Wright seems to be dividing Christ. One cannot do this because the flesh constitutes part of the person. One should also note that one is not here making the distinction that Paul sometimes makes between man's sinful flesh and his spirit, e.g., Romans 8:5. Jesus' flesh is quite simply his physical body.

When God demands the death of the sinner, it is the death of the person that is required. When Scripture speaks of the death of Jesus, it means literally what it says. When Jesus took the place of sinners, he took upon himself the penalty that should have been theirs, and, as in their case, it is the person who would have died, so it is in the case of Jesus, their substitute. Jesus' death was the punishment for sin. We see this in the case of the first man, God told him that the result of disobeying God would be death (Gen 2:17), and as Paul tells us, "the wages of sin is death" (Rom 6:23). To say that sin was punished in Jesus' flesh and not in Jesus himself is to deny the death of Christ. Death follows from sin, and at Calvary, it was not just the flesh of Jesus that died, but Jesus the person.[148]

Drawing the kind of dichotomy, that Wright does, between Christ the person and his flesh, is to divide Christ. When Jesus said, "I have come to give my life a ransom for many" (Mark 10:45) it was Jesus himself who gave his life. Another example which proves the case is Jesus' words to his disciples in Luke 23. When Jesus told them to touch his wounds he meant that they should touch his person v.39. Jesus was not distinguishing between his flesh and his true self. Likewise, when Paul speaks of sin being punished in the flesh of Jesus he means that Jesus himself, in the body prepared for him, underwent the punishment.

Some might argue that before Jesus died he gave up his spirit into the hands of his father (Luke 23:46). This then proves that the spirit of Jesus never died. This, however, is wrong because of what death is. It is essentially separation from God, the very thing that Jesus was inflicted with when he uttered the words, "Eli, Eli, lama sabachthani? that is to say, My God, my God, why hast thou forsaken me?" (Matt 27:46). Because of

---

147. Ibid.

148. I am aware of the mystery here, that Jesus was one person with two natures, a divine nature and a human nature. While the human nature died, the divine nature changes not, and, therefore, was not subject to death.

who Jesus is, the God-man, his suffering is ultimately beyond our com-
prehension. What we do know, however, is that it was Jesus Christ, the
person, who suffered.

Other New Perspective Motifs

IN THIS SECTION, I want to briefly examine some of the other aspects of Wright's new perspective. These include: the believer's destination and the function of heaven, the believer's relationship with this world, Israel's restoration and her supposed exile, the nature of God's Kingdom and Christ second advent.

THE PLACE OF HEAVEN

It seems to me that it is Wright's view and not that of Reformed theology that distorts "both passage and the doctrine."[1] Nowhere is this more obvious than in his understanding of the believer's destination. Wright has done the same as he did in regard to Romans 2:13, indeed, the very thing he charges Reformed believers of doing, namely, forcing verses to fit into a particular theological system, instead of allowing them to speak for themselves. He has caricatured the Reformed[2] teaching in the process. Wright, in the same breath, can speak of Christ's righteousness not being imputed to the believer, and of heaven not being the believer's destination. By doing this he appears to be attacking the old perspective. He must, however, be aware that no one who embraces the old perspective, who has any knowledge of Scripture, believes heaven to be the believer's final destination, and this has never been taught in Reformed theology.

Wright suggests that when we speak of the believer's destiny we have in mind some nebulous idea, where one is left in an entirely immaterial realm; floating on a cloud and listening to angels playing their harps. He tells us that "salvation does not mean 'dying and going to heaven', as so

---

1. Wright, *Revolution*, 330.

2. I say Reformed here because of the way Wright appears to lump all those that speak of going to heaven together.

many Western Christians have supposed for so long. If your body dies and your soul goes into a disembodied immortality, you have not been rescued from death; you have quite simply died."[3] To say that one has simply died is to evade the distinction that exists between spirit and body. Yes, the body may have died, the spirit, however, as we shall see, is very much alive, and upon the body's death really does go to be with Christ in heaven.

Wright seems to think that those who speak of going to heaven when they die do so because they espouse a Platonized eschatology, one that draws an unbiblical distinction between spirit and matter, where spirit is the true reality and matter reality's mere shadow and salvation means liberation from the burdensome physical body.

The Reformed understanding is, however, very different from Platonism. Matter is anything but a shadow. Yes, present matter is polluted by sin, for example, our physical bodies have been corrupted, but matter, in and of itself, is not deemed to be evil. Indeed, the Christian hope still looks forward to one having a real tangible physical body, one consisting of matter. There is so much information available which clearly explains the Reformed position on this, one is left wondering why Wright sought to present the reader with such a distorted picture.

In his recent work[4] Wright repeats, *ad nauseam*, that salvation is not about going to heaven when we die. To do this so frequently causes one to surmise that he is attempting to convince himself. Such a belief is at best but a half-truth. He nowhere mentions the fact that most, indeed, all who believe in the imputation of Christ's righteousness also believe in a bodily resurrection. In all, his assumption is far too sweeping. One must distinguish between the believer's interim and his final destination. In continually attacking the "going to heaven when you die" motif, Wright is essentially waging war against a straw man. It is not that he does not believe in the intermediate state. In his work on the resurrection, he states that "any Jew who believed in the resurrection from Daniel to the Pharisees and beyond, naturally believed in an intermediate state in which some kind of personal identity was guaranteed between the physical re-embodiment of resurrection."[5]

Wright, again caricaturing the old perspective states:

3. Wright, *Justification*, 207.
4. *The Day the Revolution Began.*
5. Wright, *Resurrection*, 164.

> The idea of "heaven" carries with it in the popular mind and even in many well-taught Christian minds the notion that this is where "good people" go, while "bad people" go somewhere else. This, of course, quickly gets modified by standard teachings of the gospel: we are all "bad people," so that if anyone "goes to heaven," it must be because our badness has somehow been dealt with and, in some traditions, because someone else's "goodness" has somehow been "reckoned to our account."[6]

This is a deliberate overly simplistic depiction of what those in the Reformed tradition believe. On examination, we find that there is not, as Wright claims, anything intrinsically wrong with believing that we will go to heaven when we die. "Good people" go to heaven because they, although sinful in themselves, have been pronounced righteous because they are united with Christ; their goodness is the result of sharing in Christ's goodness. Those who correspond to the "bad people" are those without Christ, and, yes, not being united with Christ, being still in Adam, they go to another place. Wright's allusion to those who say that "someone else's 'goodness' has been 'reckoned to our account.'" is simply a jibe against the imputation of Christ's righteousness and the Reformed position. Wright goes on to say that "the problem with this entire way of looking at things is that *the idea of moral behavior as the qualification for 'heaven' is itself a distortion.*"[7] This is somewhat ironic because it is Wright who insists in a second justification based on one's works. One is left asking if he believes that one can stand before God without having produced the necessary moral behavior? Even Israel was told that to become God's people it was necessary for it to keep all the conditions (Exod 19:5). This is only a distortion in Wright's eyes because he has rejected Christ's righteousness, his "moral behavior," that when imputed to the believer's account qualifies him for heaven.

It is true that the average man in the street who calls himself a Christian, having not read what the Scriptures teach, may well describe salvation in terms of just going to heaven. This, however, is not what Bible-believing Christians believe, and I am somewhat baffled as to why Wright appears to associate such a view with the old perspective. I don't know of any who espouse Reformed theology who would consider the final destination of believers to be in heaven, in a realm that is separate from the physical body. For the believer, there is a twofold resurrection.

6. Wright, *Revolution*, 158.
7. Ibid., 159.

The first occurs when one is regenerated, born again by the Spirit of God. This is what Jesus spoke about in John 3:3 in his conversation with Nicodemus. It involves our spiritual resurrection, where one is made spiritually alive and placed into Christ. Hence, spiritually, the Christian is even now, in Christ, having "every spiritual blessing in heavenly places" (Eph 1:3). This is why Christ said, "whoever hears my word and believes him who sent me has eternal life. He does not come into judgment but has passed from death to life" (John 5:24). The Christian presently lives in the knowledge that upon the death of his physical or mortal body his spirit will go to be with Christ, which is but a continuation of his spiritual life.

The second resurrection will involve our mortal bodies. Our present perishable bodies will be raised anew, resembling Christ's glorified body. Presently this is not the case. Paul tells us that if we belong to Christ, "the body is dead because of sin, but the spirit is life because of righteousness" (Rom 8:11). On the day when Christ returns, our disembodied spirits will be reunited with our newly resurrected and glorified bodies. Presently, our redeemed spirits groan inwardly as we wait for the redemption of our bodies (Rom 8:23). Not only will our bodies be raised, but we shall live upon a real tangible glorified world. Indeed, Paul tells us that the whole of creation, being "subjected to futility" has "been groaning together in pains of childbirth until now," looking forward to that day when it will "be set free from its bondage to corruption and obtain the freedom and glory of the children of God" (v.21–22).

Having said this, one must not exclude our intermediate state. When the body dies it goes, usually, into the earth. The spirit or soul, however, goes to be with God in heaven. This is why Paul could say, "I am hard pressed between the two, my desire is to depart and be with Christ, for that is far better" (Phil 1:23). Such a departure from his material body would mean that his spirit would be in heaven with Christ. It is why Peter could refer to the believer's desire for "an inheritance that is imperishable, undefiled, and unfading, kept in heaven for you" (1 Pet 1:4).[8] Our hope is in Christ and Christ is presently in heaven. Jesus said to his disciples: "For where your treasure is, there your heart will be also" (Matt 6:21). Christ himself is that treasure. What does Wright think Jesus meant when he told his disciples, "In my father's house there are many rooms. If it were not so, would I have told you that I go to prepare a place for you. I will come again and will take you to myself, that where I am, you may be

8. It is also important to note that Peter's reference to heaven could also denote life upon the new earth, where God will dwell in all his glory.

also"? (Jn 14:2–3). Jesus said to the thief on the cross, "Truly, I say to you, today you will be with me in Paradise" (Luke 23:43). Jesus was speaking of the thief's spirit, essentially telling him that he would enter the same place as himself, namely, heaven. This is true for all God's people who die before the second coming. The apostle speaks of our hope being laid up in heaven (Col 1:5), and he tells believers that since they "have been raised with Christ, seek the things that are above, where Christ is seated at the right hand of God" (Col 3:1). He also states that we are to set our "minds on the things that are above, not on things that are on earth" (Col 3:2). This treasure and hope resides in the place where the believer longs to be. This is why believers, quite rightly, talk about going to heaven when they die. They know that then they will know a closer communion with Christ and be finished with their struggles in this fallen world. To use a simple illustration. Imagine one is climbing a very high mountain. Two-thirds of the way up there is an intermediate resting place, a cabin containing food and a warm log fire. On the way up to the top, which, of course, is your destination, as you struggle against the wind and snow, your thoughts may focus on getting to the cabin. Heaven is something like this. Yes, believers know that one day they will dwell upon a new earth, their immediate thoughts, however, as they battle through this world's trials and tribulations, may well focus on heaven, the intermediate state, where there will be spiritual food and warmth awaiting them.

Heaven is obviously not a place that one can climb into a space rocket and journey toward. It is not to be thought of as some geographical location somewhere on the far side of the universe. It can be closer than one's jugular vein and further away than the most distant part of the universe. It is essentially an entirely different dimension. When Christ's physical body ascended into the heavens it went into the place or dimension we call heaven. It is where God is manifest in all his glory. The only means of entering is through faith in Christ. This is the place where God's people enter upon the death of their physical bodies, a place from which they await the new earth and the redemption of their bodies.

In 2 Corinthians 5:1–8 Paul touches upon both the believer's intermediate and final state. The former will be one in which his spirit will be unclothed because it will be without its future glorified body:

> For we know that if the tent that is our earthly home is de-
> stroyed, we have a building from God, a house not made with
> hands, eternal in the heavens. 2 For in this tent we groan, long-
> ing to put on our heavenly dwelling, if indeed by putting it on

we may not be found naked. For while we are still in this tent, we groan, being burdened—not that we would be unclothed, but that we would be further clothed, so that what is mortal may be swallowed up by life. He who has prepared us for this very thing is God, who has given us the Spirit as a guarantee. So we are always of good courage. We know that while we are at home in the body we are away from the Lord, for we walk by faith, not by sight. Yes, we are of good courage, and we would rather be away from the body and at home with the Lord.

    1 Cor 5:1–6.

In our final state believers will be "clothed" in their new resurrected bodies. He calls it a "heavenly dwelling," not because it will dwell in heaven, but because it will be a body fit for the things of heaven which will then exist on the new earth.

THE BELIEVER IN THIS WORLD

Wright speaks as if this fallen world is the home of the Christian, and although he refers to this world passing away, he avoids any reference to its destruction. Instead, he seems to advocate some kind of post-millennial progressive advancement of the kingdom of God/heaven; a kind of spiritual osmosis, culminating in Christ's return. He informs us that "God through the gospel puts people right so that through them he can put the world right."[9] That we "are the people who are bringing the civilization of heaven into the world in which we live."[10] He appears to be suggesting there will be a kind of meeting between heaven and earth, where the earth will have reached a point of godliness that reflects life in heaven, so much so the two become indistinguishable. The world is then being slowly transformed by the growth of the kingdom of God, to the point where God's will be done on earth as it is in heaven. We are told that: "The hope of Israel, expressed variously in the Torah, Prophets, and Psalms, was not for a rescue operation that would snatch Israel (or humans or the faithful) *from* the world, but for a rescue operation that would be *for* the world, an operation through which redeemed humans would play once more the role for which they were designed."[11]

9. Wright, Paul for Tomorrow's World.

10. Wright, On the Second coming of Christ.

11. Wright, *Revolution*, 146.

He suggests the revolution to have already taken place, whereby this world is being renewed by the people of God as they exercise their vocation, the very vocation that Adam failed to exercise:

> First, there is indeed a radical redefinition of the Jewish hope of rescue from pagan oppression, of a new justice for the peace of the world, of the ultimate return of YHWH to his temple. Once you put the crucifixion and resurrection of Israel's Messiah in the middle of that story and make it the new focus, everything looks different. Second, the Christian world has for so long clung to and taught a meaning of "redemption" that involves "saved souls going to heaven" that it takes quite an effort of imagination to come to terms with the New Testament's message, that what we are promised in the gospel is the kingdom of God coming "on earth as in heaven"; or to put it another way, for all things in heaven and on earth to be summed up in the Messiah; or, to put it yet another way, "new heavens and a new earth, in which justice will be at home.[12]

Wright is essentially confusing two worlds, and misplacing the believer's citizenship. In equating the 'new earth' with this world, one of his pivotal texts is Matthew 6:10, "your will be done on earth as it is in heaven." I would, however, argue that Jesus is not alluding to the transformation of this fallen world, but to the evangelization of his people; where those saved will honor Christ in their hearts as Lord (1 Pet 3:15). Those who are saved are to set their minds *not* on the things of the earth, but on the things that are above (Col 3:2). Jesus himself said, "I am praying for them. I am not praying for the world but for those whom you have given me, for they are yours" (John 17:9). In Matthew 6:10 Jesus is concerned with the growth of the church, with a people called out of the world. The kingdom grows as an increasing number of people hear the gospel and believe, recognizing Christ as king, and honoring him in their hearts, even as he is honored in heaven.

Wright states that "The idea of escaping from the world to a non-spatio-temporal heaven encourages an unbiblical attitude towards creation, so that anyone who engages in ecological activity, or perhaps even feeding the hungry, is seen as selling the pass."[13] Does Wright believe that this earth is going to last forever? Christians are to let their light shine. They are to behave like the good Samaritan (Luke 10:25–37). One can

---

12. Ibid.
13. Wright, *New Heavens, New Earth*, 20.

think about this in terms of a human life. Each of us knows that the death of the body is inevitable, unless, of course, Christ returns. This knowledge does not mean that we are to abuse our bodies. By the same token, the Christian knows that this world is drawing to a close. We do not then abuse the world, rather, we strive to look after God's gift, and we encourage others to do the same. The duty of Christians, however, is to preach the gospel, to point sinners to the Christ, so that they might acknowledge the kingship and reign of Christ before the impending end. When the new world arrives, it will not be because this world has been slowly transformed into God's kingdom, but as a result of this world encountering God's wrath and destruction, with a new world being created.

The church's role in this world was perfectly expressed by Lloyd-Jones:

> The deduction we therefore draw is that the church's task primarily is to evangelize, and to bring people to a knowledge of God. Then, having done that, she is to teach them how to live under God as His people. The church is not here to reform the world, for the world cannot be reformed. The business of the church is to evangelize, to preach the gospel of salvation to men who are blinded by sin under the dominion and power of the devil. The moment the church begins to enter into the details of politics and economics, she is doing something that militates against her primary task of evangelism.[14]

The church that becomes embroiled in social/political/economic programs needs to bear in mind the words of Jesus in his reply to Pilate: "Pilate answered, 'Am I a Jew? Your own nation and the chief priests have delivered you over to me. What have you done?' Jesus answered, '*My kingdom is not of this world.*[15] If my kingdom were of this world, my servants would have been fighting, that I might not be delivered over to the Jews. But my kingdom is not from the world'" (Jn 18:35–36). Those Christians who think that by their actions they can reform this world by somehow causing sinners to live a life that is more honoring to God will be sorely disappointed—as the Ethiopian cannot change his skin or the leopard his spots, so neither can one cause a person without Christ to live the life of a Christian (Jere 13:23). One might as well expect a camel to pass through the eye of a needle (Matt 19:24).

14. Lloyd-Jones, *Life in the Spirit*, 318–19.
15. Italics added.

There is a spiritual warfare going on between the world and the church, as Jesus reminds us, "I have given them your word, and the world has hated them because they are not of the world, just as I am not of the world" (Jn 17:16).[16] I am not suggesting that Christians should not engage in those activities which serve to ameliorate human suffering, e.g., provision of schools, food banks, education etc., but, as I said earlier, Christians must not through such actions believe that this fallen world is moving to some sort of millennial utopia. It is an interesting fact that nowhere in the New Testament do we find believers trying to change the political landscape or censure the world because of its behavior in the expectation of reforming it. The church's job is not to change the world with a social gospel. All we can do is behave according to what we have become in Christ; believing that others will see our good works and come to believe in Christ.

The idea that the present world is under God's curse and awaiting God's judgment is, to say the least, not fashionable, and has been subject to sanitization in order to make it fit with the present mindset. Wright tells us, in disagreeing, and in almost disbelief, concerning those who teach about "going to heaven," that "Sometimes this view is backed up by the belief that God will actually destroy the present world."[17] This world, however, possesses the seeds of its own destruction. Christians are called out of this world in the same way that Lot and his family were called out of Sodom (Gen 19). God's wrath was about to fall upon the sinful city of Sodom, but God in his grace allowed Lot and his family to escape. Again, the present world can be likened to the world of Noah's time, and as judgment and destruction came upon that world in the flood, so too a day of judgment is approaching for the present world. As Peter tells us, "the heavens and earth that now exist are stored up for fire, being kept until the day of judgment and destruction of the ungodly" (2 Pet 3:7). When that day arrives "the heavens will be set on fire and dissolved, and the heavenly bodies will melt away as they burn" (v.12).

According to Wright, we are misinterpreting this passage from Peter:

> As with the rest of the New Testament, Peter is not saying that the present world of space, time and matter is going to be burnt up and destroyed. That is more like the view of ancient

16. See also, Jn 15:18–19;
17. Lloyd-Jones, *Life in the Spirit*, 357.

Stoicism—and of some modern ideas, too. What will happen, as many early Christian teachers said, is that some sort of 'fire', literal or metaphorical, will come upon the whole earth, not to destroy, but to test everything out, and to purify it by burning up everything that doesn't meet the test.[18]

This, however, seems most unlikely. Just prior to saying this Peter had alluded to what God did previously in judging the whole world with a cataclysmic flood. This was not a metaphor or simile, but a clear statement of fact. Peter does not say, "It will be as if the heavens are being burnt up." In matter-of-fact language, he is saying that God is actually going to burn up the universe and set up a "new heavens and earth in which righteousness dwells." The apostle does not then allude to a factual case, that of the great flood, to emphasize that which is partially true or metaphorical. All non-believers perished in the flood, and all non-believers will likewise perish on the coming day of judgment. Peter uses this fact to encourage Christians to live a life befitting citizens of the new heavens and earth. Christ himself makes a similar comparison: "For as were the days of Noah, so will be the coming of the Son of Man. For as in those days before the flood they were eating and drinking, marrying and giving in marriage, until the day when Noah entered the ark, and they were unaware until the flood came and swept them all away, so will be the coming of the Son of Man" (Matt 24:37–39). As Noah and his family were safe in the Ark, so too will God's people be safe from this world's approaching destruction because they are in Christ. Every Christian is, therefore, to be a Noah, warning of the wrath to come and preaching God's remedy in Christ; we are to point sinners to Christ, the true ark of God. As Johnson tells us, "As when God destroyed the world with a deluge of water and re-established the kingdom mandate with Noah, this time God will purge the world with fire and start anew with those found in the ark of Christ."[19]

Christians are the salt of the earth, and the function of salt is to reduce putrefaction, not reverse it. The very presence of Christians seeking to please their Lord by their behavior serves this end. Our citizenship is in heaven and not of this fallen world, and we must fix our eyes there and not here. This is why Peter can call believers "sojourners and exiles" (1 Pet 2:11) upon the earth, and why God's people "desire a better country, that is, a heavenly one" (Heb 11:16). In the context of Peter's words, Christians

---

18. Wright, *The Early Christian Letters*, 119.

19. Johnson, *The Kingdom of God*, 252.

know that their stay in this fallen world is but temporary. They know they are in exile from their true home, namely, being where Christ is, as Paul expressed it, "we would rather be away from the body and at home with the Lord" (2 Cor 5:8). Again, speaking of the Patriarchs, the writer to the Hebrews tells us that "These all died in faith, not having received the things promised, but having seen them and greeted them from afar, and having knowledge that they were strangers and exiles on the earth" (Heb 11:13). To use a simple example. Imagine that one is a citizen of one country but actually living in another country, a country that is at war with your own country. Your function in the hostile country is to convince the people to change their allegiance. You do this in the knowledge that your country will win the war, and that the hostile country will be totally destroyed, and somehow replaced by one that is very different. You do not, as Wright insists, carry out your work believing that you can somehow reform the country, but, rather, that you can call people out from it, making them citizens of your own country and benefactors of what will be a newly created future world.

All of this is a far cry from that which Wright appears to argue for, where this world is one's home, and where the will of God is increasingly being done, to that point where heaven and earth will somehow coalesce.

ISRAEL'S EXILE?

The exile theme runs throughout Wright's works, representing an important plank in his theological system. He is firmly of the opinion that first century Israel still considered itself in exile:

> Most Jews of this period, it seems, would have answered the question "where are we?" in language which, reduced to its simplest form, meant: we are still in exile. They believed that, in all the senses which mattered, Israel's exile was still in progress. Although she had come back from Babylon, the glorious message of the prophets remained unfulfilled. Israel still remained in thrall to foreigners; worse, Israel's god had not returned to Zion.[20]

Israel had broken God's law and needed forgiveness. As we saw earlier, Wright believes that Jesus became a curse to ensure Israel's forgiveness in

20. *NTPG*, 268–69

order that the gospel might go to the world, where the mission Israel was given might finally be achieved:

> If her sin has caused her exile, her forgiveness will mean her national re-establishment. This needs to be emphasized in the strongest possible terms: the most natural meaning of the phrase 'the forgiveness of sins' to a first century Jew is not in the first instance the remission of individual sins, but the putting away of the whole nation's sins. And, since the exile was the punishment for those sins, the only sure sign that had been forgiven would be the clear and certain liberation from exile. This is the major national context within which all individual dealing-with-sin must be understood.[21]

The Achilles heel in Wright's position is quite simply the scarcity of evidence. There is no evidence that Israel saw itself as being in exile, as Casey points out, "We would need stunningly strong arguments to convince us that these Jews really believed they were in exile when they were in Israel. All Wright's arguments for this view, however, seem to me to be quite spurious."[22] If Wright means by Israel only those who consist of the remnant, those who exercise faith, he has chosen a somewhat strange way to show this. The lack of differentiation causes not a little confusion. On so many occasions, Wright speaks of Israel as one monolithic entity. When he here speaks of "national Israel" he appears to means ethnic Israel, the whole of old covenant Israel, although he does not actually say this. The whole idea that Jesus was about ending ethnic Israel's exile is shot through with problems. One might well ask: If Jesus did come to end the nation's exile why did this end with an even greater exile following the temple's destruction in 70 AD? Indeed, in 135 AD by Hadrian's edict, all Jews were excluded from Judaea and Jerusalem itself was renamed *Aelia Capitolina*, effectively becoming a Greek city. If it was the case that first century Jews thought in terms of their national liberation it was because they had misunderstood the nature of the message. True believers, like Abraham, were not looking for a reformation of this world, but "looking forward to the city that has foundations, whose designer and builder is God" (Heb 11:10).

Wright takes Galatians 3:13 to be an expression of the exile theme:

21. Wright, *The New Testament and the People of God*, 273.
22. Casey, "Where Wright is Wrong" 99.

> Because the Messiah represents Israel, he is able to take on him-
> self Israel's curse and exhaust it. Jesus dies as the king of the
> Jews, at the hands of the Romans whose expression of Israel is
> the present, and climactic, form of the curse of exile itself. The
> crucifixion of the messiah is . . . the *quintessence* of the curse of
> exile, and its climactic act.[23]

The problem with this is simply that, in the words of Longenecker, Wright "fails to show how the extended theology animates these verses."[24] More-over, it seems perfectly reasonable to suggest that if Paul had believed only Israel to be under the curse he would have alluded to it. Instead, he states that "all who rely on works of the law are under a curse" (Gal 3:10). Again, in Romans, when Paul speaks about every mouth being stopped because of sin, and the consequences of sin (Rom 3:19–20), he is not alluding to Israel alone, but, rather, the entire world. Both Jews and Gentiles were, and, indeed, still are unless they believe in Christ, under the original curse and separated from God. Wright's problem lies in his focus on the type instead of the archetype. Instead of making the former subservient to the latter, he appears to have reversed the order. The entire world is thus under a curse, a curse to which the Deuteronomic curse was itself but a type.

The law revealed to Israel on the two tablets of stone was simply a particular application of this universal law. Christ's work, therefore, was not concerned with ethnic Israel's exile but a much greater exile. Wright, in yet another caricature, criticizes the way we view Israel and the old covenant:

> For far too long now Christians have told the story of Jesus as
> if it hooked up not with the story of Israel, but simply with the
> story of human sin as in *Genesis* 3, skipping over the story of Is-
> rael altogether. From that point of view, the story of Israel looks
> a failed first attempt on God's part to sort out his world. "Here,"
> he says, "you can be my people. I'll rescue you from slavery and
> give you my law!" But then the people find they can't keep the
> law and the story continues to go from bad to worse. Eventually,
> God gives up the attempt to make people (specifically, Israel)
> "better" by having them keep his law and decides on a differ-
> ent strategy, a "Plan B." This involves sending his son to die and
> declaring that now the only thing people need to do is to believe

23. Wright, "Curse and Covenant", 51.

24. Longenecker, *Triumph*, 138.

in him and his saving death. This is a gross caricature of the actual biblical story, but it is certainly not a gross caricature of what many Christians have been taught, either explicitly or by implication.[25]

Although there is some truth in what he says if one is a dispensationalist, it is certainly not the Reformed position. We do not "skip over the story of Israel" but see it as an integral part of God's plan to bring forth the Messiah and to make known to Israel the promise of the new covenant. The idea that God tried one way, that of the law, to save people, and when this failed he came up with another way, namely, that of sending his own Son, seems to fit more with Wright's paradigm than with that of Reformed theology. It is Wright who maintains that Israel failed in the mission God gave her and that he had to introduce his Son to accomplish what the nation failed to do. It is the Reformed Baptist view that maintains the continuity of God's one plan to save humanity, and that puts the old covenant in its proper subservient position. Wright presents one with the possibility of Christ's work being redundant, for if Israel had been faithful to her calling, the work of Christ would have been unnecessary.

If Wright is correct in that Jesus, as the faithful representative Israelite, had honored the conditions necessary for the nation to enjoy God's blessings, one would surely have expected the exile to end and the promises to be applied to temporal Jerusalem. This is, however, not what happened. Even if Wright believes that many of the Old Testament promises are to be fulfilled, not literally, but spiritually in Christ, he still believes that Jesus, in becoming a curse, suffered on account of the old covenant curse, and this leaves him having to explain how the temporal promises that concerned geography and politics can be spiritualized away. As already alluded to, I say this because if Jesus kept the old covenant for Israel, one should expect to see Israel participating in blessings of that covenant, for, after all, Israel was God's people in that covenant. Contrary to Wright, however, the land promises etc., depended not on Christ's obedience and death under the old covenant, but, rather, on Israel's obedience to that covenant.

Let us look at this in a little more detail. Wright has reworked and redefined Israel. He maintains that ethnic Israel failed in her mission to bring the good news to the Gentile world, and this made it necessary for Christ to accomplish what the nation should have done. The problem, as

25. Wright, *How God became King*, 84–85.

I see it, lies in the way Wright presents the transition from Israel as God's people to those who believe in Christ as the Messiah. He speaks of ethnic Israel as still being in exile, then proceeds to say how Jesus ended this exile. In so doing he makes the mistake, again as a result of mixing up the covenants, of applying the consequences of Jesus' work, as the faithful Israelite, not, as one would expect, to ethnic Israel but to the church. In other words, he sees Christ's obedience to the old covenant as a prerequisite for new covenant blessings. Such a crossover is unjustifiable. Paul tells us that once a covenant has been made it cannot then be added to (Gal 3:15). This goes as much for the nature of the covenant's promises as it does for the conditions attached to the covenant. As I have said a number of times, the Sinaitic covenant was a separate covenant, one possessing its own promises and punishments. While it is true to say the old covenant spoke of the new covenant, with its many shadows and types, one cannot, as Wright as done, take the substance of the old covenant and integrate it into the new. Israel went into exile because she had broken the Sinaitic covenant. The only way this exile could end was for Israel to answer for her sin and keep the covenantal conditions. This is just what Wright believes Jesus did. He then speaks of the exile ending and the blessings being bestowed, not upon ethnic Israel but upon the new people of God. The problem is that if Jesus kept the old covenant, the promises should flow to those with whom that covenant was made. To use a simple illustration: Imagine that I make a covenant with someone, say Jill, and call it covenant A. I lay down the conditions, promising to bless her if she is faithful by buying her a new car. Beside this covenant, there is another made with Sue, call it covenant B, it is an entirely separate covenant. The blessing for faithfulness to this covenant is a round the world cruise. Now imagine that Jill fails to adhere to the conditions in covenant A, whereas, Sue keeps covenant B. I cannot then apply the blessings resulting from Sue's faithfulness to covenant B to Jill who broke covenant A, neither can I give to Sue the car that I conditionally promises to Jill. In other words, Jill can never qualify for the round the world cruise, simply because it concerned a covenant made with someone else. Substituting covenant A with the old covenant, and covenant B with the new covenant, one can see that they are two separate entities, with the former promising temporal blessings for obedience, and the latter, spiritual and eternal blessings.

According to Wright, Israel, the people of God, are redefined, and the new Israel is the result of Christ fulfilling the Deuteronomic conditions. While the Deuteronomic promises were specifically made to a nation and were conditional, one might well ask what Paul meant when he said: "all the promises of God are yea, and in him Amen" (2 Cor 1:20 KJV) Did this not include the Deuteronomic promises? I would answer this by saying the promises Paul is alluding to are those to which those in Deuteronomy are, again, a type. Indeed, all the promises relating to ethnic Israel that were dependent on her obedience for their realization were of a typical nature. A good example is provided in Ezekiel 37. The great promise, as we saw earlier, that runs throughout the Old Testament, is found in God's words, "they shall be my people, and I will be their God" (Ezek 37:23). Israel failed to become God's treasured possession, but those in Christ have become "a chosen race, a royal priesthood, a holy nation, a people for his own possession" in order that they might "proclaim the excellencies of him who called you out of darkness into his marvellous light" (1 Pet 2:9). We can then say that "all the promises find their yes in him."

Regarding salvation, the true Israel has always been under the new covenant. The old covenant which Wright asserts needs to be fulfilled before the promises can be realized was actually made after the new covenant. Before Sinai, salvation was by faith in the promise and this did not change with the giving of the law. Before Israel, God spoke to individuals, reminding them of their exile from him and pointing them to Christ, as in the case of Noah. With Israel, God used the temporal exile to speak of a far more important exile. Where the temporal exile involved Israel losing its land and being under earthly taskmasters, the greater exile speaks of humanity's separation from God and its residence in the kingdom of darkness. The temporal blessings associated with the old covenant would never be realized because of Israel's disobedience, whereas, for those who believed, all the promises of the new covenant can be entered into because they depend on Christ's obedience.

There are many references to ethnic Israel's exile in the Old Testament (Isa 5:13; 6:11–12; 32:9–14; Jer 13:19, 24; Amos 5:27). There are also the promises of her restoration (Isa 2:1–5; 30:23–26; 41:11–20; Ezek 36:8–15), in spite of her disobedience, God did bring ethnic Israel back to her land solely on account of his grace alone. This served to typify the grace of God in Christ that would be available to all who believed in the promise. Israel's failure served to make God's grace in his Messiah shine even more brightly. Throughout the old covenant, God was essentially saying, "I make this covenant with you. I promise you blessings on condition of obedience. You, however, will not keep the covenant, in your disobedience you will only reap the punishments. From this I want you to look elsewhere to find my favor. Where the old spoke of unobtainable types, the new covenant speaks of the reality itself, a reality that is available to all that believe. Look to the promise, just as Abraham did."[26]

The New Testament does not speak of God disinheriting Israel from the land, simply because Israel had disinherited itself on account of its disobedience. No one was going to come and provide what ethnic Israel could not. It was under a conditional covenant of works which it failed to keep. The promises that had been associated with that covenant were no longer available. Jesus should not be seen as one who fulfills what was Israel's responsibility. Of course, God will not cast away true Israel because this consists of those who, like Abraham, have believed in the promise becoming recipients of new covenant blessings. And, as Paul tells us, God still has those from Israel who will come to faith in the Messiah, and on the final day, he will have saved all of his elect from both Israel and the Gentile world (Rom 11:25).

Wright even equates the forgiveness of sins with the ending of Israel's exile, "*Forgiveness of sins is another way of saying 'return from exile.'*"[27] Once again, he speaks of a monolithic Israel. Ethnic Israel's exile was a consequence of her breaking the Sinaitic covenant. The exile was the nation's temporal punishment. As I have tried to emphasize throughout, the Sinaitic covenant with its temporal blessings and cursings, pointed to spiritual realities but was not itself efficacious to that end. It stopped short of spiritual realities, "it was a ministry of death, carved in letters of stone" (2 Cor 3:7). Wright, by associating forgiveness of sins with typical Israel is, to use the old saying, missing the wood for the tree. He is looking to the wrong covenant and the wrong exile. The only exile with spiritual consequences is that which occurred in Genesis, and this is the only exile that Jesus came to end by securing forgiveness of sins and a positive righteousness for his people.

One might ask: if Second Temple Jews believed Jesus had dealt with the Deuteronomic curse, why did they still insist on keeping the law, and, not only this, but insist that the Gentiles did so too? Wright's emphasis on the exile seems to be without foundation. "Cursed is everyone who hanged on a tree" (Gal 3:13), is expressed under the Deuteronomic types (Deut 21:23) to remind one that Jesus has taken upon himself a greater

26. We see the misapplication of Old Testament promises in present day Zionism.
27. Wright, *Jesus and the Victory of God*, 268.

curse, the results of which enables the redemption of God's people, both Jews, and Gentiles. The only exile that Jesus's death brought to an end was that which commenced from our first parent's sin.

I am not advocating a supersessionist[28] position. The Gentile church did not replace the people of God, it was, rather, an extension of the pre-existing church that consisted of the true Israel. The new covenant was not a renewal of anything that went before, as Wright claims, but marked the consummation of the covenant that had been available for all those with faith. Instead of renewal, we see a continuation of the one covenant and its extension into the Gentile world.

I am not diminishing the importance of the old covenant. It had come in alongside the promise of the new covenant, was juxtaposed to it, and thus served an important function in its schoolmaster role. The problem with most Jews lay in their refusal to see what was in front of their eyes. Instead, they looked to the type and thought salvation came through it. They sought to do the impossible, to descend into the abyss and ascend into heaven, instead of realizing the fact that the truth lay much closer to hand, "The word is near you, in your mouth and in your heart" (Rom 10:8).

THE KINGDOM OF GOD

Wright, again, has a peculiar understanding of the kingdom of God or the kingdom of heaven.[29] He espouses what is known as inaugurated eschatology.[30] He tells us that the gospels are about "God's kingdom being launched on earth as in heaven, generating a new state of affairs in which the power of evil has been decisively defeated, the new creation has been decisively launched, and Jesus' followers have been commissioned and equipped to put the victory, and that inaugurated new world into practice."[31] We must not teach that "Jesus died so that we can go to heaven. It ignores the New Testament emphasis on the true human voca-

28. Supersessionism is the belief that the old covenant has been replaced by the new covenant. That the New Testament Christian church has displaced Israel as God's chosen people.

29. Kingdom of God and kingdom of heaven are synonymous.

30. Inaugurated eschatology is a position that maintains Jesus' first coming marked the beginning of God's kingdom, while at the same time acknowledging its future consummation. In other words, the kingdom is and is yet to come.

31. Wright, *Surprised by Hope*, 217.

tion, to be 'image bearers,' reflecting God's glory into the world and the praises of creation back to God."[32] To do so would be to miss, or ignore "Jesus' claim to be launching God's kingdom 'on earth as in heaven' and to be bringing that work to its climax precisely on the cross."[33]

Through the church, if I correctly understand Wright, a process, or a revolution, was started, and this will continue until what is done upon the earth will reflect that which is done in heaven. As more people come to faith they will, through the work of the Holy Spirit, reflect in their lives what is done in heaven, as Paul puts it, "the righteous requirement of the law might be fulfilled in us, who walk not according to the flesh but according to the Spirit" (Rom 8:4). Christ's work and the giving of the Spirit are then "not designed to take us away from this world, but to make us agents of the transformation of this earth, anticipating the day when, as we are promised, 'the earth shall be full of the knowledge of the Lord, as the waters cover the sea.'"[34]

The word "launch" means "to start" to "set something in motion". One problem in saying that the kingdom was only launched following Jesus' completed work is that one is then left having to conclude that the kingdom of God was non-existent prior to that time, for clearly, it was not here before it was launched or started. This then leaves Old Testament saints outside of the kingdom, even though Christ was their king, reigning in their hearts by faith.

No Reformed Evangelical would disagree that Christians living in this fallen world are to be "image bearers." Believers are called to be representatives and ambassadors of Christ (2 Cor 5:20). By caricaturing the teaching Wright distorts what is believed, this distortion then becomes a foil which serves to make his own views appear more appealing. He then, against the perceived errors of other interpretations, presents an understanding that can catch out the unwary. He tells us that "The point is this: the covenant between God and Israel was always designed to be God's means of saving the whole world. It was never supposed to be the means whereby God would have a private little group of people who would be saved while the rest of the world went to hell (whatever you might mean

---

32. Wright, *Revolution*, 357.

33.

34. Ibid., 214.

by that)."[35] If by this he means that God's intention was not just to save the Jews this would be reasonable, however, he goes on to say:

> When God is faithful to the covenant in the death and resurrection of Jesus Christ and in the work of the Spirit, it makes nonsense of the Pauline gospel to imagine the be-all and end-all of this operation is so that God can have another, merely different, private little group of people who are saved while the world is consigned to the cosmic waste-paper basket.[36]

What does he mean by "the whole world"? Is he advocating some kind of universal salvation? Can one not say that the church does, when compared to those that do not believe, represent "a little group of people or a remnant? Does he expect increasing numbers to believe in the gospel, and through the Spirit put God's plan into operation to the point where the kingdom of God will cover the whole earth? One only needs to look at the present world to realize that Christians are in the minority. In the Old Testament, it was only the minority of Jews within the nation who knew circumcision of the heart. In the time of Elijah, there was only "seven thousand who had not bowed the knee to Baal" (Rom 11:4). Paul told us, concerning his day, "So too at the present time there is a remnant, chosen by grace" (Rom. 11:5). Jesus himself referred to the relatively few who will be saved, "Enter by the narrow gate, for the gate is wide and the way is easy that leads to destruction, and those who enter it are many. For the gate is narrow and the way is hard that leads to life, and *those who find it are few*"[37] (Matt 7:13–14). Where does Wright think the many referred to by Jesus are going? They are going to hell, or, as Wright calls it, "the cosmic waste-paper basket". As to this "little group" being "private," this all depends on what one means by "private." If one means they have something that others do not have, then it is indeed true because it is only believers who have access to God; access that is unavailable to those outside of Christ. The church consists of God's elect, those chosen by God out of all the nations of the world, consisting of a people who find themselves in a peculiar position in Christ. So, yes, relatively speaking, believers are a private little group of people who are saved.

Again, Wright seems to suggest that God's new creation(s) commenced only after Jesus' completed work, he states that "The new creation

35. Wright, *WSPRS*, 163.
36. Ibid., 163.
37. Italics added for emphasis.

began when Jesus of Nazareth came out of the tomb on Easter morning."[38] To suggest this is to exclude Old Testament saints as part of God's new creation, for clearly, if it did not start until Christ, one must then exclude them from those blessings we associate with God's new creation. Again we are presented with a false dichotomy between Old and New Testament believers. Such a view fails to see the unity of the Scriptures, where each believer from the beginning is a new creation in Christ. The words of Paul to the Corinthians applied as much to Abraham as they do to today's believers, namely, "if anyone is in Christ, he is a new creation" (2 Cor 17). Faith itself is the result of this new creation. The old man in Adam has gone, and the believer has become a new man in Christ. What occurred after Jesus' work, commencing at Pentecost, was an extension of God's new creation because the Gentiles were to hear the gospel in its fullness.

The question we must ask concerning the kingdom of God is: Where was the kingdom in those times before Christ appeared in the flesh? The answer is not difficult to find. The kingdom was present within the hearts of God's people who, like Abraham, looked to Christ's day and rejoiced (John 8:56). The kingdom of God is that realm in which God's kingship is acknowledged in the hearts of his people; where he is the ruler of their lives. The Lord's prayer is not meant to teach that this fallen world will be transformed through the preaching of the gospel to that point where God's will is done on this earth as it is done in heaven. Rather, it (Mat 6:10) speaks of the growth of the church; as more people come to believe in Christ, they acknowledge God's reign and subsequently seek to do God's will. There are essentially two main covenants, the covenant of works that Adam broke, and the covenant of works that Christ kept. All humanity is under one or the other. When Paul said, "He has delivered us from the domain of darkness and transferred us into the kingdom of his beloved Son" (Col 1: 13), he was not speaking of something that is only true for New Testament believers. It is true that New Testament believers possessed a greater appreciation of what salvation entails, this knowledge, however, did not alter the fact that all believers have always been *in Christ*. Abraham was a new creation in Christ, just like his New Testament counterparts. Through faith, he believed and was justified, and in his heart, he acknowledged God as his king. Like Paul, he too was placed into the new covenant and Christ's kingdom.

---

38. Wright, *The Puzzles of the Cross.*

We can conclude that if one is not in Adam one is in Christ, and if one is in Christ one is in the new covenant and in the kingdom of God. In limiting the kingdom of God to the New Testament it seems that it is Wright who fails to appreciate what the covenantal God has done for his people in Christ. None can be saved and not be in the kingdom. One should instead think about it like this: Jesus' work performed at a particular point in time legally formalized the new covenant, the blessings of which have been communicated to God's people since shortly after the Fall. Jesus did not inaugurate or launch a new kingdom but paid the price for that which started when the first man believed in the gospel. Because Christ is the guarantor, Old Testament saints could become recipients of his salvific benefits on account of the future payment being guaranteed. It is this that explains why the new creation started before Christ's completed work.

Miscellaneous Verses

HAVING LOOKED AT ROMANS chapters 1–8, there is one further text in this epistle I want to comment on, namely, Chapter 10:3–5. Having done this there are a number of texts I want to briefly examine from Paul's other epistles, these include Philippians 3:7–9; 1 Corinthians 1:30; 2 Corinthians 5:21. In regard to Romans one could have looked at chapters 9 to 11, I will, however, leave this for another occasion. Of course, there are many other texts in the Pauline corpus one could examine, but confining myself to these should suffice here.

Romans 10:2–11 is particularly important because it provides clear evidence that the old perspective on Paul is correct.:

> For I bear them witness that they have a zeal for God, but not according to knowledge. For, being ignorant of the righteousness of God, and seeking to establish their own, they did not submit to God's righteousness. For Christ is the end of the law for righteousness to everyone who believes. For Moses writes about the righteousness that is based on the law, that the person who does the commandments shall live by them. But the righteousness based on faith says, "Do not say in your heart, 'Who will ascend into heaven?'" (that is, to bring Christ down) "or 'Who will descend into the abyss?'" (that is, to bring Christ up from the dead). But what does it say? "The word is near you, in your mouth and in your heart" (that is, the word of faith that we proclaim); because, if you confess with your mouth that Jesus is Lord and believe in your heart that God raised him from the dead, you will be saved. For with the heart one believes and is justified, and with the mouth one confesses and is saved. For the Scripture says, "Everyone who believes in him will not be put to shame."

The apostle is harkening back to Deuteronomy 30:11–14 to highlight the fact that Christians must never think that the truth lies in some far off region that is impossible to reach. The Israelites were unambiguously informed of the old covenant conditions.

> "For this commandment that I command you today is not too hard for you, neither is it far off. It is not in heaven, that you should say, 'Who will ascend to heaven for us and bring it to us, that we may hear it and do it?' Neither is it beyond the sea, that you should say, 'Who will go over the sea for us and bring it to us, that we may hear it and do it?' But the word is very near you. It is in your mouth and in your heart, so that you can do it.
>
> See, I have set before you today life and good, death and evil. If you obey the commandments of the Lord your God that I command you today, by loving the Lord your God, by walking in his ways, and by keeping his commandments and his statutes and his rules, then you shall live and multiply, and the Lord your God will bless you in the land that you are entering to take possession of it. But if your heart turns away, and you will not hear, but are drawn away to worship other gods and serve them, I declare to you today, that you shall surely perish. You shall not live long in the land that you are going over the Jordan to enter and possess. I call heaven and earth to witness against you today, that I have set before you life and death, blessing and curse. Therefore choose life, that you and your offspring may live, loving the Lord your God, obeying his voice and holding fast to him, for he is your life and length of days, that you may dwell in the land that the Lord swore to your fathers, to Abraham, to Isaac, and to Jacob, to give them. Deut 30:11–20.

Israel's mistake was that it confused the word of faith which was revealed through the law with the law itself. The Jews heard the command to love God and walk in his ways, and, instead of acknowledging their inability because of sin and looking to Christ, they sought to do it themselves. Verse 11 is not suggesting that Israel could keep the law, but is essentially saying, as we read in the KJV, "For this commandment which I command this day, it is not hidden from thee, neither is it far off." Israel's disobedience was inevitable, and as a result, it inherited the curse. The Jews erroneously thought the blessings lay in the old covenant, when all along, it was closer to them than they realized. The zeal that the Jews had was their determination to abide by the requirements of the old covenant. Their problem was they were zealous for the wrong covenant and they erroneously thought it was possible to secure a righteousness through obedience to the Sinaitic requirements. They were looking to their own righteousness instead of that which God himself has provided. Although this was the case, as I have said, it did not entail them keeping the commandments perfectly, but abiding by all that the law stipulated, which included forgiveness through the sacrifices.

While these verses originally spoke of the law (Deut 30:12–14), Paul applies them to Christ. In so doing he spells out the Jewish problem in that, as far as righteousness was concerned, they were trying to do the impossible. It was equivalent to asking impossible questions like who "will descend into the abyss?" or "who will ascend into heaven?" As no man could "descend into the abyss" or "ascend into heaven" by his own efforts, so Israel could not produce a righteousness acceptable to God unto salvation by keeping the Mosaic old covenant. The law from its beginning had spoken of the promise, yet Israel saw it not. Their mindset sent them on a never-ending journey in search of what had been just beside them from the start.

Christ is said to be the "end of the law for righteousness," the law in question is the original law as revealed to all men, the natural law. This law has come to an end in Christ for a number of reasons. First, because those that believe are deemed to have fulfilled it in him; the conditionality of the law had ended with Christ's fulfillment of it. In the case of believers, no longer does the law demand a righteousness to stand before God because they have been justified, having the righteousness of Christ. Secondly, the law has ended in that the old covenant is no longer required. Christ has fulfilled the types and the old covenant was now redundant. Of course, now that the daylight has arrived the shadows disappear. Iain Murray nicely summed up the essence of this verse: "The assertion is that for all united to Christ the demands of the law, in respect to their acceptance with God, are ended by Christ's obedience. Law has been terminated—abolished—by Christ as a means to attaining righteousness. For Christ satisfied the law once and forever on behalf of believers."[1] He has himself fulfilled that which the law of Moses was patterned after. There is no need of the type when the thing typified has arrived. In Romans 7:2–3, Paul speaks of the same thing. A woman is bound to her husband as long as he lives, but when he dies, he is replaced by a new husband, when this happens the old relationship is no more.

Wright again maintains that the righteousness of God referred to in v.3 is God's faithfulness to his covenant and not a righteousness that

---

1. Murray, *The Old Evangelicalism*, 85.

can be imputed to his people. He is remiss, however, in that he does not sufficiently tell us of what this righteousness consisted. He seems to believe that Jesus kept the old Mosaic covenant, but does not explain exactly how this affects the believer. If, for example, Christ's righteousness is not imputed to believers, then in what way does Jesus' sinless life affect those that believe? It may well be the apostle, with his emphasis on righteousness, had in mind God's deliverance of his people from their captivity in Babylon. However, one must not stop with this because that deliverance was a type of a greater deliverance, where God, through his own righteousness, delivers his people from their sins. The Jews knew their history, yet failed to draw the correct conclusions. If in the first-century they still considered themselves in exile, it was because their earlier deliverance from the Babylonians was imperfect. On being delivered they were to keep certain conditions, something they failed to do. Yet all the while, through the law and his prophets (Rom 3:21) God spoke of his righteousness which only those of faith embraced.

For Wright, this passage is speaking about "the long-awaited covenant renewal spoken of in Deuteronomy," believing that it "has at last come about."[2] This is, however, to once again, misapply that particular covenant's blessings. There can be no renewal of the old covenant. What occurred was something far more profound than any renewal or reformation of what was established in times past. What would be the point of renewing that which was only unto death in the first place? The long-awaited covenant was nothing less than the legal and formal establishment of the new covenant. This is not a mere extension of the old covenant, but something of an entirely different substance. It was previously promised, and now it was being consummated in Christ. So, whilst the old covenant was patterned after the new covenant, and spoke in terms of conditional temporal blessings that failed to materialize, those blessings of the new covenant are eternal and are guaranteed by Christ's obedience. In regard to the promise, again one cannot speak in terms of renewal. Throughout the Old Testament, everything worked exactly according to God's plan. There is simply, therefore, no requirement for any renewal. What did occur was the realization of the promise in Christ.

The commandments were not too difficult for Israel to abide by, if it had the will. The problem was, because of their fallen nature, they never did possess the will, and, therefore, merited the covenant's curses rather

2. Wright, *Justification*, 216.

than its blessings. This is why this covenant is unto condemnation and death. To keep the law without the will, without a circumcised heart was impossible. Yet all the while, in the many rituals and bible readings, the answer was in their mouths and in their thoughts. They saw the promise in reading the Scriptures and thought about it in their hearts, but they failed to appreciate the one promised. Instead, they placed their faith in Moses and the sacrifices, in the means instead of the end to which the means pointed. Those Jews who realized this, and believed, were those whose hearts the Lord had circumcised so that they should love him with all their heart and soul (Deut 30:6). They believed in their hearts and confessed with their mouths the Lordship of Christ (Rom 10:9).

1 CORINTHIANS 1:30.

> And because of him you are in Christ Jesus, who became to us wisdom from God, righteousness and sanctification.

Wright gives a number of reasons why he believes the old perspective has misunderstood this verse. First, there is a scarcity of evidence, for example, the only other place (at least according to Wright) where Paul hints at imputation is 2 Corinthians 5:21. Secondly, the text does not refer to Christ's righteousness, but "the righteousness of God," and, thirdly, our interpretation, he believes, is not in keeping with the overall context of the passage.

About 1 Corinthians 1:30, Wright states:

> It is difficult to squeeze any precise dogma of justification out of this shorthand summary. It is the only passage I know where something called "the imputed righteousness of Christ," a phrase more often found in post-Reformation theology and piety than in the New Testament, finds any basis in the text. But if we are to claim it as such, we must also be prepared to talk of the imputed wisdom of Christ; the imputed sanctification of Christ; and the imputed redemption of Christ; and that, though no doubt they are all true in some overall sense, will certainly make nonsense of the very specialized and technical senses so frequently given to the phrase "the righteousness of Christ" in the history of theology.[3]

---

3. Wright, WSPRS, 123.

Wright also believes that this verse cannot possibly be speaking the imputation of righteousness because then one would have to say that wisdom
and sanctification are also imputed. He is of the opinion that the old perspective underplays union with Christ in regard to believers' justification
and the imputation of righteousness. However, nothing could be further
from the truth. It is because believers are "in Christ" that his "righteousness, sanctification and redemption" now belong to them. Justification
should be seen as the vital legal prerequisite to enable one access to the
other blessings. The believer was chosen "in him," predestined "in him,"
and redeemed at a moment in time "in him," he is being sanctified "in
him," and on the last day, he will be resurrected "in him" and presented
perfect before the Father. God has provided the believer with the wisdom
to believe; he has imputed to him Christ's righteousness, and he has set
him apart, sanctifying him both definitively and progressively. He has
purchased and liberated the believer from bondage through the redemption that is found only "in Christ."

In the words of Fesko, Wright's interpretation of this verse is guilty
of "what can only be called a literalistic Biblicism."[4] Wright's claim that
the text is not about the righteousness of Christ but, rather, about God's
righteousness, as if this excludes the imputation of Christ's righteousness,
is somewhat bewildering. Scripture makes it clear that whether one is
referring to this righteousness as being from God or from Christ makes
little difference. Paul has said in this very verse that it is "because of him"
(God) that one is in Christ. It was God the Father who was in Christ
"reconciling the world to himself" (2 Cor 5:19). It was God the Father
who so loved the world that he sent his one and only Son (John 3:16). It
was the Father who gave a people to Christ to be saved (John 6:44). All
that he has done for sinners he has done in and through Jesus Christ. The
righteousness that Christ achieved is then both from the Father and the
Son. So Paul says "righteousness of God" because it is God, the Father,
who sent his Son to do all that was necessary for salvation to take place.
Therefore, Paul is simply saying what God has done in his Son for us.

The word sanctification found in this text does not just, as Wright
maintains, speak only of progressive, but also definitive or positional
sanctification. It has the same meaning as we find in other passages, for
example, Paul starts his first letter to the Corinthians with the words:
"To the church of God that is in Corinth, to those sanctified in Christ

4. Fesko, *Justification*, 253.

Jesus, called to be saints together with all those who in every place call upon the name of our Lord Jesus Christ, both their Lord and ours" (1 Cor 1:2). Sanctification here essentially means to be "set-apart," to have been removed from one realm and placed into another. When Paul speaks of Christ becoming our sanctification he means that we have been placed into the realm and sphere of Christ, where, previously, we were in the realm and sphere of Adam. The believer in Christ has become a new man. Progressive sanctification occurs as the result of this, where the believer lives in the body according to what he has become in his resurrected spirit. The man he used to be, the old man, has been crucified, he no longer exists, but the vestiges of sin remain in our old nature. The believer has now been given the wisdom to choose those things pleasing to Christ. The decisions he now makes, e.g., how to use his body as an instrument of righteousness, are the result of his new position. He no longer expresses the wisdom of the world, but that which the world considers foolishness. The believer now has the wisdom to work out his own salvation, knowing that, because he is in Christ, God through the Spirit is working within him "both to will and to work for his good pleasure" (Phil 2:12). Being in Christ, the believer has been given Christ's righteousness on account of his having been set apart "in him." The result of all this is redemption. If one were to paraphrase this verse it would go something like this: "You have now been placed into Christ. This has affected your whole being. The decisions you now make come from being in Christ. You stand because, having been set apart in Christ, his righteousness has been given to you. He has also provided you with a new nature that enables you to use a new wisdom in making decisions about your sanctification. You have been set apart, and being in Christ, God's Spirit is in you, and he is progressively conforming you to the image of Christ. You have redemption in him, you have been and are being delivered from all evil."

I fail to see how the old perspective's understanding of v.30 fails to fit the context of the passage. Paul has been speaking about the worldly wisdom compared with that which comes from God; how God chooses those things which the world finds foolishness. Not many believers were wise or of noble birth (v.26), indeed, many were by the standards of the world, considered weak (v.27). Verse 30, contrasts the position of believers with that of the world. Where the world likes to boast of its own achievements, believers boast only in the things of Christ. The world is what it is in and of itself, whereas, believers are what they are because they are "in him." They are not their own but have been bought at the price of God's own blood (1 Cor 6:19–20). By referring to more than righteousness in v.30, Paul is emphasizing the fact that everything believers have has been received from another, even Christ. If any do boast, they need to heed Paul's rebuke, "what do you have that you did not receive? If you then received it, why do you boast as if you did not receive it?" (1 Cor 4:7).

2 CORINTHIANS 5:20–21

> Therefore, we are ambassadors for Christ, God making his appeal through us. We implore you on behalf of Christ, be reconciled to God. For our sake he made him to be sin who knew no sin, so that in him we might become the righteousness of God.

Hodge summed up the old perspective's understanding of this text:

> There is probably no passage in the Scriptures in which the doctrine of justification is more concisely or clearly stated than in [2 Corinthians 5:21]. Our sins were imputed to Christ, and his righteousness is imputed to us. He bore our sins; we are clothed in his righteousness . . . Christ bearing our sins did not make him morally a sinner . . . nor does Christ's righteousness become subjectively ours, it is not the moral quality of souls . . . Our sins were the judicial ground of the sufferings of Christ, so that they were a satisfaction of justice; and his righteousness is the judicial ground of our acceptance with God, so that our pardon is an act of justice . . . It is not mere pardon, but justification alone, that gives us peace with God.[5]

This understanding, according to Wright, is wrong because the text has nothing to do with the imputation of righteousness:

> The key text, which is 2 Corinthians 5:21, has been read for generations, ever since Luther at least, as an isolated, detached statement of the wondrous exchange . . . I can see how frustrating it is for a preacher who has preached his favorite sermon all these years on the imputation of Christ's righteousness from 2 Corinthians 5:21 to hear that this is not the right way to understand it but I actually think that there's an even better sermon waiting to be preached.[6]

5. Hodge, *An Exposition of the Second Letter to the Corinthians*, 150–151.
6. Travis Tamerius, "An Interview with N. T. Wright."

It is "not about justification, but about his own apostolic ministry."[7] He states:

> What Paul is saying is that he and his fellow apostles, in their suffering and fear, their faithful witness against all the odds, are not just talking about God's faithfulness; they are actually embodying it. The death of the Messiah has taken care of their apparent failure; now, in him, they are 'the righteousness of God', the living embodiment of the message they proclaim.[8]

Again, he tells us that: "What the whole passage involves, then, is the idea of the covenant ambassador, who represents the one for whom he speaks in such a full and thorough way that he actually *becomes* the living embodiment of his sovereign."[9] In other words, Paul is effectively saying, if I may paraphrase: "God has appointed us ministers of the message that declares his covenantal faithfulness, the manifestation of his righteousness. We represent him in such a way that we can be considered as the embodiment of his righteousness." The message is declared through the ambassador, one who is then identified with the message he has been entrusted with.

Again, Wright argues that this text says nothing about the righteousness of Christ. It is all about God's righteousness. This argument, as in 1 Cor 1:30, does not hold water. Christ's righteousness is God's righteousness. It was in and through the work of Christ that God made known his righteousness and his covenant faithfulness. This is because the righteousness has been achieved on account of Christ having kept the covenant of works.

The traditional understanding is deemed to be wrong because "The verse has been traditionally read as a somewhat detached statement of atonement theology."[10] Wright appears somewhat bemused that the apostle, when speaking about his apostolic ministry, should make reference to what Christ has achieved for his people. He sees such a reference as being somewhat incongruous.

It would, however, have been remiss of Paul not to have made a reference to the efficacy of his gospel message. One must not forget that Paul's entire ministry was but a means to an end; the end being the salvation

7. Wright, WSPRS, 104.
8. Ibid., 105.
9. Wright, "Becoming the Righteousness of God" 206.
10. Ibid., 203.

of sinners and their perfection in Jesus Christ. In this chapter Paul stops and reminds his hearers of this essential fact, for example, in vv.14–15 he tells his readers why the love of Christ controls his ministry, namely, "because we have concluded this: that one has died for all, therefore all have died; and he died for all, that those who live might no longer live for themselves but for him who for their sake died and was raised." Again in v.17, he states: "Therefore, if anyone is in Christ, he is a new creation." So Paul is an apostle of reconciliation, having said in vv.18-19, that God "who through Christ reconciled us to himself and gave us the ministry of reconciliation; that is, in Christ God was reconciling the world to himself, not counting their trespasses against them, and entrusting us with the message of reconciliation." Here Paul states that his message is one of reconciliation, and what reconciliation entails; how it affects those who believe. It then seems perfectly logical that in v.21 Paul should do something similar in telling us something more about why Christ died and the consequences of his death for all who believe. So, yes, we died with him; we are a new creation because, "for our sake he made him to be sin who knew no sin, so that in him we might become the righteousness of God." Far from being what Wright calls "detached" it is an integral part of the text as understood by the old perspective.

One cannot separate the first part of verse 21 from the second part. We have, in the words of Piper, "the parallel between the two halves."[11] The forgiveness of sin and the imputation of a righteousness must go together, and this applies to all believers because of their union with Christ. In the first half, Paul speaks of Christ, who, although himself being without sin, was made to be sin for us, whilst the latter half speaks of the sinner, who, having no righteousness, is enabled to become the righteousness of God. So, we have Christ's being "made sin" and its consequence, the sinner becoming righteous. Wright, disassociating the latter part of the verse from the former, appears to be saying that Christ became sin in order that the gospel might be preached, rather than referring to any righteousness that may have been imputed to God's people. Did Christ die on the cross of Calvary so that men like Paul might preach the gospel? No, Christ died so that men and woman might be saved. Wright makes preaching the gospel the consequence of Christ's being made sin. However, the entire point of preaching, or being a minister of reconciliation, is that sinners might believe and be forgiven of their sin and receive Christ's righteous-

11. Piper, *The Future of Justification*, 174.

ness. Wright's interpretation seems to be along the lines: "Jesus was made to be sin for us so that we might preach the gospel of reconciliation." The second part of the verse, however, does not refer to the ministers of the gospel, but to what the gospel achieves for the believer. It's this that Isaiah expresses, "out of the anguish he shall see and be satisfied; by his knowledge shall the righteous one, my servant, make many to be accounted righteous, and he shall bear their iniquities" (Isa 53:11). The believer can say, with Ladd, that:

> Christ was made sin for our sake. We might say that our sins were reckoned to Christ. He, although sinless, identified himself with our sins, suffered their penalty and doom-death. So we have reckoned to us Christ's righteousness even though in character and deed we remain sinners. It is an unavoidable logical conclusion that men of faith are justified because Christ's righteousness is imputed to them.[12]

Who was the apostle referring to by "ours" and "us"? Was he simply referring to those entrusted with preaching the message, or all the Christians at Corinth? It seems that Paul was identifying with those to whom the letter was written. So he is essentially saying that for all who are in Christ, sins have been forgiven and righteousness imputed.

It should also be noted that no reconciliation can be achieved from the forgiveness of sin alone, for, as we have seen, the preceptive requirements of the law of God must be kept perfectly; this is why the righteousness secured by Christ is so important. Furthermore, this righteousness does not consist of our works (even if it's Spirit working within us), simply because God demands a perfect righteousness, one that Christ alone can supply.

PHILIPPIANS 3:7-9.

> Look out for the dogs, look out for the evildoers, look out for those who mutilate the flesh. For we are the circumcision, who worship by the Spirit of God and glory in Christ Jesus and put no confidence in the flesh though I myself have reason for confidence in the flesh also. If anyone else thinks he has reason for confidence in the flesh, I have more: circumcised on the eighth day, of the people of Israel, of the tribe of Benjamin, a Hebrew

---

12. Ladd, *A Theology of the New Testament*, 491.

of Hebrews; as the law a Pharisee; as to zeal, a persecutor of the church; as to righteousness under the law, blameless. But whatever gain I had, I counted as loss for the sake of Christ. Indeed, I count everything as loss because of the surpassing worth of knowing Christ Jesus my Lord. For his sake I have suffered the loss of all things and count them as rubbish, in order that I may gain Christ, and be found in him, not having a righteousness of my own that comes from the law, but that which comes through faith in Christ, the righteousness that depends on faith. That I may know him and the power of his resurrection, and may share his sufferings, becoming like him in his death, 11that by any means possible I may attain the resurrection from the dead.

When Wright approaches this passage he makes a mistake concerning the position from which Paul had been saved. About Paul, the Pharisee, he states:

> The keeping of the law was not a way of earning anything, of gaining a status before God; the status was already given in birth, ethnic roots, circumcision and the ancestral possession of Torah. All that Torah-obedience then-does-it's a big 'all', but it is all-is consolidate, to express what is already given, to inhabit appropriately the suit of clothes ('righteousness') that one has already inherited.[13]

While the law is holy, the Jews, however, were quite the opposite. Yes, they were commanded to be righteous (Ex 19:5), but the *ought* did not imply the *can*. The only status Israel possessed was its membership to the old covenant, a covenant from which there could be no true salvation. Wright is once again imposing an efficacy on the type, rather than focusing on the antitype. He tells us that:

> The 'works of Torah' were neither an attempt to earn the covenant membership he already had by God's grace, nor an attempt to add his own merit to the grace he had been given. They were an attempt, he would have said, to do, out of love and obedience to Israel's God, the *works which would function as a sign in the present that he was part of the people who would be vindicated in the future, on the last day, when God would act in his long-promised judgement and mercy.*[14]

---

13. Wright, *WSPRS*, 122.
14. Ibid., 125.

Paraphrasing verses 7-9 Wright states: "Paul is saying, in effect, 'I, though possessing covenant membership according to the flesh, did not regard that covenant membership as something to exploit. I emptied myself, sharing the death of the Messiah, wherefore God has given me the membership that really counts in which I too will share the glory of Christ.'"[15]

Yes, Paul did possess covenant membership, but it was membership of the old covenant, the very covenant that demanded obedience to God's statutes and commandments in order to become God's true "chosen race, a royal priesthood, a holy nation." Wright maintains Sinai to have been a covenant of grace, with the new covenant being another administration of this same covenant. It is then reasonable to suppose that if Paul was a member of the former covenant he was already considered a member of the covenant of grace, hence, being in the new covenant did not alter this pre-existing fact. He would then have already possessed those blessings referred to by Peter (1 Pet.2:9). It, therefore, stands to reason that Paul would require no change of clothes because he was already suitably attired.

On the Damascus Road Paul underwent a change far more radical than that imagined by Wright. He was born again by the Spirit of God and placed into Christ, becoming a member of the new covenant; one that is radically different from the conditional old covenant. In failing to recognize the Adamic, Abrahamic, and Mosaic covenants to be of works, and even refusing to recognize the typological aspects of the old covenant, Wright has constrained all into one overarching covenant of grace. This has effectively caused him then to force square pegs into round holes.

The idea that works could be a sign of who was going to be justified on the last day is partly correct. True believers do good works as a consequence of what they have already become; they arise spontaneously from out of the new nature. Effectively then, the Christian's good works arise from their living according to what they truly are—a new creation in Jesus Christ. One could not, however, have expected the Israelites to have done such works as a consequence of their temporal redemption, e.g., Paul, prior to his conversion, while he may have gloried in the idea that he belonged to a people to whom the law had been given, certainly had not received the grace one associated with God's true spiritual people.

15. Ibid., 124.

Paul, in this passage, has in mind the old and new covenants. He is under no illusions about the old covenant, and "the righteousness under law," reminding the Philippians that if anyone could be saved for rigorously trying to keep the law it would have been him. In terms of the covenant's outward requirements, he had considered himself "blameless" (v.6). He possessed all of the necessary credentials. Yet, like the scribes and Pharisees whom Jesus addressed in his Sermon on the Mount, he lacked spiritual understanding. If one were to ask Paul (or Saul as he was then known) if he had coveted, he would respond with an emphatic "No". He was looking only to externals, not realizing the essential fact that sin goes much deeper, affecting one's very thoughts, and that what occurs in the mind can be as much of a sin in God's sight as committing the actual act. It was only when he truly saw the spirit of the law that he became aware of his true condition. Following his encounter with the risen Christ, he then understood that there was no spiritual salvation to be had under the old covenant. No matter what one did, the old covenant was impotent to save. It was essentially a covenant in which the righteousness of Christ was unavailable. The covenant's mediator was Moses, and the way in which he was given the law, with thunder and lightning (Ex 19:1), was a foreboding as to the covenant's purpose. It is for this reason Paul takes such an emphatic stand against those who want to hold on to the old covenant, calling them "dogs . . . who mutilate the flesh" (Phil 3:2).

During Old Testament times, Christ's righteousness was only for those who, although being under the old covenant externally, exercised faith in the coming Messiah. Paul came to see that compared to the righteousness of Christ, any so-called righteousness under the law was considered "rubbish." The only thing Paul could now boast about was the fact that he was "found in him," being in possession of that righteousness which came from his union with Christ. He, like all Jewish believers, knew fleshly circumcision, but now he knew the very thing it spoke about, namely, spiritual circumcision of the heart. Only such as these "worship by the Spirit of God and glory in Christ" (v.3) because only these constitute God's true people who had been born from above, born of the Spirit of God.

Penal Substitution and/or Christus Victor

IN HIS RECENT WORK, *The Day the Revolution Began*, Wright seems to have nailed his colors to the mast, so to speak. Any ambiguity has gone. He makes it perfectly clear that he does not support the Reformed understanding of penal substitution. The idea that it was God the Father who vented his wrath upon his own innocent Son he considers to be the result of importing ideas associated with medieval paganism rather than with anything revealed in the Scriptures.

In his denial of penal substitution in *TDTRB*, he employs one caricature after another in an attempt to discredit Reformed teaching. Not only does he not consider the arguments of those who espouse the Reformed understanding of penal substitution, men like J. I. Packer and John Stott, Leon Morris etc., he does not even mention them. All too often he seems to be battering a straw man, where he provides but a superficial caricature, says it is wrong, and then moves on to his next point. An example of this concerns his allusions to the blood of the sacrifice, maintaining that the blood of the sacrificed animal does not represent death but a life released. He makes such assertions without actually engaging with the arguments.

Penal substitution is often compared with the *Christus Victor* model as if it is a case of either/or. About the tendency to chose one theology of the atonement to the exclusion of others J. I. Packer said, "It is a pity that books on the atonement so often take it for granted that accounts of the cross which have appeared as rivals in historical debate must be treated as intrinsically exclusive. This is always arbitrary, and sometimes quite perverse."[1]

---

1. Packer, *Tyndale Bulleting* 25, 1974, 3–45.

I am persuaded that both penal substitution and *Christus Victor* atonement models should go together and that it is penal substitution that brings about *Christus Victor*. Wright maintains that he is eclectic in this matter, not accepting one model to the exclusion of others. Yet, he appears to completely reject the Reformed understanding of penal substitution, even believing it to be harmful, "While I believe large parts of it are harmful to our understanding of God as a Father and it misses the main point of God's eternal purpose, that doesn't mean I see no value in it, especially in the substitution aspects of the theory."

The term, (not the idea), *Christus Victor* was first coined by Gustav Aulen in his book, *Christus Victor*, published in 1931. It presents a view of Christ's work that eschews penal substitution in favor of Jesus' triumph over evil and death. It is something akin to this view that Wright appears to embrace.

So what exactly is the *Christus Victor* model? An example often used is the victory of Aslan, the lion, in C. S. Lewis's allegory, *The Lion, the Witch and the Wardrobe*. Aslan, the lion, does not find himself afflicted by a punishment from God, but by all the evil powers of the Witch's kingdom. The consequence of Aslan's victory was that life and warmth returned to the ice kingdom. So too with Jesus' "death, the climax of his work of inaugurating God's kingdom on earth as in heaven, was the victory over the destructive powers let loose into the world not simply through human wrongdoing, the breaking of moral codes, but through the human failure to be image-bearers, to worship the Creator and reflect his wise stewardship into the world."[2] Jesus took upon himself the "consequence of Israel's rebellion, idolatry, and sin, so that Israel and the world may be rescued. He will draw unto himself the actual results of Israel's sin-the pagan hostility against God's people-in order to exhaust it and so make a way through."[3]

Wright maintains that when Jesus died at Calvary, the evil forces had a field-day by inflicting their evil deeds upon him. When he says that he believes in penal substitution he essentially means that Jesus was punished, not by his Father, but by impersonal sin and its effects. By voluntarily taking this punishment upon himself Jesus effectively exhausted sin. It did its worst to him in order to spare us. As we saw earlier, the idea that God in any way punished the person of his own Son is rejected. In all,

2. Wright, *Revolution*, 148.
3. Ibid., 339.

one feels that Wright has essentially presented us with a lopsided atonement, one that leaves out the most important element. A truly biblical understanding of salvation embraces both the Reformed understanding of penal substitution and Christ's victory over "principalities and powers." The latter results from the former.

One of the principal weapons in Satan's arsenal consists in undermining the believer's assurance, and inducing feelings of guilt, even though his sins have been forgiven. Justification removes the guilt of sin, whereas the pollution is removed through progressive sanctification. Henri Blocher, commenting on Colossians 2:14–11, Hebrews 2:14 and Revelation 12 states:

> [Col. 2:14–15] connects [Christ's] triumph to the cross and precisely to the cancellation of the bond of our debt (as defined in the ordinances of the law) when Jesus was crucified . . . Then and there were the principalities and powers, the chief of whom is called Satan, 'disarmed.' The action concerns judicial claims. Since God can be expected to uphold the rules he has set, we can also expect that the cancellation was obtained through the payment of the legal debt. This appears to be confirmed by the many *ransom* sayings that state that the life or blood of Christ *was the price paid to free human beings from bondage* . . .
>
> Satan was the accuser, and he prevailed as long as he could point to their sins. But the blood of the lamb was the price paid for the cancellation of their debt. The blood of the lamb wipes out the guilt of their sins forever, and the devil was disarmed. Similarly, Hebrews 2:14 stresses that Jesus deprived the devil of his power . . . through death, and we are told that 'he has died as a ransom to set them[those who are called] free from sins committed under the first covenant' (Heb. 9:15), his blood obtaining the remission of their sins (Heb.9: 22; cf. 27-28).[4]

Having been translated from the kingdom of darkness into that of Christ, the believer has been lifted out of the realm of the devil and his minions. All the principalities and powers that the devil employed to carry out his works have, through Christ's work, effectively been rendered impotent. All too often, however, the Christian forgets what he has become in Christ, and thereby makes himself susceptible to Satan's cunning stratagems.

---

4. Blocher, "*Agnus Victor*" 86–88.

The individual requires forgiveness because he has done something wrong in God's eyes. John tells us that for those that do not believe the wrath of God rests upon them (John 3:36). The reference to *wrath* here implies God's anger. It burns against the individual who rejects the message, and it is against the individual that this wrath will be directed. People are said to be forgiven and rescued because Jesus has, in some abstract way, suffered, and released them from the satanic powers that were against them. While, of course, this is true, it by-passes the essential fact that the individual stands condemned and is subject to God's wrath and that the only means of achieving reconciliation is for another, a middle person, to take this wrath upon himself. That Jesus, the Christ, took this wrath upon himself is made evident in his shed blood which signifies death. As God demands the death of the sinner, so too did he demand the death of the sinner's substitute. The wages of sin is death and it is God himself, through the work of his Son, who pays the wages.

As referred to earlier, when Wright was presented with a videotape by an evangelical that supported penal substitution, he gagged when mention was made to the fact that "someone has to die." The question one must ask is simply this: If the wages of sin is death (Rom 6:23), how can it be possible for someone to take the punishment upon himself without suffering death? The whole point of Jesus being a ransom is that he must pay the price, and the price is death. Again, it is no use trying to say that any wrath that may have been displayed in Jesus' suffering concerned only his flesh and not his person. The body cannot be separated from what the person is, and to punish the body or flesh, is to punish the person. To then maintain that Jesus paid the ransom price while excluding God's wrath, which manifests itself against all sin, is, to say the least, something of a contradiction.

In the case of the first Adam, although he was without sin, there was the possibility of his falling into sin. This he did because he listened to the devil. The very fact that the devil could bring about his fall highlights something of his power. If Satan could do this when Adam was in a state of righteousness, then one can but imagine his power over those who are ungodly and unrighteous. Those who stand outside of God's sheltering love are fully exposed to the principalities and powers. However, for those who are in Christ, sharing in his victory over sin's power, there is no possibility of a fall because Christ has elevated the believer to a position that is higher than Adam ever knew. Because of Christ's penal substitution, believers are back in the Father's fold and subject to his authority and protection, subsequently, everything that the devil and his minions had at their disposal has been defeated.

In Colossians 2:13–14 Paul states that God, "having forgiven us all our trespasses by cancelling the written record of debt that stood against us with its legal demands. This was set aside, nailing it to the cross. He disarmed the rulers and authorities and put them to open shame by triumphing over them." It is important to bear in mind that the 'rulers and authorities" have been divested of their power because the debt of the law's "legal demand" has been cancelled. This applies to believers, not because the law has not been honored, but because it was honored by Christ. This "written record" is God's broken law. It stood against Adam after he had transgressed, albeit, in an unwritten form, and, also, in its written form it stood against Israel. Today, in both its unwritten and written form, the law stands against all those who refuse to believe in Christ. However, in the case of believers, God has saved them from his own wrath by redirecting it onto himself in his own Son, so that the consequences of his broken law should not fall upon them.

We see Jesus' triumph over the powers every time a sinner comes to faith, as John Stott states, "every Christian conversion involves a power encounter in which the devil is obliged to relax his hold on somebody's life."[5] The believer is released from the prison house of sin because God has through Christ shed his own blood which canceled God's wrath. Hence, "those who were far off have been brought near by the blood of Christ" (Eph 2:13).

One should also consider Jesus' victory over sinful powers in his journey to the cross. Satan did all he could to undermine Jesus' mission, from promising to give him all the kingdoms of the world to encouraging Judas in Jesus' betrayal. As Stott tells us, "If he had disobeyed, by deviating an inch from the path of God's will, the devil would have gained a toehold and frustrated the plan of salvation."[6] Jesus, however, overcame, and through his obedience, even unto death on the cross (Phil 2:8), he has defeated the powers that railed against him. In doing this he fulfilled all righteousness.

A simple illustration might help to show how the believer's justification by faith, with God himself paying the debt to overcome all the forces of evil, lies at the heart of *Christus Victor* theology. It's important to again

5. Stott, *The Cross*, 236.
6. Ibid., 235.

remember that all illustrations fall well short of that which they serve to illustrate. It's, therefore, important that one does not caricature the illustration. Imagine that a boy's father is a very powerful person and that in virtue of the boy living in his father's house he is protected from the people who are determined to do the household harm. Now suppose the boy does some heinous act, for example, stealing the money that was in his father's safe, and is consequently banished from his father's presence, i.e., he is thrown out of the house and estate. The boy will now, being on the outside, find himself exposed to the forces that are against his father. He will effectively be without protection and fall easy victim to these forces. If the boy wants to escape these he must first make amends with his father by repaying what he had stolen. Imagine then that a stranger gives the boy the money to pay back to his father, for only in this way can he be reconciled. Once he is reconciled, having put right what was wrong, he will be able to go back to the protection of the father's home, to a place that will shelter him from all that he was exposed to on the outside. Of course, in reality, it is God himself (the boy's father) who pays the debt. Penal substitution works in a similar fashion. When man was exiled from God he was subject to evil powers because he had lost God's protection and had effectively put himself at the mercy of Satan, as Calvin put it, "while we are out of Christ, all is under the dominion of Satan."[7] It is only when the price has been paid, when sin has been punished and a righteousness secured, that one can be at peace with God, and know the deliverance from the evil forces in the world, i.e., the flesh, the world and the devil. It is only then that one can come under the Father's protection.

One must remember that the believer is one who has been translated into an entirely new realm and is spiritually speaking even now seated with Christ in heavenly places. Christians need to realize what they have become "in Christ," that the old has passed away and all things have become new. The *Christus Victor* theme is, of course, important, it should, however, be viewed as the consequence of the believer's reconciliation with his Father and his new position in the kingdom of God. In substituting penal substitution with the *Christus Victor* model, Wright has effectively jettisoned the very thing that brings about *Christus Victor*.

7. Calvin, *Sermons on Ephesians*, 309.

Conclusion

THOSE OF THE NPP, including Wright, are, to quote Fesko:

> beckoning us to look through their telescopes to see that the
> universe does not revolve around soteriology but rather ecclesi-
> ology. Are we at a nexus in church history where a Copernican
> revolution is underway and the advocates of the old perspective
> on Paul will soon wear the red faces of chagrin because they
> have refused to peer into the telescope and see the truth? Quite
> frankly, the answer to this question is, No.[1]

NPP proponents believe themselves to be initiating a theological revolution that is on par with the discovery that the earth is spherical, or with
Luther's rediscovery of justification by faith alone, and, I am sure, that
Wright sees himself as the new Copernicus or new Martin Luther, ushering in a new reformation.

I have tried to emphasize throughout this work that I see the error
of the NPP as having its roots in the misidentification of the various covenants. Nowhere, at least to my knowledge, has Wright explained what
the redemption of Israel in the exodus actually means. By this, I mean
simply that he has not distinguished between spiritual and fleshly Israel.
For example, when he deals with Paul's Damascus Road experience, as I
said previously, he believes the apostle to have already been a recipient of
grace and justified because of his membership to ethnic Israel.

Again, Wright depicts Jesus as being the true Israelite, the one who
achieved in his own flesh what the nation failed to do, namely, keeping
the old covenant. I have tried to show why Jesus did not keep this covenant, which is but a type, but a new covenant, the antitype. From this
we saw that it is wrong to do what Wright has done, namely, look for the
fulfillment of the old covenant's temporal promises in the new covenant.

---

1. Fesko, *The New Perspective on Paul.*

The NPP follows the standard Presbyterian position. It too believes that the new covenant in regard to its blessings and efficacy only became applicable from the time of Christ. In doing so it fails to appreciate the fact that the truly saved in the Old Testament were participators in the new covenant. I believe it is only this understanding that allows one to avoid the all too familiar mistake of believing all Israel to be a truly redeemed people, confusing the type and the antitype, and wrongly applying their respective promises and blessings.

Wright's position is a good example of galloping through the Scriptures with a desire to 'make fit' a preconceived idea; one taken not from the Scriptures but from first century Judaism that had to a large degree misunderstood the old covenant. Jesus himself demonstrated just how wrong the Pharisees and scribes were in their understanding of the law. It is, therefore, unlikely that one would find in their writings an understanding of the law that one can then apply to the Scriptures. Yet this is what the NPP has tended to do in regard to Second Temple Judaism. Wright does not appear to have stopped to consider whether there were different types of first century Judaism and whether he has identified the right type when it comes to the interpretation of Scripture. Furthermore, the Scriptures are the inspired infallible Word of God that are opened up to the believer by the supernatural work of the Holy Spirit. If Wright is correct one would have to ask why the Spirit did not reveal his particular interpretation to the church earlier than the late 20th century.[2]

One also feels that Wright has an ecumenical agenda. He depicts Christ's victory over sin in a way that is readily acceptable to Roman Catholics. "'Justification' in the first century was not about the establishment of a relationship with God, but about God's eschatological definition, both future, and present, of who was, in fact, a member of his people."[3] The advocates of the NPP want to show that any disagreements between Roman Catholics and Protestants were all due to a misunderstanding in regard to justification by faith. By maintaining the doctrine to be about ecclesiology rather than soteriology, Roman Catholics and Protestants can then sit at the same table, acknowledging that their differences on justification were the result of a misunderstanding.

For the old perspective justification, far from being a subsidiary crater or a kind of secondary doctrine, forms a vital part of the primary

2. I am aware that one could ask the same question concerning the Protestant Reformation's rediscovery of justification by faith alone.

3. Wright, *WSPRS*, 119.

crater, and it is from the resulting peace with God that other blessings flow. Justification must be viewed against the backcloth of the covenant of works, a covenant that demands obedience and the punishment for sin. Christ has dealt with both. He became a propitiation. He suffered the wrath of his Father, shedding his blood in death so that the ungodly might be forgiven, and he also, by his thirty-three years of perfect obedience to the original covenant of works achieved a righteousness for his people. Those for whom he died have been since the first person after the Fall believed, been justified through faith. This faith was not a later badge but, rather, the only badge of membership where the new covenant is concerned. Believers are pronounced righteous, not simply because the judge finds in the sinner's favor; but finds in the sinner's favor because he sees the actual righteousness procured by Christ. All that was achieved by Christ's redemptive work becomes the believer's because of the insoluble union he has with him. There is much more one could say about the differences that exist between the old perspective and the NPP, but what I have said should serve to show that the differences are not trivial, but concern those doctrines that lie at the very heart of Reformed theology.

I have tried to show something of the simplicity that lies at the heart of God's covenantal redemptive schema. All humanity is in one of two possible positions; either one is in the first Adam and under the covenant of works, or one is in Christ and in the new covenant. To be in Christ, united to him, is to be in the kingdom of God. There is no other possibility. The appearance of the old covenant did not change the fact that one is by nature under the original covenant of works but was itself an explicit revelation of the demands of this first covenant. Salvation, from first to last, is the result of believing in Christ, be this in the form of a promise awaiting its fulfillment or looking back to what occurred, as we do today. There is one Christ, one new covenant, one mediator, and one true redemption that all believers have received.

The controversy generated by the NPP is not going away soon, but I'm sure that with time it will gradually become less significant, and, no doubt, be replaced by something else. It is my hope that this brief work, although imperfect, will at least cause the reader to think about what has been said and not be afraid to question his/her own position to make doubly certain it conforms to what the Scriptures teach.

Bibliography

Augustine. *Contra Julianum* 1.6.22. cited in Martin Luther, Lectures on Romans, trans. Jacob A. O. Peeus. LW 25 St Louis: Concordia, 1974.

Barth, Karl. *Church Dogmatics, II:I: The Doctrine of God.* T & T Clark, 1957.

Bainton, Roland. *Here I Stand: A Life of Martin Luther.* New York: Penguin, 1955.

Blocher. "*Agnus Victor*: The Atonement as Victory and Vicarious Punishment", in John G. Stackhouse (ed) *What Does it Mean to be Saved?* Grand rapids: Baker, 2002, 86–88.

Berkhof Louis. *Systematic Theology.* Edinburgh, The Banner of Truth, 1979.

Bloesch, Donald. *The Future of Evangelical Christianity" A Call for Unity and Diversity.* Colorado Springs: Helmers & Howard, 1988.

Booth, Abraham. *Paedobaptism Examined.* As cited in Kingdom, *Children of Abraham,* Carey Publications 1977, 38–39.

Buchanan, James. *The Doctrine of Justification.* Grand Rapids: Baker, 1977.

Bunyan, John. *The Doctrine of the Law and Grace Unfolded*: The Works of John Bunyan Vol. 1 Edinburgh: Banner of Truth, 1999.

Cara J. Robert. *Cracking the Foundation of the New Perspective on Paul.* Ross-shire: Christian Focus Publications (Mentor), 2017.

Calvin, John. *Institutes of the Christian Religion.* Ed. T. John McNeill. Philadelphia: Westminster Press, 1960.

———. Institutes of the Christian Religion, trans. Henry Beveridge, Grand Rapid: MI: Eerdmans, 1953.

———. *Sermons on the Epistle to the Ephesians.* trans. A. Golding; Edinburgh: Banner of Truth, 1973

Campbell, Douglas. *A Faith To Live By: Understanding Christian Doctrine.* Ross-shire: Christian Focus Publication, 2010.

Carson D. A. "Atonement in Romans 3:21-26: 'God Presented Him as a Propitiation'", in C. E. Hill and F. A. James III eds. *The Glory of the Atonement,* Downers Grove: IVP; Leicester: Apollos, 2004, 119–139.

———. *Justification and Variegated Nomism: A Fresh Appraisal of Paul and Second Temple Judaism – Vol 2: The Paradoxes of Paul.* ed. D. A. Carson, Peter T. O. Brian and Mark A. Seifrid, Baker: Grand Rapids, 2004.

———. Carson, review of N.T. Wright "Evil and the Justice of God" in *Review of Biblical Literature 2007.*

Casey, Maurice. "Where Wright is Wrong: A Critical Review on N. T. Wright's Jesus and the Victory of God," *Journal for the Study of the New Testament* 69: 95–103, 1998.

Chalke, Steve. *The Lost Message of Jesus.* Michigan, Grand Rapids: Zondervan, 2002.

Coxe, Nehemiah. "A Discourse of the Covenants That God Made With Man Before the Law." In *Covenant Theology: From Adam to Christ*, Ed. Ronald D. Miller, et al. 29–140. Palmdale, CA: Reformed Baptist Academic Press, 2005.

Cranfield C. E. B. *On Romans and Other New Testament Essays*. Edinburgh: T.&T. Clark, 1979.

Dabney, Robert. *Lectures in Systematic Theology*. Michigan, Grand Rapids: Zondervan, 1976.

Dale, Robert William. *The Atonement*, London, 1909.

Denault, Pascal. *The Distinctiveness of Baptist Covenant Theology*. Birmingham, Alabama: Solid Ground Christian Books, 2013.

Denney, James. *The Death of Christ*. Quotation from Alan Stibbs, His Blood Works, 30, Ross-shire, Christian Focus, 2011.

Duncan, Ligon. "The Attractions of the New Perspectives on Paul" 3; Robert Smith, "Justification in "The New Perspectives on Paul'" *Reformed Theological Review 58* 1999.

Dunn D. G. James. "The Theology of Galatians: The Issue of Covenantal Nomism." *In Pauline Theology I: Thessalonians, Philippians, Galatians, Philemon*, Ed by Jouette M. Bassler, 125-46. Minneapolis: Fortress, 1991.

———.*The New Perspective on Paul*, Grand Rapids: Wm. B. Eerdmans, 2007.

Enns, Peter. "Book Review of N. T. Wright's *Crown of Fire* and *Following Jesus*," *Westminster Theological Journal* 58/2 (1996).

Eveson H. Philip. *The Great Exchange*. Kent: One Day Publications, 1996.

Fesko J. V. *Justification: Understanding the Classic Reformed Doctrine*. New Jersey, Phillipsburg: P&R, 2008.

———."John Owen on Justification and Union with Christ" in *Themelios* 37.1 (2012): 7–19

Fisher, Edward. *A Marrow of Modern Divinity*. Swengel, PA, Reiner Publications, 1978.

Fitzmyer. J. *Romans Anchor Bible Commentaries*. Yale University Press, 2007

Frame M. John. *Systematic Theology: An Introduction to Christian Theology*. Phillipsburg: P&R, 2013.

Gathercole, Simon. "The Doctrine of Justification in Paul and Beyond: Some Proposals," in *Justification in Perspective: Historical Development and Contemporary Challenges*. Ed. Bruce L. McCormack, Michigan: Baker Academic, 2006.

Gentry J. Peter & Wellum J. Stephen. *God's Kingdom through God's Covenants*. Illinois: Crossway, 2015.

Grant, George. "Books: Revisiting the Apostle," *World Magazine*, 1 Nov 1997.

Grudem, Wayne. *Systematic Theology*. Nottingham: Inter Varsity Press, 1994.

Hamer, Colin. *The Bridegroom Messiah*. London: Apostolos, 2018.

Hodge, Charles. *Commentary on the Epistle to the Romans*. New York, A. C. Armstrong and Son, 1896.

Hoekema, Anthony. *The Bible and the Future*. Grand Rapids, Eerdmans, 1979.

Holland Tom. *Contours of Pauline Theology*. Ross-shire: Christian Focus Publication, 2010.

———. Tom Wright and the Search for Truth: A Theological Evaluation, London: Apiary Publishing, 2017.

Horton, Michael. *Covenant and Salvation: Union with Christ*. Louisville: Westminster, John Knox Press, 2007.

Hutchinson, Edward. *A Treatise Concerning the Covenant and Baptism.*

Jeffrey, et al, Steve, Ovey; Andrew M. Sach. *Pierced for our Transgressions: Rediscovering the Glory of Penal Substitution*. Wheaton, Ill: Crossway, 2007)

Johnston D. Jeffrey. *The Kingdom of God, A Baptist Expression of Covenant & Biblical Theology*. Conway, AR: Free Grace, 2014.

———. *The Fatal Flaw*, USA: Free Grace Press, 2010

Johnston, Robert. *Lectures on the Book of Philippians*. Minneapolis: Klockond Klock, 1977 [1875]).

Lloyd-Jones, Martyn. *Studies in the Sermon on the Mount*. Grand Rapids: Wm. B. Eerdmans, 1976.

———.Romans: Exposition of Chapter 1. Edinburgh, Banner of Truth, 1985.

———. *Romans: Exposition of chapters 3:20–4:25*. Edinburgh: Banner of Truth, 1978.

———. *Romans: Exposition of Chapters 2:1–3:20*. Edinburgh: Banner of Truth, 1989.

———. Romans: *Exposition of Chapter 5, Exposition of Chapter 5 Assurance*. Edinburgh: Banner of Truth, 1976.

———. *Romans: Exposition of Chapter 6, The New Man*. Edinburgh: Banner of Truth, 1979.

———. *Romans: Exposition of Chapter: Exposition of Chapter 7:1–8:4*. Edinburgh: Banner of Truth, 1975.

———. *Romans: Exposition of Chapter 8:17–39*. Edinburgh: Banner of Truth, 1975.

———. Romans: *Exposition of Chapter 10, Saving Faith*. Edinburgh: Banner of Truth, 2004.

———. *life in the Spirit in Marriage, Home and Work*. Edinburgh: Banner of Truth, 1973.

Lillback A. Peter. *The Binding of God*. Grand Rapids: Baker, 2001.

Lofthouse W. F. *Ethics and Atonement*, London, 1906, 161.

Longenecker W. Bruce. *The Triumph of Abraham's God*. Nashville: Abingdon, 1998.

Luther, Martin. Luther, *Lectures on Galatians*, 1535, Chapters 1-4, vol. 26, of Luther's Works, ed. Jaroslav Pelikan, St. Louis: Concordia, 1963.

———. *What Luther Says: An Anthology*, ed. Ewald M. Plass, St. Louis: Concordia, vol. 2, 1959.

———. *The Babylonian Captivity of the Church*.

Macleod, Donald. *Christ Crucified: Understanding the Atonement*. Nottingham: Inter-Varsity, 2014.

McGrath E. Alister. *IUSTITIA DEI: A History of the Christian Doctrine of Justification*. Cambridge: Cambridge University Press, 2005.

Moo J. Douglas. *Romans: The New NIV Application Commentary*. Grand Rapids: Zondervan, 2000.

Morris, Leon. *The Apostolic Preaching of the Cross*. London: Tyndale Press, 1972.

———. *The Cross of Christ in the New Testament*. Exeter: Paternoster, no date.

Murray, John. *Redemption Accomplished and Applied*. Edinburgh: Banner of Truth, 1979.

———. *The Epistle to the Romans*. Grand Rapids, MI: Eerdmans, 1959.

Murray H. Iain. *The Old Evangelicalism: Old Truths for New Awakening*. Edinburgh, Banner of Truth, 2005.

Meyer C. Jason. *The End of the Law*. Nashville, Tennessee: B&H, 2009.

Neill, Stephen and Wright, Tom. *The Interpretation of the New Testament. 1861-1986* New York: Oxford University Press, 1988

Owen, John. *The Works of John Owen*, Vol. 5. Edinburgh: Banner of Truth Trust, 1976.

————. *The Works of John Owen*, Vol.10. Edinburgh: Banner of Truth, 1978.

————. *The Works of John Owen*, Vol. 22. Edinburgh: Banner of Truth, 1991.

Packer, J. I. *Knowing God.* London: Hodder & Stoughton, 2013.

————. *Tyndale Bulleting* 25, 1974.

Pink W. Arthur. *The Divine Covenants.* Memphis: Bottom Hill, 2011.

Piper, John. *The Future of Justification: A Response to N. T. Wright.* Nottingham: Inter-Varsity, 2008.

Robinson, Brian. *Banner of Truth Magazine.* Sept, 2002.

Sanders E. P. *Paul and Palestinian Judaism: A Comparison of Patterns of Religion.* Philadelphia: Fortress, 1977.

————.*Paul A Very Short Introduction.* Oxford: Oxford University Press, 1991.

Schreiner R. Thomas. *Faith Alone – the Doctrine of Justification.* Grand Rapids: Baker, 2015.

————.*Romans.* Baker Exegetical Commentary on the New Testament, Grand Rapids: Baker, 1998.

Seifrid A. Mark. Christ, our Righteousness: Paul's theology of justification. Leicester: Apollos: 2000.

Seyoon, Kim. *Paul and the New Perspective: Second Thoughts on the Origins of Paul's Gospel.* Grand Rapids: Eerdmans, 2004.

Shedd G. T. William. *Dogmatic Theology.* New York: Charles Scribner's Son's, 1889.

Smeaton, George, *The Apostles Doctrine of the Atonement*, Edinburgh, 1870.

Stendahl, Krister. "The Apostle Paul and the Introspective Conscience of the West," in *Paul Among Jews and Gentiles and Other Essays.* pp 78–96. Philadelphia: Fortress, 1976.

Stibbs, Alan. *His Blood Works.* Ross-shire: Christian Focus, 2011.

Stott, John. *The Cross of Christ.* Leicester: IVP, 1986.

Tamerius, Travis. "An Interview with N. T. Wright," *RRJ 11/1* (2002): 129–30.

Truman R. Carl. "The Portrait of Martin Luther in Contemporary New Testament Scholarship: Some Casual Observations." Lecture delivered at Tyndale Fellowship in Christian Doctrine, 2001.

Turretin. *Elenctic Theology,* Vol.2. George Musgrove Giger, ed. James T. Dennison. Jr, Phillipsburg, NJ: P&R, 1994

Venema, P. Cornelius. *The Gospel of Free Acceptance in Christ.* Edinburgh: Banner of Truth, 2006.

Waters, Guy Prentiss. *Justification and the New Perspective on Paul.* Phillipsburg: R&P, 2004.

Watson, Thomas. *A Body of Divinity.* Edinburgh: Banner of Truth, 1958.

Wells F. David. "Forward" in *By Faith Alone: Answering the Challenges to the Doctrine of Justification.* Ed., Gary L. W. Johnson and Guy P. Waters, Illinois: Crossway, 2006.

————. *God in the Wasteland.* Grand Rapids: Wm. B. Eerdmans, 1994.

Westerholm, Stephen. *Justification Reconsidered.* Grand Rapids: William B. Eerdmans, 2013.

————. *Perspectives Old and New on Paul: The "Lutheran" Paul and His Critics.* Grand Rapids: William B. Eerdmans, 2004.

White, R. James. *The God Who Justifies.* Minneapolis: Bethany House, 2001.

Wellum J. Stephen. "Baptism and the Relationship Between the Covenants" in Believer's Baptism ed Thomas R. Schreiner and Shawn D. Wright, Nashville: B&H, 2006.

Wilhemlus a Brakel. *Our Reasonable Service*. trans. Bartel Elshout, Ligonier, PA: Soli Deo Gloria, 1992.

Witsius, Herman. *The Economy of the Covenants Between God and Man*, Vol 1 Phillipsburg, New Jersey: P&R, 1990.

Woolsey A. Andrew. "The Covenant in the Church Fathers." Haddington House Journal, 2003. 25–53.

Wright N. T. "On Becoming the Righteousness of God 2 Corinthians 5:21" in *Pauline Theology*, Volume -II, ed. D. M. Hay: Minneapolis: Augsburg Fortress 1993, 200–208.

———."Curse and Covenant Galatians 3:10–14." Pages 137–56 in *The Climax of the Covenant" Christ and the Law in Pauline Theology*.

———. *Climax of the Covenant: Christ and the Law in Pauline Theology*. Edinburgh: T&T Clark, 1991.

———. *Evil and the Justice of God*. Downers Grove, III.: InterVarsity, 2006.

———. *How God became King*. SPCK, 2012.

———. *Jesus and the Victory of God: Christian Origins and the Question of God* Minneapolis: Fortress, 1996.

———. *Justification: God's Plan and Paul's Vision*. London: SPCK, 2009.

———. *New Heavens, New Earth*. Cambridge: Grove Books, 1999.

———. *New Perspectives on Paul*. 10th Edinburgh Conference, Rutherford House, Edinburgh.

———. "New Perspective on Paul," in Justification in Perspective, Reprinted in N. T. Wright, Pauline Perspectives, 26. Essays on Paul, Fortress, 2013.

———. Paul and the Faithfulness of God. Minneapolis: Fortress, 2013.

———. *Paul for Everyone* 1 Corinthians. SPCK, 2003.

———. *Paul for Everyone Galatians and Thessalonians*. SPCK, 2002.

———. *Paul for Everyone Romans, Part: Chapters 1-8*. London: SPCK, 2004.

———. *Paul and his Recent Interpreters*. Minneapolis: Fortress, 2015.

———. *Paul: In Fresh Perspective*. Minneapolis: Fortress, 2006.

———. "Romans" *The New Interpreter's Bible: Acts-First Corinthians*. Vol.10, ed. Leande E. Keck, Nashville: Abingdon, 2002.

———. "Romans and the Theology of Paul" in *Pauline Theology* pp 30–67. ed. David M. Hay and E. Elizabeth Johnson, Minneapolis: Fortress, 1995.

———. *The Day the Revolution began*. London: SPCK, 2016.

———. *The New Testament and the People of God*. Minneapolis: Fortress, 1992, reprint 2013.

———. *The Climax of the Covenant: Christ and the Law in Pauline Theology*. Minneapolis: Fortress, 1991.

———. *What St Paul Really Said*. Oxford: Lion Hudson, 1997.

CONFESSIONS OF FAITH

The Baptist Confession of Faith 1689. London: The Wakeman Trust, 1981.

The Westminster Confession of Faith. Publications Committee of the Free Presbyerian Church of Scotland, 1976.

INTERNET

Augustine, Proceedings on Pelagius www.preteristarchive.com Accessed 09/03/2017.

Craig, W.L. N. T. On Wright's View of the Second Coming. www.youtube.com Accessed 25/11/17.

Duncan, Ligon. The Attractions of the New Perspective (s) on Paul. www.ligonier.org/learn/articles/attractions-new-perspectives-paul/

Eusebius, Demonstio Evanglica 10:1, Trans. W. J. Ferrar, http://www.earlychristian writings.com/fathers/eusebius_de_12_book10.html Accessed 27/03/17.

Fesko J. V. The New Perspective on Paul: Calvin and N.T. Wright. -Fesko J. V. The New Perspective on Paul: Calvin and N.T. Wright. http://www.ligonier.org/ Accessed 03/03/2017.

Hodge, Charles. http://www.ccel.org/ccel/hodge/theology2.iv.vii.vii.html Accessed 08/04/2017.

MacArthur, YouTube, John MacArthur on N. T. Wright, pub. 22 March, 2017. Accessed 07/06/2017.

Trueman R. Carl. A Man More Sinned Against than Sinning? The Portrait of Martin Luther in Contemporary New Testament Scholarship: https://www.crcchico.com/covenant/trueman.html Accessed 05/04/2017.

———. NT Wright on the Second Coming, Youtube. Accessed 03/07/2017.

———. Sounding the Alarm: N. T. Wright and Evangelical Theology by Travis Tamerius, originally appeared in Volume 11.2 (Spring 2002) of The Reformation & Revival Journal. Accessed via www.thepaulpage.com 05/28/2017.

———. "The Law in Romans 2" in Paul and the Mosaic Law. Ed. James Dunn. Mohr Siebeck, 1996. 131–151

Wright N. T. "The Cross and the Caricature: A Response to Robert Jenson, Jeffrey John, and a New Volume Entitled Pierced for Our Transgression," http://www.fulcrum-anglican.org.uk/news/2007/20070423wright.cfm?doc 205. Accessed 03/10/2017.

Wright, Transcript of interview by Trevin Wax, 19th November, 2007. Accessible from Monergism.com.

———.Jesus and the People of God https://www.youtube.com/watch?v=1AukgNlAgiI Accessed 05/05/2017.

———.Wright, ntwrightpage.com/2016/07/12/new-perspectives-on-paul/ Accessed 03/01/2016.

———. Paul for Tomorrow's World Part 1 – lecture. "Glorification does not mean going to heaven, it means being put in charge." Accessed 15/10/2017.

———. Paul in Different Perspectives: Lecture 1. Delivered at Auburn Avenue Presbyterian Church (Monroe, Louisiana). Ntwrightpage.com

CPSIA information can be obtained
at www.ICGtesting.com
Printed in the USA
LVHW081301110219
607131LV00018B/445/P

9 781532 649196